OPENING CINEMA

SU TONG

Translated by (in order of appearance)
Olivia Milburn, **Nicky Harman**,
James Trapp and **Haiwang Yuan**

SINOIST

ACA Publishing Ltd
University House
11 13 Lower Grosvenor Place
London SW1W 0EX, UK
Tel: +44 (0)20 3289 3885
E mail: info@alaincharlesasia.com
Web: www.alaincharlesasia.com

Beijing Office
Tel: +86 (0)10 8472 1250

Author: Su Tong
Translated by *(in order of appearance)* :
Olivia Milburn, Nicky Harman, James Trapp and Haiwang Yuan

Published by Sinoist Books (an imprint of ACA Publishing Ltd)

Chinese language copyright © 露天电影　苏童散文 *(Lu Tian Dian Ying: Su Tong San Wen)* 2014, by Zhejiang Literature & Art Publishing House, Hangzhou, China

English Translation text © 2021 ACA Publishing Ltd, London, UK

ALL RIGHTS RESERVED. NO PART OF THIS PUBLICATION MAY BE REPRODUCED IN MATERIAL FORM, BY ANY MEANS, WHETHER GRAPHIC, ELECTRONIC, MECHANICAL OR OTHER, INCLUDING PHOTOCOPYING OR INFORMATION STORAGE, IN WHOLE OR IN PART, AND MAY NOT BE USED TO PREPARE OTHER PUBLICATIONS WITHOUT WRITTEN PERMISSION FROM THE PUBLISHER.

This novel is entirely a work of fiction. The names, characters and incidents portrayed in it are the work of the author's imagination. Any resemblance to actual persons, living or dead, events or localities is entirely coincidental.

Paperback ISBN: 978-1-83890-524-8
eBook ISBN: 978-1-83890-507-1

A catalogue record for *The Open Air Cinema* is available from the National Bibliographic Service of the British Library.

OPEN AIR CINEMA

SU TONG

Translated by

(in order of appearance)

· OLIVIA MILBURN

· NICKY HARMAN

· JAMES TRAPP

· HAIWANG YUAN

Sinoist Books

- The Bicycle Song
- Rain on the Roof Tiles
- The Secret of the River
- Sankeshu
- A Sandstorm
- Open-Air Cinema
- Goldfish Mania
- Our Lovely Ladies
- The Seamstress
- Women's Voices
- In Winter
- A Street in Summer
- The Bridge North of the City
- Boats
- Talking About the Past
- The Events of My Childhood
- Going to School
- A Bedridden Child
- Born in the 1960s, a Label
- A Second Hometown
- My Eight-Hundred-Metre Hometown
- Girls From Twenty Years Ago
- An Autobiographical Moment
- My Alma Mater
- The Cave
- Memories of the Water Tank
- Singapore's Chinatown, Durian and Other Things
- Beiju in Suzhou
- The Soul of the City
- What is the South?
- The Uses of Childhood
- A Diary of Seven Days in Leipzig

PART 1

Reminiscences of the South

translated by
Olivia Milburn

My only firm faith has been in literature, which has freed me from many unspeakable sufferings and worries. I love it and feel a deep gratitude for it. I am grateful that such a profession could exist: it has provided me with a livelihood and filled my existence with wonderful things.

THE BICYCLE SONG

On a wide, featureless road, apart from the occasional bus, Dongfeng or Jiefang truck, cars are a very rare sight, and the main component of the busy traffic is bicycles. On many of the bicycle wheels the chrome has peeled off, exposing patches of rust and many people in gray, blue and army green clothes can be seen riding these bicycles in a constant stream down both sides of the road. This is how a Western movie would depict Beijing in the 1970s—a clumsy but accurate shorthand. As everyone knows, when you see a sea of bicycles, you are looking at China.

I'm going to add some of the details that are missing from this image. Most of these bicycles are black, with a 26 or 24-inch frame. The latter is usually considered a woman's bike, but women's bikes are pretty butch and the frame is just as simple and solid as the men's. Occasionally, the odd red or blue racing bike might appear, whose brake lines are not exposed straight steel wires but cross lines in a nylon housing, forming the fashionable logo in front of the handlebars—just like the logo of CCTV today. The owners of these brightly coloured bicycles are often unusual young people from rich or powerful families. When such a bicycle passes in front of other youngsters, it might encounter some deliberate obstruction. There were various different reasons for their behaviour: some acted out of pure jealousy and were deliberately out to make a little trouble; but sometimes teenagers can be tiresome, they'd force the rider to get off their bike and then fight to climb on top themselves, going for a spin on their borrowed ride.

We are now going to turn our attention to the ordinary black bicycles, of the kind that can be seen everywhere. They mainly consist of three brands: Forever, Phoenix and Flying Pigeon. Flying Pigeon is produced by a bicycle factory in Tianjin, so they are rare in the south. Round us, ordinary families dreamed of having a Forever or Phoenix bicycle made in Shanghai; people who already owned a Forever would tell others about how they hoped to lay hands on a Phoenix; and those who had a man's bike were greedy enough to seek out relatives who worked in shopping malls to see if they could get hold of a 24-inch women's bike. However, in an era of material scarcity such requests simply annoyed people: it would be like telling people nowadays that you wanted to borrow money to speculate on the stock exchange.

Occasionally some hot-heads who'd just acquired a new bike would race them in the streets to show off their bicycles and skill in riding them. Seeing these guys careering across the narrow streets, the bolder women would shout after them: go to hell! The cyclists didn't hear: they were enjoying the pleasures of speed too much— just like racing drivers today. There were also people who went far too slowly, which was also eye-catching. I will never forget one middle-aged man wearing an old military uniform. Maybe he was too careful of his new bike, or he was a poor cyclist, but his posture in the saddle looked very strange, his body bent so that his head was almost lying on the handlebars. He probably wasn't expecting that a whole load of people would be interested in watching him cycling. Unfortunately, he always came by our street at dusk, when we kids were out messing around in the street. I don't know why the man's posture aroused our childish disgust but we decided that he looked like a bastard. One day, we suddenly started yelling at him: Bastard! Bastard! I remember him looking back at us and then ignoring us. But the attitude he adopted did not change our inexplicable aversion to this cyclist. The next day we were waiting in the street. When he passed our territory at the usual time, the same voices as yesterday pursued him but louder and clearer: Bastard! Bastard! In the end, the poor man got angry. I remember him jumping off his bike and running towards us with fury in his eyes. Everyone fled to their homes. Of course, I ran away too, but once I got inside the front door to my house, I glanced back at him and saw him stop suddenly. He too was looking back. It was obvious that he was worried about the fate of his bicycle leaning against the wall. I'll never forget how he stood hesitating in the middle of the street. At last he turned and ran to his bike. That poor man just had to put up with our insults, in order to protect his bicycle.

My father's bicycle was a 1960s Forever. From the time of my earliest memories until I left home to go to university in the 1980s, my father rode off on it in the morning and returned in the evening. Every Sunday morning, I could watch my father in the yard wiping his bicycle over with a cloth. Nowadays I think of that bike with gratitude, because it saved my life. I was a sickly child, and many is the day that I sat perched on my father's bike on the way between home and the hospital. Once my father carried me twenty miles on that bicycle out to some village in the countryside to find a barefoot doctor in possession of some secret family herbal remedy. That twenty-mile journey was unforgettable: the first ten miles or so were through the cobbled or bluestone slab-set roads in the city centre in Suzhou (at that time, asphalt was only to be found gracing the main thoroughfares through the city), and the next ten miles was over the kind of undulating mud track found in rural areas. I was bumping along behind my father like a dinghy and my father was the experienced mariner, keeping us on an even keel. Just as he was confident in his own driving skills, he expressed complete faith in my ability to hang on. He said: It'll be fine! Don't worry! Just sit still, we'll be there soon!

How many Chinese people have a strange affection for their father's bike? How many children would get on their parent's bicycle and sneak out on a Sunday? What were they up to? Why nothing, they were just out for a ride! I remember the first time I cycled around Suzhou, I went to a small square in the centre of the city. There were three cinemas and a shopping mall around the four sides of the square. I inspected the posters in the windows of the three cinemas. They all illustrated the same model opera, *Azalea Mountain*, with its heroine Ke Xiang. However, in some of the depictions Ke Xiang had a round face and in others a long one; that allowed me to judge the quality of the posters quite quickly. Then I went into the mall and wandered around but the empty shelves didn't interest me at all. When I came out of the shopping mall, I was suddenly dumbstruck, and it was the bike that caused me this wave of panic: I discovered that the square had now become a sea of bicycles. There were thousands of them crammed together, all black, and every single one of them was as peas in a pod to my family's bike. I could remember just where I had parked it but the attendants were always moving the bicycles about. I walked round and round in a daze, the key in my hand, and in my terror, I felt the pain of the Chinese bicycle industry: they all looked the same! The colour and shape of the frame was identical—sometimes they even had exactly the same locks on! I couldn't find my bike: no matter how many times I put my key in a lock, I couldn't turn it. The attendant standing off to one side put a stop to my clueless search; she kept shouting at me: Check that it's actually your bike and then unlock it! But I had lost the ability to distinguish one from another; this was not my fault but because amazing things always happened whenever I got on a bicycle. I felt that any number of the newish Forever bikes could have had their saddles and racks imbued with my father's spirit and with mine—so how could I not be confused?

The story of every bicycle involves not being able to find it; this was not the fault of the attendants but the result of having too many bikes. I am sure that there must have been plenty of kids like myself who were constantly pestering their parents with the question: If it's so hard to get hold of a bike, how come there are so many of them about? This question is easy to answer but the answer has nothing to do with bicycles. The answer is: China has too many people.

By the end of the 1970s, Golden Lion bicycles made in Changzhou came on the market. People said that Golden Lion bikes weren't as good quality as the made-in-Shanghai Forever and Phoenix but, in any case, a new bicycle had appeared at long last. If you wanted to buy a Golden Lion, you still needed to have a ration ticket. It was pretty hard to get hold of a ticket with the 'Golden Lion' sign. One of the neighbours had a daughter whose boyfriend worked in a bike shop. That made him an object of interest to everyone in the surrounding area. They were all envying her for her marriage prospects and they kept asking what he would give his parents-in-law to be when the wedding was announced. His future father-in-law was perfectly open about it; right then and there he fished a piece of paper with blue printing on it out of his pocket and said: Oh, he didn't give us anything much, just a Golden Lion!

The glory days of the bicycle still continued but now there was a revolutionary motto: Overcome all difficulties and strive for victory. Many families in our street later tasted the victory of owning a bicycle—at least they could have a Golden Lion. However, my father pulled all the strings he could thanks to his long career in the civil service and bought a third bike for our household; he didn't want any Golden Lion, though this was mainly because of his inbuilt distrust of any such newfangled nonsense. He put his faith in

Forever and Phoenix and was prepared to redouble his efforts to secure one.

My father bought this third bike for me. It was on the eve of my graduation from middle school in 1980. They said: If you fail to get into university, you can use this bike to get to work. But I made the grade. My parents then said that the bike should stay at home: after you graduate, you can use it when you come back here to get a job. However, when I graduated, I didn't go back to my hometown to work. So my parents looked disappointed and said: We'll send the bike to Nanjing. At least it'll be useful for you there.

On a sultry early autumn afternoon, I went to a warehouse attached to the Nanjing West Railway Station to look for the bicycle that had arrived from Suzhou. The triangular frame of the bike had been carefully wrapped to prevent it suffering damage if the porters were rough in loading or unloading. I touched the tyre, which proved to be bulging: it must have been pumped up just before it was consigned for transport, and that was a sign of my parents' care and attention. I hopped on my first bicycle and left the station warehouse. The early autumn sunshine on that road in Nanjing was still hot and my heart was burning because I knew that from this day on, my life would change. Getting my bike was like hearing the starting gun that would set me racing towards a new life and it was time for me to begin running.

I used that bike for five years: a black 26-inch Phoenix. It was very similar to my father's Forever. Parents in cycling countries always choose a strong and durable bicycle for their children because they think it will be with them for most of their lives. Five years later, my bike was stolen. I felt almost as if relieved from a burden and rushed round to the nearest bike shop to pick out a ten-speed racing bicycle of the kind that was fashionable in those days. It was blue. It was a beautiful, majestic bicycle that would have been beyond my wildest imaginings as a child.

The world is changing fast—including our bicycles, and our lives. All these years later, I still like to go out for a ride on my bike and scope out young people's fancy new bicycles. Sometimes you'll see an old Forever or an old Phoenix go past in the traffic and just as an old person's face will make you think of the vicissitudes they've endured, they make you think of some of the stories about bikes in days of yore. I once rode after just such an old Phoenix for a long time. The owner was a man in his fifties. Beside him was a girl with a backpack, also on a bike, but she was riding a Giant—a very popular brand right now—an orange mountain bike. Clearly they were father and daughter. I was on my way somewhere so I wasn't paying attention to what the father and daughter said as they cycled along. But I can assure you that the two bicycles were whispering to each other as they moved along side by side. What did they say? As I am sure you can guess, it was a very simple message:

    The black old Phoenix said: Slow down! Think about the past!
    The orange Giant said: Speed up! Think about the future!

RAIN ON THE ROOF TILES

Rain twenty years ago sounded different to today. As the rain fell on the old blue roof tiles, people inside the building would hear a crisp beat like the sound of a bell. Without any exaggeration, the sound of rain on the tiles was really like music but the invisible musician was of a cranky, moody disposition. Suddenly, it would lose patience, and the rain would come down with a noise like exploding firecrackers. You might wonder if such violent rain was not a sign of worse to come but then suddenly it would get tired of that and quit. Then we would only hear the rain dripping down from the eaves, streaming down past the window, carefully, with a sense of guilt. At this time, the silent street would begin to come to life again. People wearing raincoats or umbrellas stepped out into the tail end of the rain and headed for home. There would be a voice somewhere calling out happily: The rain has stopped! Let's go home!

    The Chilean poet Pablo Neruda is a lover of rain. He said: Rain is a sensitive and terrifying force. His observation and analysis of the rain makes me feel at a loss. What makes rain sensitive? What makes rain terrifying? I'm very interested in these meaningless questions. Please imagine that a heavy rainstorm has driven all the pedestrians to seek shelter beneath the eaves of a house. Please imagine that these same people enter the building, for then even the biggest raindrops won't be able to wet your clothes and things: so what is it that experiences the sensitivity and terror of rain in our stead?

Twenty years ago, I was living in a run-down traditional house of the sort you find in the south. I was not happy with the boring architecture and construction: indeed, I was full of disdain for my house. But one summer I climbed up onto the roof of the warehouse of the cement plant across the river to practice my diving, and for the very first time, I noticed the dark blue tiles on my roof. They were arranged as neatly as fish scales, showing an unexpected magnificence. It's a special memory for me and the weather that day was also special: there was a sudden rainstorm and some of the boys practicing diving with me braved the driving rain to stay up on the roof of the warehouse. We watched the rain tumbling from the sky, washing the hot streets and houses on the opposite bank and scrubbing our own bodies clean.

It was the only time I saw my roof in the rain. The heavy rain fell on the blue tiles and what came splashing back was not spray but a kind of grey mist. When the power of the rain had been somewhat reduced, the mist dispersed and the tiles showed their simple, smooth outline again. I realised that the competition between the rain and the roof tiles was proceeding at high tempo and it was impossible to tell who was falling behind. What you could see with the naked eye was the rain washing the dust off the tiles because afterwards these old tiles suddenly recovered the gloss they would have had when new—after this sudden storm had washed them clean, they shone and the lichen on the eaves showed again the bright green colour that plants should have. For the first time, I carefully observed the way in which the rain was making music on the roof and made a new discovery: it was not the rain that made the music but the resistance of the tiles against the force of the rain.

It sounds most peculiar but from this point onwards I thought of the sound of rain as being the sound of roof tiles: I dare say this is a very personal interpretation and nothing to do with the knowledge of the natural world. However, it is bound up in my memories. All that memory gives us is our memories. I remember my home of twenty years ago. In addition to the roof in the rain mentioned above, there are also our open windows. Far in the distance, through the curtain of rain, I could see my mother through the window. She was at home, hunched over the sewing machine, working on some shirts for my older brother and I.

Now I don't remember what happened to those shirts and my mother has been dead for many years. But that rainstorm twenty years ago gave me a special affection for rain. If there's a roof covered with blue tiles, I don't think rain is a terrifying thing; if your mother ever sewed new shirts for you to the sound of the rain, I don't think you will ever truly be lonely.

This is what I know about rain.

This is what I know about tiles.

THE SECRET OF THE RIVER

For the people who live by the river, the river is a mystery.

The river bed feels the weight of the river every day but it is covered by water and constantly receives its favours. How can it reveal the secrets of the river? The fish in the river know its characteristics and their physique reflects the quality of the water. However, you know how long-suffering fish are, how taciturn and solitary. They are happy enough to blow pointless bubbles but are never going to tell the people by the river anything.

The river's secret remains a mystery.

"My love, I'll never tell you why

The river flows so slowly."

This line is from a poem by Garcia Lorca—a tease on the part of a poet who loves rivers. In fact, it is easy enough to find out why the river flows so slowly: whether it is out of exhaustion or anxiety, is it a gesture of obedience or a harbinger of resistance, whether it is because it is sleepy or because the river is making plans...

The banks are shackles for the river. The ruthless power held by the river over its bank means that the latter cannot be bothered to consider the river's true feelings. The bank shows its friendliest face to the fields, wharfs, restaurants, real estate industry and walkers but it is merciless to the river. Obviously, this tension is at the heart of the relationship between river and bank. The bank thinks it has complete dominion over the river but the river doesn't agree. People who live by the river will sooner or later discover that the river is a very complicated companion; even if the water is as clear as a mirror, there is an unfathomable mind at work. The power of the river is incalculable and in summer and autumn it may burst out in violent revolt at any moment, obliterating the arrogant banks. At this time, the usual relationship between river and bank is inverted and, because of this, everything is thrown into disorder. The people living by the river are in a state of panic and they use all the building materials they can find to block the river's door-to-door visits. No wonder they are in such a state—they are used to being the guests of water and are not prepared to welcome the river as a visitor in their own houses. In summer, residents of the riverside talk about flooding with pale faces: they say that with one rainstorm the flood beat down their doors; some people's furniture has been carried away by the river; and on such-and-such a road the cars went floating off like boats, bobbing along on the waves. They complain that the flood has ruined their lives and they don't realise that being washed out should be considered part of their everyday lives. The relationship between the river and people was established unilaterally by people, and the river wasn't asked its opinion, so it is not surprising that many people were suffering from misapprehensions. In fact, it is easy enough to understand the river's behaviour, just based on the principle of fair play. If you go to someone else's place for a party often enough, you might expect to be required to give a return invitation. Asking someone back is only polite. The character of the river and its poverty determine the hostess-gift it brings: water brings more water. The river gains in dignity in the flood season, as every few years, it reminds people that it is not to be despised. Then the flood season passes. The residents along the river find the late autumn water-level in the river to be very high. The large volume of rainwater entering the river makes it run fresh and clear. In autumn, the relationship between river and the trees on the bank becomes ever more polarised. The trees wither and the leaves fall, whipped by autumn winds, as the river looks ever more radiant and vigorous. If you're standing on a bridge across a river looking down at the waters flowing past, you'll be aware of the speed of the current—its enthusiasm is quite shocking: it is the galloping of wild horses; it is a long speech given by a political prisoner at the moment of his release; it is the annual outpouring of the river to the world, telling the bank that water is free and cannot be held back, no dam will stop it, no embankment retain it, you must let it go by. The river tells the people on the banks: none of you have the level of conviction shown by water and none of you are as lucky. The river puts its faith in the ocean and what a simple faith it is! The ocean is reliable, its broad and deep embrace is safe; the ocean accepts rivers without asking for incense or money; it does not set up a cross or promise Heaven. It just says: Come! So the river goes. When the river runs to the sea, it sings the national anthem of water, in which there are just four words. It sounds loud and devout: Head for the ocean! Head for the ocean!

Who can convey the song of the river in each of the four seasons —at once so gentle and so imperious? I can't; and I'm afraid you can't either. I have always enjoyed reading all the poems and essays about rivers that I can lay my hands on. Everyone who loves rivers and pays attention to rivers has a certain mental fluidity. Sometimes their minds can be compared to a fisherman's lantern; it can't illuminate the dark sky on the shore but it bathes the waters in a friendly light—that's worthy of respect. Whose pen is bold enough to cut straight to the heart of the river? Mine isn't, and I'm afraid yours isn't either. I mentioned before that the secret of the river is not one that can be communicated to humankind. How can praising the river dispel the growing hostility and estrangement between it and the rest of us? A person who loves a river will often say that they envy the fish. A fish belongs to the river, so it can explore the depths of the river and visit its very heart. However, who could have imagined that the relationship between fish and river has now become increasingly tenuous? News media report that fish numbers are rapidly decreasing and all of the problems with water and fish boil down to one thing: pollution. But how can the one word 'pollution' explain the revolution that has taken place in the depths of the river? Who knows whether the fish have betrayed the river or the river has expelled the fish?

Now I suddenly call to mind the back window of my childhood home. The window faced the river: please allow me to use the solemn word 'river' to designate one of the small streams so common in the south, meandering through the suburbs that fringe the cities. This waterway has a name recorded in the local chronicles but it is not one that anyone would ever use. People talked about it in accordance with a rough, informal tradition: there was the river, the riverbank, and the other side of the river. Such a river might dream all day long of meeting the Yangtze or the Yellow River but thanks to the vast distances and inhospitable terrain it could never achieve any such ambition, which left it looking miserable and attenuated. Such rivers have been subject to many years of management, and they are overburdened with mandatory tasks such as connecting urban and rural water transportation networks and dredging for water conservancy. All the signs of human development—houses, factories, docks and garbage dumps—can be found crowded along its banks and these ensure that the river feels abandoned and neglected. Of course, this is not appealing but I find this unappealing aspect of the river quite unforgettable.

As far back as I can remember, what I saw from the window was a depressed river, a polluted river, a river suffering from homesickness. It is not difficult for a child to judge whether a river is happy or not, since one just listens to its voice and looks at its running waters. But I never heard the sound of the river flowing by, for it was mostly silent. It was only when a heavily-laden barge was moored by the shore that it made a slight mumbling noise. Even a child could easily tell that it was not a happy sound. It was not the tone of a river welcoming a boat; on the contrary, the kid could easily imagine that it was the river saying go away! Leave now! In that child's eyes, much as he hated school, the river was even lazier and more negative. It was overtly hostile, and shirked its responsibilities and duty as a river. Take a look at the filthy waters in spring and you will understand—the river's attitude towards the muck floating around in it can make it seem like an annoying child. Oil, rubbish, plastic, dead cats, condoms—do what you like, I don't care! The child soon realised that there was floating garbage to be seen every morning by the embankment: the river hadn't washed the old rubbish downstream but simply returned it to the residents of the riverbank: the waters were saying: This is yours and I'm giving it back to you—nothing to do with me! As I remember it, the river's secret is an immoral one. I remember that in summer when the waters were relatively clean, I used to wash and go swimming in the river like all the other residents along the bank. Right up to the present day, I still remember the first time I opened my eyes underwater. I looked inside the river and saw the waters stretch out like a blurred sky. It was just like the sky except that, unlike air, water will prick your eyes and make them sting. This is one of the river's rules: it loves fish eyes but hates human eyes. People like to say that eyes are the window to the soul, so perhaps the river has a particular dislike of these windows.

I'm sorry that I have to describe a river of this kind in order to explore the heart of the river. In fact, the river's heart is always much richer and deeper than you can imagine, as you will see from the way my mother described the selfsame river, the stream we could see from the back window of our house. It was a wonderful story—one winter when the river was frozen, my mother rushed to the factory on the other side of the river and, being in a hurry, she went over the ice. My mother said that after the first couple of steps she really regretted it because the ice formed a very fragile and thin crust and she could hear the dangerous sound of cracking under her feet. She hesitated but it would have been even more dangerous to go back. So my mother prayed to the river and walked straight across. Guess what, she made it over to the other side safe and sound! For me, that's just a fable and I don't believe a word of it. I asked my mother how she prayed to the river and she said with a smile: How could I pray? I begged the river, let me pass… let me pass… and then the river let me across!

If you come south in winter and see the kind of rivers they have there in that season, would you believe my mother's story? You'd be as skeptical as I am about it. But perhaps the story about the river is competing with people's conceit and it may be perfectly true. Please think about how this same river became so wonderful and magnificent when my mother described it!

The heart of the river is floating in the water. No matter what kind of net you weave, you won't be able to catch it. This is the biggest secret about the river. For many years, I have been unable to forget the stories about water ghosts they have in my hometown. I have always been quite sure that those wet and shining water ghosts have mastered the secrets of the river. The reason is very simple. Those unfortunate drowned people have in the end exchanged their souls for the waters. They have seen the heart of the river and that's why these ghosts are free to go in and out of the water without being drowned again. They have obtained a key and with that they can open the secret door to the river.

But outside such legends, we will never meet water ghosts, whether on the bank at night or on a boat sailing along the river. If water ghosts are emissaries of humankind, they must have betrayed their origins and given their loyalty to water. They no longer go ashore and this is to ensure they keep the river's secrets. These ghosts have been assimilated by water and even now they must be lurking in the depths of the river, holding high their proud green heads, sending out the final cry for their motherland: people on the shore, you may have conquered the moon and space but please remember, water is invincible!

SANKESHU

Many years ago, I liked to walk along the tracks of the Beijing-Shanghai railway. At set periods, a train would appear and then it would mercilessly leave me as it sped northwards. At about one o'clock in the afternoon, the train from Shanghai to Sankeshu would come past. I looked at the white sign under the windows, reading: Shanghai—Sankeshu. I looked at the strangers through the window as they rushed past at high speed and my heart was filled with jealousy and sadness. Then the train to Sankeshu vanished as the tracks disappeared into the distance and I began to imagine the scenery at their destination: a small railway station in the north. In front of the station, there were many animals that were rare in the south, including black donkeys, white horses and big jujube-red mules. There were some deeply-tanned farmers squatting on the ground or perhaps riding around on their carts, with white sheepskin caps on their heads. There would also be trees—the three trees commemorated in the name Sankeshu, standing all by themselves out on the plain.

The three trees would be very tall and straight. I could imagine their green canopy and brown trunks but, since I didn't know what they were called, I've never been sure what kind of trees these were.

Trees make me feel frustrated, and this feeling has been repeated over and over again during my life because I've never really got to grips with trees. The children in Xishuangbanna have tropical rain forests; the descendants of the woodcutters in Daxing'anling have Korean pines and white birch trees; while kids in the countryside have tallow and locust trees. But I never had a tree. I grew up walking up and down a narrow lane, never climbing trees to look for eggs. I cannot blame growing up in a city for my lack of experience with trees because there were plenty around—avenues of paulownia and willows growing on both sides of the road—but I happened to live on a street without any trees. There were also quite a few houses along the lane that had trees: there'd be a fig or a couple of mulberry trees standing quietly in the garden outside their window but my house didn't have a garden, just a covered courtyard. There wasn't any place there to put a tree, so I grew up without one.

I tried growing my own tree. I once transplanted a Chinaberry seedling which I'd dug up at a nearby factory. I planted it in a flowerpot—not my fault. I knew that trees were different from shrubs and that one could be planted in pots but the other had to go into the ground but I couldn't plant my seedling in the ground. The fault lay in what I had to work with: the courtyard, our house, the wide step by the back door—everything was either cement or slate. That was fine for shoes, boxes or even chairs but there was absolutely nowhere for a little Chinaberry seedling to go. I could only put it in a flowerpot. I was a primary school student at that time and I brought the tree home with me. There it was in its pot—my tree—and since it was my responsibility, I put it out on a stone slab overlooking the river. A little five-inch tree was growing by my side and as spring turned to summer, it didn't get any bigger but just put out new leaves. I knew exactly how many leaves it had; not one could escape my eye. Then it was winter and I felt how the sapling's uneasiness increased day by day. The wind was strong by the river and my tree trembled in the wind, just like a crying child. I thought it was asking me for sunshine and warmth. I moved the flowerpot to the windowsill, the only place in my parents' house that got any sunshine in the winter. It was an absolute tragedy: there was a gale that very night. At the height of the storm I was snug in my warm room, fast asleep, but my sapling was out on the windowsill, bearing the brunt of the icy blast. Anyone can understand how the wind torments a tree but who could have imagined how it would humiliate me and my Chinaberry tree? It plucked my sapling from the windowsill and hurled it to the stone paving slabs, then it pulled the Chinaberry out of the pot and tossed it into the river. All that was left behind on the bank was shards of flowerpot and a heap of earth.

This is one of my memories of trees. One winter morning, I stood by the river and looked deep into the river, and saw my tree indistinctly, struggling in the water. After fighting for a while, my tree began to sink. I vaguely saw it land in the mud at the bottom of the river, swaying and trembling. Finally, it was still. I realised sadly that my tree had gone home and was gone forever. My tree had been looking the whole time for somewhere to sink its roots, only for the wind to coldly dump it in the water. Or perhaps my tree was different from other trees and could only grow in the river.

I have never had a tree and this is a source of pain and regret for me. Like many people, as an adult I have traveled to see various famous mountains. I have seen the dark green primeval forests of Xishuangbanna; I have seen Korean pines and beech trees covered in snow at Daxing'anling. I have seen countless rare trees which I had only ever heard the names of before in the National Forest Park in Western Hunan. But those trees grow out where anybody can see them, so they aren't my very own.

Where is my tree? Since it won't tell me, I can only wait for time to reveal all.

1988 was a memorable year for me. In the autumn of that year, I got my own place to live: the attic of a dilapidated building. When I collected the keys to inspect the place, I spotted two trees in front of the building. What do you think they were? Two fruit trees; a pomegranate and a loquat! The autumn afternoon sunshine glittered on the two trees, shining on the most precious gift I have ever received. Years of anxiety and melancholy disappeared, that autumn afternoon there was an answer for everything: Yes, I have a tree, two of them in fact, and the wonderful thing is they are both fruit trees!

Fruit trees are compassionate to people and pomegranates are particularly affectionate. Its luxuriant branches and leaves, brilliant flowers and abundant fruit all go to prove it. Loquats are reserved and quiet trees; when my visitors mistook it for a magnolia, it didn't care. But then in early summer it would make it quite clear that this was no magnolia, as it put out loquat fruit. Those trees were very kind to me. Now there were two trees outside my window: a pomegranate and a loquat. I felt intensely grateful to the unknown former owner who'd planted those trees. I was told their age... about fifteen years old. I thought back to my experience of planting a Chinaberry in a flowerpot fifteen years earlier and decided that none of this was a coincidence—destiny had brought me these two trees, two much bigger and much better trees. I have always suffered from depression, I worry about what is going to happen, I feel suspicion more than trust. My parents told me how lucky I was and I didn't believe them; my friends told me how lucky I was and I didn't believe them; but now those two trees told me I'd been lucky in the end and I believed it.

I am a lucky man. Those two trees closed the chasm that gaped between me and the rest of the world. Especially the pomegranate... every morning in spring and summer I would open the window and the pomegranate leaves and flame-red flowers would dance before my eyes; the flexible slender branches would not hide their desire to enter the house. If I had kept the window open, within three days, I'm sure the pomegranate would be right there by my bed, on my desk, talking to me all night long. Pomegranates are so friendly, and it would say to me: I am your tree, your tree!

The trees brought the birds with them, and the birds left their gray droppings on my windowsill. The fruit brought out any passing children: they would climb the tree to pick the fruit and the leaves would rustle. Sometimes I would appear in the window shouting at the children to get out of my trees and the children would leave with loud complaints while unripe little pomegranates would lie scattered across the ground. I could see the pomegranate putting its branches and leaves back together as if nothing at all were the matter: it reminded me that this was an accident and not an injury; it reminded me that trees offer a boundless generosity. I am not just your tree; I also belong to the children passing by!

For seven years in all, I slept in the attic of an old building up amongst the trees, and the attention the trees and I paid to each other gradually became one-sided: it was the trees watching me. Once I had my own trees, I gradually came to ignore them. Trees are always so tolerant and compassionate; they will never make up their minds to betray you. During the course of those seven years, there was precious little that the two trees didn't know about me, including my private affairs but they didn't say a word and nobody else found out about it. The trees watched over me and those seven years were enough to make up for anything. The two trees became a little tired but I didn't notice it. Later on, the two trees outside the window were even more tired and the spring rains found it easy to knock all the flowers off the pomegranate and spread them across the ground. I walked across a carpet of pomegranate petals and didn't even realise that the tree was saying goodbye. I had no idea that my trees had finished their mission and that after seven years they were about to say farewell to me.

The blueprints for urban regeneration resulted in the destruction of many people's homes, not to mention their trees. In the summer of 1995, bulldozers razed the district called Shangcheng'an. My attic, my pomegranate and my loquat tree disappeared among the twisted girders and broken bricks. The demolition workers could have preserved my two trees, at least for a few more days, but I couldn't ask them to. I understood that the two trees would have to go. I had spent seven years in a dream; that pomegranate, that loquat… neither of them was my tree.

Now there are no trees in front of my window. I still don't have a tree—in fact, trees puzzle me. Where is my tree? I have had a pomegranate and a loquat but I always thought I should have three trees, just like the name of that far-away railway station that I recall from my childhood. It was called Sankeshu—the three trees—so where is the other one? I asked this question of myself and then I heard the response from the river near my childhood home. I heard the Chinaberry sapling that had been carried away by the wind many years ago calling out to me: I'm here, I'm in the water!

A SANDSTORM

André Gide's prose-poem entitled *Les Nourritures Terrestres* records a journey through North Africa in warm, gorgeous and self-satisfied words. The beautiful scenery and the beautiful young men were equally his targets. Shepherds under palm trees, overgrown Arab gardens, beehives balanced on grayish red boulders and cool wells in the oases—an innocent heart beats behind the overwhelming praise heaped upon exotic customs. Gide, pale and sickly, is filled with lust and love under the scorching North African sun, which bathes everything in a golden glow.

Then he wrote about the desert.

"The next day, my heart was filled with love for the desert." The next day belongs to the desert. The beautiful Arab youth in his white robes got ready to leave and the desert appeared. Gide's eyes widened. It was obvious that the desert made him feel solemn, as if in a sacred place. He exclaimed: "My soul, what do you see in the desert?"

What do you see in the desert?

The desert is a sea of yellow sand. The shifting sands form billows, the ever-moving dunes. If you climb up one sand dune in the hope of being able to look to the horizon far in the distance, all you will see is another dune. The desert is a sea of yellow sand. Life is extinct but it quivers with the wind and heat waves. In the shade, the sand is extremely soft; it is burning hot in the evening and cold in the morning. Riding through the desert gorges, the horse's hooves are immediately buried in the sand—this is the desert Gide saw and it is also all that any traveller through the desert remembers, as their footprints are buried in the sand.

But the memory of the desert is eternal, the only truly golden memory those travellers will ever have.

Any mention of the Sahara reminds me of the Taklamakan Desert. I think that's the only desert travel I've ever done. We passed through the Taklamakan along the new Cross-Desert Highway, from northern Xinjiang to Hotan in the south. There was a lot of sand. It was just one sand dune after another. We were buffeted by hot winds and heat haze. No matter how I try, it is difficult to find anything that does not appear in Gide's description of the desert, apart from the tamarisks and saxauls. I don't know if those two plants are unique to the Taklamakan Desert, but it was seeing them growing in the sand and flourishing there that reminded me that there is always life in the desert, just as there are always fish in the sea. It is only fair that plants should grow here. If the desert is bleak, there are nevertheless limits to how bad it is going to get; if the desert is alien, that is not the fault of the desert but the people who insist on traveling through it. Why should tourists be tramping through the desert when they are neither merchants on caravans along the Silk Road nor nomadic tribesmen leading their camels in search of the next oasis? These people come from coastal areas far away from the desert and they cross vast expanses of sand just to see more sand.

What do you see in the desert?

The desert caravans have already disappeared over the horizon. The camels and merchants who once trekked across the desert are gone. Like a mirage in the desert, they have simply vanished. "Some caravans went east in search of sandalwood, pearls, Baghdad honey cakes, ivory and embroidery. Some caravans went south in search of agate, musk, gold and ostrich feathers. Some caravans went westward, setting out at dusk and disappearing in the dazzling sunset." The caravans finally found what they were looking for, so they disappeared from the desert, not caring how much the desert would miss them.

There can be no doubt that the desert misses and cares for people. I think of those days in the desert, the wind-blown sands, each grain riding on the breeze. The sands raced across the road, forming wavy ripples on the surface; these are the sand wreaths, guiding the car. The wind blew the sand so that it slapped against the windows of the car; the gentle movement has no hostility, if it's not a kind of welcome ceremony, then what is it? Looking at the desert through the window, the desert is monotonous and the travellers are rendered soporific by a kind of yellow haze. But then the driver is due his break and the travellers jump out of the car, and soon discover that they are surrounded not by desolation but by the hospitable and kind sand. Sand creeps into men's sneakers and women's high-heeled shoes, so soft and warm, so full of love. If you want to understand just how much the sand cares about people, try picking up a handful; you will feel the heat of sand is similar to your own body temperature, and the lightness and smallness of the grains will surprise you. The magnificent huge dunes rolling across the face of the desert and these dear little grains of sand: they are cause and effect—what a wonderful combination!

Holding a handful of sand in the desert, I thought of the sentimental André Gide's question, when he asked: "Sand, do you remember what life is? Do you remember from what kind of love you were created?"

How can the sand answer this difficult question? The real problem is that it can't speak up for itself, for life, for love. From what kind of love was the sand created? Maybe it's the secretion of love between the sea and the earth's crust when the world was young. On the other hand, maybe it's not. Sand doesn't remember the past: it only thinks about its own love affairs. Sand has loved every single traveller that traversed it, but they never return, so it is left to the sand to prove its love. Sand is helpless; the witnesses to its affections are far away and forgetful, while material evidence is so unfavourable to the desert. The old bones to be found there are proof of death; whether they were once the bones of camels, or merchants or shepherds, they are silent now. They cannot tell us whether the desert killed them through heat and desiccation or if it took them in with passionate embrace. The desert has been much distressed, so it sighs sadly at night. My travelling companions and I stayed overnight at headquarters in the desert oil fields. We could clearly hear the sand whipping through the night sky outside the window. The sound of the singing sands made the desert night seem damp and depressing and it was hard to sleep. When I went over to the window, I could see the moonlight bathing the sand dunes far and wide. The dunes were completely still but it seemed to me that this solemn and dignified pose did not conceal their concerns. The desert suffers when it is abandoned by its visitors and the sound of the sandstorms at night are its moans.

How can I prove the desert's love for travellers?

Will the yellow sand in my trouser pocket suffice? I was preparing to buy some souvenirs in a jade shop in Hotan, when I felt that there was sand in my pocket—a whole handful of yellow sand. At that time, we'd said goodbye to the Taklamakan Desert two days earlier but the sand was still hidden in my pocket, refusing to leave! Will the sand in my backpack prove the desert's feelings? I found it a week after I returned to Nanjing. I was going out and grabbed my backpack, and there was another handful of yellow sand! I don't know when it worked its way into my backpack but it proved exceptionally devoted: it followed me all the way home! But I don't want to just use these two handfuls of yellow sand to prove a great love. I have to tell you about what happened to me in May this year —an unforgettable May afternoon. As I watched, the sky in Nanjing suddenly turned yellow and the wind rose. Without so much as a phone call or letter to warn me, yellow sand filled the sky outside my window, hurling itself against the glass in a gesture of ecstatic reunion between old friends, a kind of dream come true. I saw a spectacular miracle as the roiling sands, like a galloping wild horse, fulfilled the dream of so many thousands of years and came to the city to visit all those who had travelled through it, never to return. I welcomed that bizarre sight and, as the sandstorm swirled, I could hear the voice of the desert: travellers, we've come to see you!

Meteorologists had their own explanation for that afternoon in May: a sandstorm hit the city. But many of those who had travelled through the desert said something else: The sands came visiting relatives and arrived outside the window at 5 p.m. It's flying sand on a mission from the desert. Only friends of the desert can recognise its smell in the air.

Living by the sea, André Gide understood the soul of the desert; he noted that sand wanted to be praised. Then in a moment of inspiration, he thought of Saul in the Bible. Thus he said: Saul, you searched for a donkey in the desert but you didn't find it; instead you found the throne that you did not seek.

There is no donkey in the desert; instead there is a secret throne. How can travellers understand such a mysterious story? Maybe we should ask Saul. Unfortunately, Saul has been buried in the desert by the sands of history.

OPEN AIR CINEMA

Even today, I still remember the cinema screen that was regularly set up on the threshing floor. A white screen with purplish-red edges would be propped up on two bamboo poles and the moment the lights went on in advance of a performance, it became a bright and cheerful window in the dark, lonely nightlife of the countryside. If you were still hurrying along the paths through the fields heading to the threshing ground; if you were coming from the city; if the newsreel had already started, the pace of the pedestrians picked up anxiously. The bright screen on the threshing floor seemed to them a window onto paradise. It opened, and the previously empty and boring night was thoroughly enriched.

Farm tractors, threshers and haystacks vanished beneath the crowds. Most of the farmers in the nearby villages were sitting in the front row. They would have brought benches and stools from home. On such nights, they enjoyed the rare privilege of being VIPs. Most of the viewers were kids and young people like me, of unknown origin. We were standing in among the crowd, squeezing into the front row to the sound of curses, or sitting on the ground in any unoccupied space, ignoring the pushing and complaining from all around. There were also people sitting on the opposite side of the screen: they were more aloof and preferred to watch the movie in reverse so as not to have to push and shove along with everyone else. Once the movie began, the commotion on the threshing ground gradually died down. The familiar Li Xiangyang would come on brandishing his pistol; followed by the straight-haired female guerrilla party representative Ke Xiang; the greasy-faced traitor Wang Lianju; and the sinister Japanese Captain Matsui. The children would announce their arrival in advance, only to be shushed by their parents but the fact remains that this was a reunion between the crowd and their old friends, the movie characters. The people on the threshing floor were just waiting for their friends to stop by: whether heroes or villains, they would treat you equally and enthusiastically announce your name. If it was winter, the northwest wind would play unpleasant pranks: the people who appeared in the film, men and women, would have their faces distorted by the wind. This didn't just happen to bad people; good people—even heroes—had their features mangled by that icy blast. I remember that on one windy night, the beautiful heroine Ke Xiang sang the whole of the aria 'Storm Clouds Gather' with her mouth askew.

The happiness we all enjoyed at the threshing ground finished when the words 'The End' appeared on the screen, and then there was chaos. Some women suddenly found that their kids were missing, so they shrieked their children's names. Some of the young men would suddenly start punching each other, so people had to move out of the way to avoid them. When asked what had happened, they'd say they got angry trying to watch the movie. Who had their head in the way the whole time and refused to move? Well, when it's all over, let's make them pay. At that time, I was still just a little kid. I'd go with the slightly older children of one of our neighbours to unfamiliar threshing grounds and when the movie was over, I could never see where they'd got to. Therefore, my memories of open-air movies also include those frightening walks back through the darkness.

I remember those nights when I went home alone, following the flow of people along the paths through the fields and gradually the people with me turned off to other villages, until I was the only one walking along the pitch-black ring road. The air in the country smelled quite different from the industrial zones—the fragrance of hay and the smell of farmyard manure mixed together and filled your nostrils. The open-air movie now lay far behind you and then you would realise just how long the road home could be: then a tiresome child would begin to pay the price for going to a movie he'd already seen many times. The price might be walking five miles —sometimes even ten miles—through the darkness. There was no light, just the pointless flickering of some fireflies flying aimlessly around the middle of the fields. Several times, I ended up walking alone past the largest graveyard in the suburbs and saw with my own eyes what people called 'ghost candles' (now I know that it is the phosphorus in the bones that give rise to these unearthly lights), and the trees and overgrown grass of the cemetery deepened my fears. The way I conquered my terror was by not facing up to it. I would look over to the other side of the road and run with my head turned away. I heard the wind whistling across my face as the graveyard gradually receded further and further behind me. When the dense housing in the suburban estates loomed up like mountains before me, I felt the lighted windows were like the cinema screens on the threshing floor—these were my new goal. I rushed towards the windows of my own home as eagerly as I had run towards the screen set up on the threshing floor two hours earlier.

GOLDFISH MANIA

Back in the 1970s, the monarch of a certain Southeast Asian country once visited our city for three days and when he left, he took away with him a jar of the very finest goldfish. I heard people talking about the king and the goldfish. I don't remember what variety of goldfish was involved but I do remember very clearly that it was an ordinary member of the public who presented the goldfish to the king. Some people knew him and said he was pretty stupid but he made a good thing out of his fish. They chatted not only about the king and the goldfish but also gossiped about how this man had made good.

Such were the quiet beginnings of goldfish mania.

All of a sudden, I realised that the city was full of people raising goldfish but I didn't have a single one to my name, which made me sad. It was an age when it was easy to lose but hard to gain possession of things. Goldfish just weren't available for sale, any more than flowers were. I spent ages staring with covetous eyes at the beautiful fish in a neighbour's pond: children's biggest concern is that they can't have the things they want and even my family gradually came to know of my obsession. My sisters must have told people more than once: He wants some goldfish! My mother told her colleagues in the factory: My son is just crazy about goldfish!

My ecstasy on being given my first goldfish lasted only five days. It was my older sister who brought back four beautiful 'coloured pearls'. I remember the four goldfish with white spots on their red backs and how one of the neighbour's kids told me that 'coloured pearls' are a good variety. I remember the four goldfish with silvery-white spots on their red backs and the five-day delight they brought me. During those five days, I wandered around the ponds and canals where fish breeders were to be found, trying my best to lay in stocks of ant eggs, hoarding food for my goldfish. I didn't know that my goldfish were on the verge of death from overeating.

I always remember that I had those 'coloured pearls' for just five days. On the afternoon of the fifth day, I came home from school and saw my four goldfish lying belly-up. I'm still embarrassed to mention the scene I made at that time. With all my earth-shattering wailing, I forgot to investigate the cause of the goldfishes' death. I'd never seen a dead goldfish before: they were so ugly and their transformation from beautiful to ugly seemed almost like a magic trick. I felt that I had been ridiculed—it wasn't just that I'd lost my fish but I'd been injured in the losing. My parents must have been shocked by my reaction. I remember my mother behaved most uncharacteristically, assuring me that she'd help me find a new goldfish.

Later on, my mother brought a little goldfish with a crooked tail back home, a modest and humble fish mixed in with several larger goldfish of the variety called 'Red-jade'. None of the goldfish had yet changed colour and the one with a crooked tail was only half a digit in size and so dark it was impossible to see what variety it was. It was so hideous, especially with its crooked tail, quite the opposite of what is normally considered beautiful in a goldfish. In a moment of disgust, I named it 'Crooked Tail'.

My fish-farming career came to a half-hearted end later on, not because I stopped thinking goldfish are cute, but because with the arrival of puberty I had other more important concerns. Goldfish mania gradually ebbed away across the city and my batch of 'Red-jades' were gone in the space of a few months. However, it was then that I realised the vitality of my 'Crooked Tail'. Growing up hungry and alone, it was more and more the boss of my fish tank, as its body slowly turned red and its eyes grew bigger and bigger in its head. Its reserved attitude seemed to tell me: I'm not just some crooked-tailed creature, I'm a pedigree 'Soaring Dragon'!

My story is all about this crooked-tailed 'Soaring Dragon'. After all the pretty goldfish had deserted my tank, after I had lost any interest in goldfish, it stayed with me for another four years. Four years later, I was far away from home, studying at a university in Beijing. I never thought about my crooked-tailed goldfish at all. However, one day I received a letter from my elder sister, which mentioned my last goldfish and said that Crooked Tail was dead. She'd concluded that what killed Crooked Tail was a comb. Combing her hair, she'd accidentally dropped it into the fish tank. The comb stayed down there with the goldfish for a while. The comb was OK but the goldfish died.

I admit that it was the death of Crooked Tail that made me review my brief fish-farming career. In the final analysis, I let those poor little things down badly. But everything is predestined: I was never going to get anywhere keeping goldfish. I would never have been able to give a pedigree goldfish to any king since I couldn't even look after my one Crooked Tail. It was a very determined little fish, and when it decided the time had come and I no longer deserved it, the comb was how it went.

OUR LOVELY LADIES

The three of them left such a deep impression on me just because they were living an alternative lifestyle—though, of course, we didn't use words like that more than twenty years ago. In the conservative yet worldly-wise streets of my old hometown, people would call them glamour-girls but with an ambiguous tone of voice. (Please note that 'glamour' can mean either conspicuously fashionable or promiscuously sexy, so men would use this term with pleasure while most women would speak of them through gritted teeth).

So what kind of women were these glamour-girls? Obviously they were very good-looking. Going by their appearance, the three of them could be divided into the Classical, Western and Shanghai schools. The Shanghai school needs some explanation. She was originally from Shanghai, where she grew up in one of the modern housing estates, and she had the typical laziness of a metropolitan beauty. Her languor would be a nuisance in a lesser woman, but it gave her a wonderful charm. This Shanghainese glamour-girl had married an overseas Chinese guy from Holland, and he worked in a nearby cement plant, but really you'd never have guessed—she just ignored the mundane details of everyday life. She'd carry a blue and white rattan basket with her when she went out shopping to buy her daily vegetables but, more often than not, there'd only be fruit inside. Her interfering neighbours would peer into her basket and ask: Why didn't you buy any vegetables? What on earth are you going to eat today? Our Shanghainese glamour-girl would say: Who cares? The vegetables weren't fresh so I'll just be eating fruit!

When discussing women, of course, we have to talk about their clothes. In the 1970s, beautiful women certainly weren't finding it easy but, as I remember it, none of these three women were willing to let themselves go. They dressed themselves with the utmost care, and they were three bright spots in the gray and dreary streets. At a time when everyone else wore overalls or military uniforms, they were dressed in high-collar sweaters and white bell-bottomed trousers; when high collars and bell-bottomed trousers became fashionable among the young, they wore cheongsams and woollen skirts; when other women's hair was cut in a short bob to the ears, their hair was permed into all manner of waves; when other people began to go in for perming, and women's hairdressers were full of customers, their hair hung loose in the newest 'natural' style. In this way, the three of them were almost cruel in the way they made the clothing and hairstyles of other women look frumpy. They were very proud and always presented a united front, they would occasionally meet in the street and say hello, exchanging a few words but, unlike beautiful peacocks, they never competed in front of the public. This was no doubt facilitated by the different life experiences of the three: Shanghai school and Western school were married but our Classical glamour-girl was much younger than the other two and she wasn't even engaged yet.

The story behind our Western school glamour-girl was something like a French film, romantic, sentimental, and deep. You can imagine what Western school looked like from her name. She was born and raised in our street but, somehow or other, she looked almost Italian. Out of the three of them, she was the most vulgar in character and would often swear: that made the teenagers who worshipped her feel excited and also a little nervous. Her legend was born with her love story, with the face of the thin, pale man behind her. When she stood in the doorway dressed in her nighty on a summer afternoon, inspecting the street with a bored gaze, her sluttish eyes gave male passers-by quite the wrong impression—they thought that their luck was in. But there would always be a man lurking behind her in that dark narrow lane; the sexy woman watching the street, the silent man watching his wife... that is an image I've never forgotten. As we all knew, when she was still a girl, she got into endless difficulties because of her behaviour—she was what would now be called a troubled teen. She often ended up at the police station and there she was interrogated by a young household registration officer who fell madly in love with her and had followed her around ever since. As you may have guessed, she ended up marrying the young officer—he was her husband. Of course, in those days, marrying a woman for no other reason but her beauty was bound to be the subject of criticism. He took a lot of cold-shouldering because of their relationship and in the end he was forced out of a highly desirable job in the police because of it. When you saw how pale his face was, well, it was pale for a reason.

Last of all, I'm going to talk about Classical school but her story is one that I hate to think of. Every day on my way to school, I would pass her door and I often saw her. She really was incredibly lovely but she was embarrassed by her own beauty—she seemed not to know what to do with herself. When she went out for a walk she'd stare down at her feet; the reason why she was considered such a classical beauty was because of her reserved manner. What's more, she was known to be very filial. Her father, who used to run a butcher's shop, said that his daughter always put dinner on the table before she went out to meet her friend. And who was this friend? The son of a retired general. People gossiped that she and the general's son were engaged in 'bourgeois corruption' (that was how people at the time talked about any relationship between a man and a woman, and shouldn't be seen as particularly critical). But in this case, 'corruption' came with consequences, as some of the local women started a venomous rumour: "The butcher's daughter's got herself knocked up!" That story put a new light into the eyes of her admirers but they were to be disappointed. Who could have imagined that so modest a girl would take her boyfriend out to a bamboo forest in the suburbs to try and force him to marry her and then end up giving him three slaps across the face! Later, it was said that those three slaps ruined everything, which is frankly idiotic. The general's son was a strapping young man who ought to have been able to cope with a slap from a girl. However, he was insisting that even if she was pregnant he was still going to break up with her and that was what made her angry enough to hit him. When she started slapping him he grabbed her by the neck—that was the end of this unfortunate affair, because she was strangled to death by her boyfriend in a bamboo forest out in the suburbs on a cold winter's night. In fact, her boyfriend worked in a factory not far from the bamboo forest. Well informed people privately said that they'd had sex that night (even if this was what the forensic examination said, it was still shameless).

People's fates, including those of the beautiful, can be utterly incalculable. I wrote this piece one afternoon many years later, bringing together some scattered memories. I never saw any of these women again but I still remember one afternoon more than twenty years ago when I went to the grocery store on my street and saw our Classical school glamour-girl leaning on the counter chatting with the saleswoman. That would have been the last autumn before she died. She was showing some colour photos to the salesgirl. They'd been sent to her by the Shanghainese glamour-girl, who'd just moved to Hong Kong. I took a glance and saw her leaning against a tree, still smiling lazily. It seemed like she was in a garden and the photo was particularly gorgeous because it was still rare to see colour pictures at that time. I still remember how Classical school sighed as she leaned over the counter. "Oh, how lovely Hong Kong is!" she said. "Look at her... Isn't she gorgeous!"

THE SEAMSTRESS

The seamstress was a little strange—her job was making clothes for other people, and the majority of her work took the form of traditional Chinese cotton padded jackets and overcoats, and as a sideline she also sewed shrouds. My mother once invited her to come to our home to make clothes and she produced my father's Chinese-style camel-hair padded jacket and my grandmother's shroud. At that time, the seamstress was about sixty years old and her hair was already gray but it was combed up into a neat, glossy bun and she wore a double-breasted black coat with a white orchid pinned to her buttonhole. She came to work with a basket on her arm every morning and my father set up a door-leaf to make a work table for her. She sat there sewing, wearing a pair of bifocal glasses, and she would open her mouth slightly, as if matching the rhythm of the thread. I noticed that her front teeth were gone, so no wonder she wheezed when she spoke. That whistling was loud and made it difficult to understand what she was saying. She wasn't the sort of old woman who likes to chat; she seldom spoke while she was at work but she liked to hum a tune or something. The seamstress, thanks to her superb craftsmanship, could also demand a really expensive lunch from her employers—she asked for meat every day. That was wonderful for me: for the couple of days when she was working at our house, I too ate braised pork. One time, I noticed a yellowed old magazine at the bottom of her basket and when I took it out, it turned out to be a 1930s movie magazine with pictures of all kinds of female stars unknown to me posing in strange getups. The magazine seemed really exotic and special, and I asked her for it. She took hold of the magazine and shook it a few times but nothing fell out, so she said generously: Take it.

Although the seamstress gave me an unexpected gift, my mother didn't like her because when she paid her she was short fifty cents and the seamstress absolutely refused to accept less than full payment. This made her seem cold and demanding.

The seamstress lived in Kunshan. I don't know why she came as far as us or where she rented a house. She often appeared in our street and several times when I went to school, I saw her sitting like a child at the gate to the chemical plant, letting another old woman comb her hair, sweeping it up into that over-neat bun. Her basket with its sewing box, scissors and ruler was tucked away under the bench. There was a sewing box, a pair of scissors and a ruler. I guess this must have been one of her days off, when nobody had hired her to sew.

The next year, the seamstress rented a room in a neighbour's house, so she was living next door. Every year, during the winter and summer holidays, there'd be two Kunshan dialect-speaking children joining her in her rented room and they wouldn't play with the other kids in the street. The two of them—brother and sister— would be locked up in the room, squabbling and making a racket. A very fine looking old gentleman would be looking after the two kids in between reading his newspaper: apparently the children were the seamstress's grandkids and the old man was her husband. From this point on, the seamstress's life aroused a great deal of interest in us. What did it mean when an old couple are so very different from each other? Someone asked the seamstress about this. The seamstress waved her hand and said: They're so annoying, I can't stand living with them. In another couple of days I'll make them go back!

In fact, we didn't know whether the seamstress was really tired of her family but after the holiday, her husband and grandchildren went back to Kunshan, leaving behind the seamstress walking up and down our street with her basket. Perhaps it was because she was getting on and her eyes weren't what they used to be but at some point (and I can't remember which clear-sighted housewife it was) someone noticed that her sewing skills had deserted her. She'd managed to make the sleeves of a jacket different lengths, and the women started talking about it behind her back, saying: What on earth does this look like! I'll never employ her again!

After that, it seemed that no one asked the seamstress to come and work for them at home and she became more and more frail. Once I saw her go out to the communal kitchen to get hot water and she was hobbling along as if she were on her last legs. Besides, she had two red medicinal plasters pasted on her forehead, left and right. Her expression as she looked at the passers-by was full of disgust but she did not know that her own appearance was quite hideous.

On the eve of Chinese New Year, she had some visitors come from Kunshan. One was a middle-aged man wearing glasses; the other a middle-aged woman who was obviously a Party cadre. They turned out to be the seamstress' son and daughter-in-law. With wooden, set faces they bundled the crippled old seamstress and an indigo-printed bundle of her belongings onto the back of a bicycle rickshaw and carted her off down the road, heading for the railway station. The seamstress was so wrapped in a scarf that only a pair of eyes could be seen. Her eyes were filled with resentment but this was not directed at her son or daughter-in-law, or even at us onlookers. She didn't even say goodbye.

When everyone was gone, we children broke into the room rented by the seamstress out of sheer curiosity. What we found in that dark and humid room was just piles of garbage, and Chairman Mao's portrait had been blackened by smoke. Under the bed there was a heap of newly-burned paper money. One sharp-eyed child found a copper censer, a candlestick and two red candles of a kind rarely seen on the market in those days. Guess what that strange old woman must have been doing yesterday? She was burning incense and worshiping Buddha—she was practicing feudal superstition!

Confronted with the evidence at the scene of the crime, we kids were deeply indignant. We all felt that it was a very serious matter… it would have been quite right to have a struggle session against her, and perhaps she should even have been paraded through the streets. Unfortunately, she'd gone now, which meant that she had got away with it.

I always thought that there must have been more to know about that old seamstress and I've often found myself recalling the expression in her eyes that last time I saw her. Hatred is always mysterious. One day I asked my mother about her, and she said the seamstress kept herself to herself and was never willing to talk about her past. But according to my mother, she'd had a colleague at the factory who also came from Kunshan and knew all about the seamstress: she'd originally been a nun!

I still find it hard to believe that amidst the turmoil of the 1970s, among all the weird and wonderful folk I met then, there could be such a person as the old seamstress. It's strange to say that whenever the seamstress's face appears in my mind's eye, I always think of the street in the twilight twenty years ago and an old woman clutching a basket, walking home alone in the twilight. Moreover, I always think of two lines from one of Chairman Mao's poems:

"*The rolling hills sea-blue,
the dying sun blood-red.*"

WOMEN'S VOICES

I only lived in Suzhou for eighteen years all told. I grew up on a street with a strong market atmosphere. There were no big mansions on our street, so I never got to know any upper-class girls. Some of the local families did have pretty daughters but that kind of girl would be shy. She'd spend her time shut away in her room and God alone knows what she was doing in there all day. So if I talk about the women in Suzhou, the only ones I am confident about depicting are actually market-women but then I have always maintained that the difference between these women and the rest is nothing but a matter of language and voice. Maybe some of my more conservative readers won't like it but I am going to talk about voices: a story about three Suzhou women's voices.

The first woman: her voice is concerned with the famous art of Suzhou *pingtan*...

If you walked down the road and happened to meet Min'er's mother, you'd never guess that she was a *pingtan* performer. But if someone told you: that Mrs Yan, the woman over there with the white silk scarf on, she used to be a *pingtan* artiste... you'd say: Oh, sure, she must've been a *pingtan* performer. How can you tell whether someone was a performer or not? I can't explain but I guess it was because her voice was so clear and there was a kind of sing-song note to it. She also had eyes that could speak to you and, even more important than that, there was a kind of smile in them, the way that professional artistes have.

As I remember it, Mrs Yan loved bright sunshine and manifested this through her extreme enthusiasm for drying quilts, sweaters, radishes... and she would even put her slippers out in the sun to bake. She adored the sunshine, but her husband preferred to ignore it, sitting by the door of his house with a teacup in his hand, playing chess with his cronies. Mrs Yan would be running back and forth past her husband with a rattan carpet beater while her mother-in-law would also be sitting at the door, neither playing nor watching the chess game in progress. She'd turn an indifferent gaze on her daughter-in-law as she rushed around, from time to time straightening the blanket across her knees. It seemed as though the old woman thought it was natural for her daughter-in-law to be so busy; her eyes were saying: I've been busy all my life. Now it's your turn. Mrs Yan just gritted her teeth and got on with it. I remember her beating the quilt all over as it hung from a pole up in the air, telling her neighbours in her unique sing-song voice: The weather is so good, just right for sunning our quilts!

This *pingtan* artiste had two sons: one of them had been sent down to the countryside and was working on a farm in Northern Jiangsu Province—he came back once a year for New Year's. He looked very much like his mother, a really handsome guy but somehow he was too pale and always seemed depressed. Min'er was her younger son, another good-looking child but he was known to all as a problem youth and spent his whole time getting into trouble. The parents of other children would come to the door, wanting to complain and then Mr Yan, as always, would retreat to one side and shout into the house: Come out! Come out right this minute! Mrs Yan would then emerge from behind the door curtain to deal with whoever had turned up... but she didn't come out like ordinary people would—she came out as if she were appearing on a stage, walking forward with a smile on her face like an artiste greeting her audience when, in fact, she was confronting a couple of irate neighbours. It was always the same: she'd begin by enumerating all her son's faults and then move on to analyse what had happened—sometimes she'd just be guessing but this would make the neighbours feel that she was keeping a close eye on the faults of the younger generation. When you began to nod and agree, the former *pingtan* artiste would get to work soothing you down with a word here and a word there: she was terribly persuasive. The burden of her remarks was that it takes two to quarrel, what she meant was that boys will be boys—it's normal for them to get into fights. Their parents shouldn't be making a mountain out of a molehill: all this quarrelling just made good neighbourly relations impossible. Her professional narrative techniques made sure that every word was spoken in a calm and good-natured tone so that even if the complainants were not really convinced, they simply couldn't keep up the argument, so they'd always end up slinking off shamefacedly. Because of her outstanding achievements in dealing with such matters, other women in the street often gathered around to study how she got rid of these people. However, as I am sure you can predict, it was quite useless; this was not a skill to be learned by any amount of observation. Besides which, it is not every woman who could have made it as a *pingtan* performer like Min'er's mother.

In those days, all of our local *pingtan* troupes would have been disbanded. I don't know where Mrs Yan worked—every so often I'd see her rushing down the street carrying a cloth bag, greeting people with her clear voice all along the way. I wondered to myself, what did she look like when she was performing in the theatre and who was her partner? Did she know how to sing Yu Hongxian's famous aria: "I lost my proud poplar, and you your willow"? Of course, I don't know any details about her career as a *pingtan* artiste. I know that many singers have to exercise to train their voices but she never did, so her wonderful voice was wasted in talking with the neighbours about the sunshine and her quilts. Isn't it a shame to live like this? I couldn't ask her this question, and she just spent her days basking in front of her house, and walking up and down the street. Many years later, the local *pingtan* troupes started performing again and there were posters up outside the theatres in the city centre with the names of the artistes—when I went past, I could not help looking for Mrs Yan's name. However, as the programme listed one performance after another, I never saw the name of Min'er's mother. I asked my mother: Wasn't Min'er's mother supposed to be a famous *pingtan* artiste? How come she isn't performing? My mother didn't know the reason but she speculated that Mrs Yan must have left the troupe.

Pingtan later came back into fashion in our city. It wasn't just in the theatres any more, you could hear it over the radio loudspeakers and even in some of the teahouses; there would be a famous or unknown artiste chattering away and then singing an aria, blah, blah, blah... but Mrs Yan wasn't one of them: she just stayed at home the whole time. Strangely enough, she was no longer busy sunning her possessions all over the place. I once saw her standing by the door wearing a black woollen coat, directing her husband to collect a basket of dried turnip strips. Her husband was unable to manoeuvre the bamboo basket through the narrow door. Her mother-in-law was trying to help but she shook so much that her assistance was worse than useless: the dried radish fell all over the ground. What surprised me was Mrs Yan's response to this. It was completely out of character. With her willow eyebrows slanting upwards, she shrieked in ringing tones: How stupid you are! You can't even move some dried radish without me!

Mrs Yan wasn't angry about the dried radish—it was her illness. I later learned that she was far too sick by then to be out sunning her quilts: she had breast cancer. I heard that she'd had one of her breasts removed by the doctor. Her singing voice was also lost to the disease. The neighbours grabbed hold of her son—that was Min'er—in the street one day and asked: How is your mother? Min'er twisted his head round and said: She's sick. What's that got to do with you? The neighbours all stuck their tongues out in amazement.

"Mrs Yan is such a nice woman," they declared. "What could she possibly have done to deserve a son like that?"

Later on, Mrs Yan died. A coloured photo of her taken in the 1960s was hung up on the white cloth as a commemorative portrait, and she looked very beautiful and charming in that picture, with the corners of her mouth full of humour. In Suzhou, funerals are open to anyone who would like to attend, so everyone went to offer their condolences. We could see that her husband, mother-in-law and even her annoying son were all crying. How could they not? The pillar of the house was gone; even the neighbours were crying, how could they fail to do likewise? In the future, no one would ever use such a wonderful voice to talk about housework and their children again.

To be honest, standing by her coffin, I was more curious than sad because I was distracted by looking for evidence of this woman's artistic career. High up on the snow-white gable I noticed a pipa; it seemed that it had been hanging there for many years. With the wailing and lamentation of her funeral, the pipa had been forgotten by all. I thought someone might have considered putting it beside the dead woman. But what would that avail? I couldn't explain. I just felt that one half of this woman's life had been spent on our street but that was just the shell and shadow of her real life which had escaped us. Where had it gone? Perhaps it was to be found on the stage of a theatre, buried in the dust. I tried to imagine that other life… how she would have held that pipa in her hands and how she would have sung—I never even heard her perform *pingtan* once. I decided that my imagined picture of her was absurd. It is true enough that she was a *pingtan* artiste and she also lived right by our house… so why is it that I never once heard her perform?

There is no answer to this question, so I will have to let it rest. Let me now describe the voice of the second woman—this has nothing to do with *pingtan* but is concerned instead with a loudspeaker.

The woman I am talking about now also had the sweetest voice, so it was not surprising that she was employed at the factory opposite our house to broadcast announcements over the loudspeakers. Her voice had to be sweet, otherwise it would have been unfair. There were so many young women workers in that factory who could speak mandarin perfectly, so why should she be making the broadcasts? She had a slight lisp after all and pronounced 'yes' as 'yeth' while 'class enemies' became 'clath enemith'.

In the morning, I was often roused from sleep by her voice: I don't say woken up because I am trying to be factual and that soft, gentle tone would never wake anyone up. Her voice would emerge from the loudspeaker opposite with the breathy buzz of an industrious honey bee and you would slowly be roused from your sleep. I heard her say: The article says... and what would follow would be a text taken from the newspaper. There were loads of broadcasts of that kind in those days but since at that time I was a silly boy, I liked to take things literally and when I heard her say "the article says..." I would wonder what on earth she was talking about. Articles aren't people, they don't talk, so how can they say anything?

I always thought that the woman broadcaster was wrong in what she said but that was entirely the result of my own mistakes and prejudices. My mother worked in the same factory and sometimes I would go there to have a bath or eat lunch. On the road running through this industrial area, I would occasionally see a slim young woman with her hair done in two braids. She'd also be wearing blue overalls but both the shirt and trousers had obviously been modified to fit the curves of a woman's body. Moreover, her overalls were free of any dust or oil. Instead of working tools or machine parts, she'd be carrying a rolled-up newspaper or a magazine. She looked as lovely as a lotus floating on the surface of a clear pond. I knew that she was the one I could hear over the loudspeakers: "The article says..." When "the article says" went for a walk through the factory, many people—men and women—would go over to greet her, from which it can be seen that she was a popular figure, which was also perfectly normal. As far as I know, no matter whether in a factory, out in the countryside or at school, at that time anyone making announcements had to be rated 'excellent' in all regards. If her relationship with the masses wasn't great, then you'd have other people complaining about why should she be sitting in the broadcasting room reading articles and grasping the revolution when we have to sweat it out promoting production at this cement kiln? You also had to have a high level of knowledge, otherwise you might misread and thus misunderstand the spirit of the pieces in the *People's Daily* and *Red Flag*! If your ideological awareness was not high, that would be even more dangerous. Suppose that you made use of your position to proclaim reactionary slogans—then where would we be? So I was quite sure that the female broadcaster would be an outstanding member of the Party but I still had reservations about her "the article says..." Could she really not put it another way?

One autumn, the loudspeakers of the factory on the other side of the river suddenly went silent for a few days and then a strange girl's voice took over. This girl stammered, showing that she was a new recruit on the broadcasting front. She said in a nervous voice: Next, please listen to some revolutionary songs. After waiting for a long time, the revolutionary songs still weren't playing and the silence went on and on. She couldn't get the music to play. The nervous voice returned and in even more tense tones proclaimed: Today's broadcast is over. Goodbye comrades.

This new broadcaster seemed quite depressing. Nobody likes to make invidious comparisons but I reckon in those days when "the article says" suddenly disappeared from the broadcasting station, there must have been plenty of people like me in the area covered by the factory's high-pitched loudspeakers, wondering: Where is "the article says"? What's happened to "the article says"?

My connection with the broadcasts coming from across the river was suddenly severed. Without really being aware of it, I had become used to and relied on a woman's voice... I didn't know that before. It's not true to say that I missed her voice but certainly I hated the new girl's sharp and harsh tone. I also now started to hate the factory broadcasting station. Every morning when the prelude of 'Sailing the Seas Depends on the Helmsman' woke me up, I would cover my ears in pain, yelling: "What is this racket?"

I'd better explain what happened to the woman broadcaster, since it's not much of a story. That New Year's Day—or was it the Spring Festival? I can't remember—anyway, on the occasion of a holiday in the early 1970s, my mother took me to a theatre to see a performance. Any performance in those days would involve a model play being performed again and the performances were always built up out of the same materials. First, there'd be a vigorous choral number and then there'd be a model play. If it was difficult to put together a whole model play, then let's have a few individual acts. The battle-of-wits scene from the play *Shajiabang* began… and who was that playing sister-in-law Ah Qing, standing under the sign of the Chunlai Teahouse? I felt she looked familiar and then suddenly I heard the audience next to me frantically and proudly sing out her name, saying, "That's the announcer from our factory! She's playing sister-in-law Ah Qing!"

It was indeed the woman broadcaster who had disappeared for so long. It turned out that she'd gone to join a propaganda team, which was a promotion. Out of habit, I was happy to be part of her audience. I heard her sing the line: "this useless man may yet come good…" and I started to hum along; I saw her pointing her finger at Hu Chuankui and Diao Deyi, and thought this gesture was more heroic than Hong Xuefei's. At that moment, she was sister-in-law Ah Qing! I forget her shortcomings when broadcasting over the loudspeakers: she wasn't "the article says" any longer—she was perfect in every way. But that was nothing. After *Shajiabang* came an excerpt from *The Legend of the Red Lantern*. Li Tiemei, with her long braid and red coat, came onto the stage. What I remember most is the roar of approval from the audience, then I heard some people say in amazement: "Wow! First she's playing Ah Qing and then little Tiemei! That's amazing!"

It was her, the woman broadcaster! Sitting in my seat in the theatre that day, I suddenly understood the inevitability of her disappearance from the radio station. She was amazing! In the 1970s, people didn't talk about how so-and-so was gifted and I didn't know what it felt like to worship a woman. But from then on, I understood that a woman can indeed be highly talented. Was "the article says" a broadcaster? Was she sister-in-law Ah Qing? Or was she Li Tiemei? Who the hell was she? I guess she was like a kaleidoscope; shake her, and she'd turn into someone else.

Now please recall Diao Deyi's comments on sister-in-law Ah Qing in *Shajiabang*. Diao Deyi says in startled and admiring tones: This woman is remarkable… Whenever I hear a falsetto voice singing I remember that woman broadcaster. Of course, I am talking about her in her youth. What happened later on? Someone is sure to ask. I don't want to go into what she is like now. The edges and corners of now are so sharp and so boring, just like the fate of most of us. Sometimes the brilliant limelight kisses your forehead only once and then disappears; that was the case with the female broadcaster I'm talking about here.

When I write a story, I like it to be perfectly consistent but what happened to her is far from that. Later on, she got married and her husband was another of the key workers in the propaganda team. When they got married, they lost the chance to perform on the same stage. It was not that they weren't working hard and getting better all the time but the propaganda team was disbanded and everyone returned to their jobs. Somehow or other she didn't go back to the radio station again, so she ended up doing various odd jobs for the union. Then she had a daughter and, a few years later, another daughter. After a few decades passed, she became a grandmother. In the 1990s, she was still as slim as ever but her face was deeply wrinkled, giving people a weather-beaten impression. This did not do much for her charms. She would go out to buy vegetables and take her grandson to the bathhouse for a wash, and her voice was still clear and sweet, but all she ever talked about was family matters and boring things like that. All of this goes to show that the female broadcaster of my story belongs to the past because now her life had become utterly mundane. The former female broadcaster now walks through a desolate and dying factory; an industrial zone where production has ceased is shockingly quiet. But no matter how quiet it gets, she cannot hear her own voice as it was in her younger days, echoing through the factory: "The article says..." There are more and more newspapers being printed nowadays, and more and more articles appear every day; "the article says..." but what has that to do with her? Nothing; she's out of work now.

The article in the newspaper says that competition will lead to the creation of new jobs. I don't know who she's supposed to be competing with and I don't know whether she is wondering where she should be going to find another job.

I don't want to talk about being laid off and trying to find another job because I want to talk about the third woman—her life also depended on using her voice but in a more vulgar and secular way. Her voice was not beautiful and, indeed, a lovely voice would have been useless for her purposes because it was mainly used to sell vegetables and fish.

She stood out among the women in the neighbourhood. What made her outstanding was nothing to do with her appearance: her face was quite ordinary, even a little vulgar-looking; and it wasn't her clothes either, since what she wore was the same as everyone else. Whatever the majority of women her age had on, she'd be wearing too. Her unique qualities lay in her occupation. In the era when the urban population was strictly prohibited from engaging in private economic activity, she still made a living by selling vegetables. She was a market hawker!

She was a market hawker, which ensured that all the local kids were quite sure there was something fishy about her. Knowing that she was the subject of constant speculation gave her a furtive, guilty look. But strangely, no one ever actually saw her selling any produce. People said she would go far away to collect vegetables and then went to the farmers' markets to sell them. These ideas about her business practice were nothing but conjecture; they were never confirmed by seeing it with their own eyes. This was the most remarkable feature of this hawker and the focus of a lot of comments from her neighbours. Some people who knew her well said that she was shy and easily embarrassed. She didn't like the idea of her neighbours getting into her business.

Her husband was a factory worker who spoke with a terrible stammer. He'd found her in some farming village out in the countryside and married her, and they had three children together but he'd never been able to wangle a proper job for her. Bringing up a family when you only have one person earning is very difficult. Although this woman was born a peasant, she wasn't willing to lead the simple and hard life of her kind. When she saw a watch on someone else's wrist she wanted one too... and she'd also like a sewing-machine such as she'd seen in one of the neighbours' houses. Other women thought that she was too competitive but if you are going to compete you have to get off your arse, so that's what she did. She started selling vegetables.

As a market hawker, her movements were uncertain. Sometimes she'd disappear for days on end. This would often happen in the golden season, when she could make a good profit on her trade. She went out early and came back late, and the only people to catch sight of her would be her own family. Not that there was much point in seeing her. In general, she moved through the streets empty-handed (I don't know where she kept her baskets of vegetables) and from the dust she was covered in, you would think she'd just returned home from work in a textile mill. But at other times she'd stay at home idle for several days at a time, with a needle and thread in her hand, sitting at the door and chatting with her neighbours about this and that. As a market trader, of course, she had the same interests as the rest of them: she liked to watch any fun that was going. If there was a couple quarrelling or a father beating his son, she'd be right there front and centre. She never said much, obviously, because she was worried about getting into a slanging match. But you could learn a lot from looking at her expression; you could see at a glance who she was sympathising with or blaming and which side she'd come down on. Later, we understood that this was a great way to put a stop to the worst of the gossip about her own activities—she wouldn't do anything, she'd just stand in her own doorway looking at other people airing their own dirty laundry: that was very clever!

She was illiterate but good with numbers. When any of her neighbours were selling off stuff they didn't want, they'd all drag her over to run through the figures, to make sure they weren't being cheated somehow. Such arithmetic skills were undoubtedly beneficial in her career as a hawker. She was very popular and never offended anyone except her husband and children (she often scolded them for their stupidity and obstinacy). Therefore, for all that she was engaged in criminal activity, she received due respect and understanding from her neighbours. On one occasion, we kids heard a lot of racket coming from her house, which was terribly exciting. We all rushed to her door to see what was going on. However, her two sons and a daughter stood staunch, blocking the door like iron generals: only adults were allowed in, children could not enter, and they were pretty foul-mouthed about it too. They seemed to understand the humiliation their mother had just suffered. She had been brutally maltreated at the market by law enforcement officers. The scales had been broken; the vegetable baskets trampled on; and their mother had been beaten up. As she cried inside the room, her children very sensibly sent the adults in to comfort their mother. They were hoping that some of these well-spoken and thoughtful women would find a way to cheer her up. However, they soon discovered that her sorrows were complex and not easy to resolve. She suddenly screamed: "What a hard life I've had!" This kind of shrill cry just confused the children but the adults understood exactly what she meant. Although her daughter was only fourteen or fifteen years old, she must have understood how much her mother suffered in being a market trader. So she stood behind her two brothers, helping them to block the door, crying about her mother all the time.

This brings us to the subject of her children. There's nothing much to say about her daughter. She was a bit stupid but very sweet-natured. Later on, she married an honest, hardworking young man. His family was poor so, as a result, even the furniture in their new house was bought by the woman market trader. The generosity of the dowry the girl was provided with surprised everyone. They said they had no idea that she'd got so rich from selling vegetables over the years. All sorts of unexpected things happened to her family. Her oldest son grew up and just when he was getting ready to be sent down to the countryside, suddenly one day he got sick with a heart problem and then next thing anyone knew he was found dead in his bed. The woman hawker got seriously ill but eventually she recovered. She said to one of the neighbours she was friends with: "I can't stay lying on my back. My elder son's gone but the younger one is still with us. I've got to go back to work." The neighbour understood just what she meant, "going back to work" meant selling vegetables. That poor woman! She went back to work for the sake of her younger son when she was still wearing mourning for her older boy.

Her younger son was a handsome and likeable kid but difficult. He was one of those classic teenaged boys that won't learn anything and is forever getting into fights. There was an endless stream of parents coming to the door to complain that their children had been bullied by him. When the woman wasn't at home, her husband dealt with it, and his technique was to slap his son across the face. After many years of boxing his ears like this, suddenly one day, the father's hand was firmly grasped and his chest was hit by a heavy punch. "Fuck you," the son said, "if you hit me again, I'll kill you."

That's what her only surviving son was like. Everyone predicted he'd come to a bad end. Only his mother blindly constructed a blueprint for her son's happiness. In the end, however, that blueprint was ripped in two by her son himself when he got into serious trouble. He stabbed a watermelon seller in the guts with his pocket-knife and was arrested by the police at the scene of the crime. When the woman heard the news and rushed over to find him, people showed her the blood in front of the watermelon stand. The woman ignored the blood; she just wanted them to let her son go. Of course, the police ignored her. That brainless kid ended up being sent off to a Reeducation Through Labour camp.

The neighbours remember that afterwards the woman hawker had another serious illness. She was bedridden for a while and even her husband wondered whether she'd survive the blow. However, as I've already mentioned, she was an unusual woman, not just in the profession she'd adopted, but in her strength of mind and faith. After visiting her son, she soon regained her confidence in life. She complained to her neighbours that the law was unfairly enforced by some people. There were kids who got into fights and killed people, but they weren't sent to prison—it was all a matter of connections. She didn't have connections, so her son had to suffer. The neighbours didn't have the heart to question her selfless maternal love, so they asked her what she was going to do in the future. The woman wiped away her tears and a tough, positive smile appeared at the corners of her mouth as she said: "What can I do? I have two hands, so I'll go out and make some money. When he comes out, I'll make him the money to get married and have a family!"

The woman miraculously continued her career. As the Reform and Opening Up policy expanded, she too grew her business. Afterwards, her neighbours said that she didn't just sell vegetables any more but also fish and shrimp. In autumn, she also travelled to Yangcheng Lake and even Hongze Lake, selling the big crabs that were fashionable right then. Another neighbour saw her buy gold rings and necklaces in a department store, though she turned around and denied it straight away. She flat out lied and said that she couldn't afford it and was only looking to see what they had.

When her son was released from the Reeducation Through Labour camp, the bad boy who disappeared for a few years had grown up into a tall and handsome young man. All of the maternal love she'd been storing up for years finally had a focus and the lucky young man got to open a corner shop with his mother's money. Having been through a process of reeducation, he'd lost interest in fighting but he had a powerful craving for money and fun. In any case, he now seemed to have embarked on a safer road. Because of his outstanding appearance, he quickly found himself a girlfriend. He didn't object to his girlfriend's demand that he marry her and told her very honestly that his mother had five hundred thousand yuan in hand, all of which was his. Her son, that lucky young man, let us hear how he planned to apportion his mother's lifetime savings:

Two hundred thousand yuan is enough to get married on. The remaining three hundred thousand yuan we'll put on my Great Wall debit card, so I can spend it later. What? She won't hand it over? How dare she? If she doesn't give me the money I'll kill the bitch!

IN WINTER

The El Niño phenomenon does exist; one of the most obvious proofs is that the winter is not as cold as it used to be. In the last couple of years, winter passed almost unnoticed, which made people wonder whether they should be happy or worried about it. In winter, I am responsible for taking my daughter back to school after lunch. Occasionally, I can see that the ice on the puddles on the ground hasn't quite melted. The thin layer looks very fragile, not like ice, but like a sheet of plastic. I asked my daughter if the ice was thicker when her mother took her to school in the morning but she didn't notice. In fact, she's never seen the ice lying thick and solid across the ground her whole life.

When northerners come to Jiangnan for the first time in winter, almost everyone stares at you with disappointed eyes and says: Why is it so cold? How come it's so cold here? I don't know where their illusions about winter in Jiangnan come from. It's the same as my family worrying about whether I could withstand the severe cold up there when I went to study in the north, but I found that one day in November, even the radiator in the dormitory toilets in the campus of Beijing Normal University were buzzing, which made my fear of the severe winter disappear.

In my memory, winters were always cold. The northwest wind howled outside the window for three days in a row and then the coldest part of winter began. Mother took out our cotton padded clothes from the camphorwood chest: things for each of the six members of the family. All of our cotton padded clothes, winter shoes, hats, and scarves, whether we liked it or not, we had to wear winter clothes which smelled of camphor. Whether you wanted to or not, you had to go out onto the street to greet the arrival of winter.

When winter came, people on both sides of the street closed the wooden doors that had been opened through the other three seasons. A street without secrets had no choice but to show its mysterious side. Indoors and outdoors were equally cold, and people with nothing to do could be seen anywhere that caught the sun. I am speaking about sunny weather but many winter days were overcast, with humid air, and the sky a leaden gray. Everything seemed to be leading up to even colder weather and the forecast on TV confirmed this again and again. From their anonymous studio located who knows where, the weather person announced in a calm voice that a strong cold front from Siberia was moving south and would arrive in Jiangnan tomorrow.

The streets were very clean in winter and there was hardly any garbage like melon peel or shells lying around on the ground. Moreover, the smell of industrial effluent would be blown far away by the strong winds. Therefore, breathing deeply, I think I can smell winter's own smell. The smell of winter may not be a real scent; it is clear and pure, and sometimes brings a prickling sensation to my nostrils. The potholes in the pavement are capped with a thick layer of ice, especially in the days after snow. People came up with all kinds of tricks in order to deal with the ice and snow on the road, like tying straw rope around the soles of their rubber shoes to prevent slipping, while the children used the ice and snow on the road to amuse themselves. They would slide across the frozen road in their cotton shoes, thinking that they were skating. There is a saying in Jiangnan that dogs are happy when it rains and snows. I don't know whether there is any truth in this. Very few people living on our street had dogs and I never saw any of them doing anything special when it rained or snowed. I always thought this proverb is more suitable for children. Kids feel dreary and sad in the winter but a heavy snowfall often suddenly transforms the boring nature of the season. After heavy snow, children rush out of their homes and schools, just like the rock star Cui Jian sings about in his song. They run wild in the snow, making a festival for themselves. Snow in the south of the Yangtze River is somewhat like family planning: it's very restrained. It happens once or twice a year and all the adults complain while, for a short space of time, the kids don't completely hate winter. My first memory of snow isn't of building a snowman nor a snowball fight—actually it's more than a little boring. I grabbed a big heap of snow with my hands and squeezed it into an ice lump, which I kept in a broken teapot. I had a vague idea in my mind to keep that piece of ice until spring when it would be a unique treasure. As you can imagine, a few days later, I fished the teapot out of the coal-heap and saw that there was nothing inside it, not even water from the melted ice, because it had seeped through a hole in the teapot into the pile of coal.

Snowmelt weather is hateful; the sun is shining but everything is sopping wet, the ice on the eaves is always dripping down onto the street. The road is black and white, with the filth gradually flowing towards the gutters, while the remaining patches of snow struggle to survive. The street looks like a warzone: completely wrecked. Also annoying are those over-diligent housewives who rush out to air clothes, sheets, diapers and the like as soon as the weather clears up, making the whole place even more chaotic.

Winter is sandwiched in pre- and after-snowfall; but sometimes when a big snow is imminent, people in Jiangnan will quote the proverb about how a wet winter solstice means a dry year. They are prepared to sacrifice the winter solstice, if that means by Chinese New Year they'll have good weather without rain or snow. The gods are often ready to meet people's demands. As I remember it, the streets on the day of the winter solstice were always deep in mud. People in Jiangnan have the winter solstice as a holiday, and every household will celebrate by taking a tot of whisky with their mutton stew—but I have no idea where this comes from. Once I went to the grocery store to get a bottle of whisky and since it smelled so good, I stole a few sips on the way home. When I got back, my face and ears were bright red and the back of my cotton padded coat was splashed with mud, for which I was severely reprimanded by my mother. I don't remember now whether my mother scolded me for coming back stinking of alcohol or because I shouldn't have made my new cotton padded clothes so dirty. Anyhow, I felt deeply misunderstood. I went to my room and sat down on the bed. There I was overcome by all the whisky I'd been drinking and fell asleep on the bed.

Everyone says that Jiangnan is a wonderful place but no one says that the winter in Jiangnan is any fun. Personally, I am not very sensitive to the changes in the seasons, but if I had my way, one day the climate here would be like Kunming in Yunnan, the city of eternal spring. I don't like winter but then I think of that one winter when I was on my way to school hanging my head. Suddenly, I heard the sound of music coming from the teahouse on our street. Walking over and looking through the glass window at the overheated room within, I could see a bunch of old men sitting around a greasy table, holding cups of hot tea, listening to a man and a woman giving a *pingtan* performance. It wasn't cold at all in here. At the time I admired the way those old people were enjoying themselves. Now when I remember the fun they were having on that cold winter's day, I think it might be interesting to spend the winter like that.

A STREET IN SUMMER

The counters of fruit shops were not like the others; they were set at an angle and separated by wooden bars into several frames of the same size. Some measly peaches and a few sour green apples lay inside, as if reposing on a desolate hillside. The saleswoman in the fruit shop was a kind and beautiful young girl and she did a good enough job, but who's going to go there to buy that horrible fruit just because she's a nice person? As a result, people got used to the idea that summer fruit is inedible: they went straight past the lonely fruit shop and its single saleswoman, heading for the candy shop by the bridge. The three middle-aged women who kept the candy store were busy shouting at each other behind the counter all the year round, and they were relentlessly rude to their customers. One of them had an ugly scar above her eyebrow. Whenever a child walked in, she'd demand in a hoarse voice: What do you want? That livid scar would wriggle too: what do you want? But even so, the candy store was packed with children all summer.

The freezer at the candy store had been in use for many years, and every summer it was there making a dreadful racket. A blackboard stood on top, on which was written the list of products for sale: red bean ice lolly 4 *fen*; cream ice lolly 5 *fen*; ice cream brick 1 *jiao*, soft drink (not including bottle) 8 *fen*. In summer, over and over again the saleswomen would angrily throw open the lid of the chest freezer and lift up the insulating cotton mat. The child would then crane its neck to inspect the items laid out neatly under the mat. They would soon see that there were very few red bean ice lollies left but a lot of cream ice lollies and ice cream bricks, which lay there in a cold fog, enviably sheltered from the heat. Any child could grasp the cause of this phenomenon. It wasn't that cream ice lollies and ice cream bricks weren't popular but they were a few *fen* more expensive. When a child carefully peeled back a corner of the paper to see if there were lots of red beans in the ice lolly, they'd be shouted at by the saleswomen. "What are you looking at? It's all made by machine. Do you think we are trying to cheat you? All you do is eat ice lollies and more ice lollies: it's a wonder your stomach hasn't frozen to an icicle!"

With one ice lolly plugging his mouth and holding tight to his lunch box, the child ran desperately along the hot afternoon street. The other ice lollies in their lunch box rattled about, under threat from the fierce sun, so the kids knew they had to run home as quickly as possible, so that the family could enjoy this cold treat at its best.

On the very hottest days, the whole street seemed to shimmer. People walking down the street would feel the heat of the pavement burning under their plastic sandals and if they touched the wall of one of the houses, it would be hot too. Walking down the street, people wondered if the whole world were not dizzy with heat. It was so hot that it seemed as if the air itself were gasping for breath: there was almost a faint sibilant sound humming in my ear. The talkative, loud and fussy locals now all shut their mouths. They lay about on bamboo reclining chairs, trying to beat the heat. In this furnace, they forgot about modesty: the only thing that mattered was getting to feel any cooling breeze around. They sprawled by the door facing the street, snoring intermittently with their big mouths agape. They didn't notice that their fans had fallen to the ground. The men wore their trousers so loose that everything was hanging out and they didn't even care. The radio was on as usual and the crisp voices of *pingtan* artistes emerged, reciting the wonderful story of Wu Song's drunken attack on the door god Jiang Menshen. However, they did nothing but snore, completely ignoring the performers' efforts.

At three o'clock in the afternoon, the sun altered its tactics from frontal assault to regional defense. The houses along our street took the opportunity to create a '38th Parallel' formed from their own walls, and this '38th Parallel' gradually crept over: one side of the line was hot and bright, the other cool and dark. Pedestrians were resolute in walking along in the shade. This reminded us of the North Korean film that was being shown in the cinema right then: *The Fate of Geumhee and Eunhee*. People cried bitterly over the tragic fate of Eunhee, caught on the wrong side of the 38th Parallel. However, in summer, they all chose the route without sunshine and preferred to hide in the darkness with Eunhee.

It seemed to take forever for the sun to set in summer but in the end it would have to disappear behind the mountains. In the summer holidays, children pay attention to the movements of the sun, so they can jump into the moat at the earliest possible opportunity and enjoy the greatest pleasure of the summer season. At dusk, all the boats plying the canals were particularly cautious, because at any moment a boy might launch himself into the water with a cry from any of the docks, roofs, windows or doors in the city. They even needed to be careful about watermelon peel floating down the river because some of those 'half watermelons' were kids' swimming caps. Those annoying children, with half a watermelon on their heads, would go and grab onto the boat's anchor chains. When they were messing about in the water they wouldn't want to exhaust themselves, so they'd ask the boatman to take them upstream or downstream. So the mothers doing their washing on the stone slab steps outside the house would see the most terrifying sight: their children holding onto the anchor of a boat as it powered up the river, riding high on the waves. In a flash, their kids would disappear from sight, and then even if their mothers shouted themselves hoarse, what would be the good?

When the night came, people treated the street like an open-air canteen. Many people moved their dinner tables out onto the road. Adults and children would sit on the street with their mouths full of food and watch late-comers ride by on their bicycles. If you eat in the street, you provide a certain amount of entertainment for interfering old women who like to find out what other people are having for dinner today. These old women would walk up and down among the dining tables along the street, pausing here and there, waving a palm-leaf fan. They felt that what was going on at every table was their business. "What are you going to have to eat?" one of them asked.

"Oh, nothing special," the housewife replied. "Salt fish and fried radish."

"What do you mean nothing special?" the old crone demanded. "Is salt fish not good enough for you?"

It was getting dark and almost everyone was out on the street. Here, someone had cut open a watermelon and the whole family now had their heads down over a broken basin, spitting out the seeds. There, they were holding off eating dinner because the kids weren't back yet. When the children returned, they'd be soaking wet. An angry dad would ask his son: Where've you been? And the kid would answer back impatiently: Swimming. Didn't you know? The dad would glare at his son's developing body and ask: How far did you go hanging onto the boat? Likou, the kid replied. Now the father would be so irate his eyes would practically start from their sockets: I've told you over and over not to do that; are you trying to get yourself killed? It would end up with the dad boxing his kid's ears resoundingly and then the neighbours would come clustering round. There'd be angry voices and mumbling ones, serious and plaintive, and they'd blend into a noisy quarrel which could be heard far and wide. So people would come running over, maybe still even carrying their rice-bowls, because even in the hottest summers everything recovers energy at night.

THE BRIDGE NORTH OF THE CITY

Ever since ancient times, Suzhou has proverbially had six gates, but Qi Gate in the north of the city is not one of their number. However, I am from Qi Gate. To be precise, I am from outside the Qi Gate of Suzhou.

The street where I grew up runs north of the Qi Gate drawbridge. When I crossed the bridge, I would walk northward along a narrow street with densely packed houses, passing my own front door. If you went about a mile further, the city would suddenly disappear. You would be right out in the countryside, with fields of vegetables, rice paddy, haystacks, ponds and flocks of farmyard ducks. Therefore, the place where I grew up was actually the edge of the city. However, for all that it was out on the edge of the city, the street beyond the Qi Gate was still full of southern features. By living there for all those years, I got the full flavour of the south. When I remember that street, I remember the south.

The Qi Gate bridge was originally actually a wooden drawbridge, put in as a defensive measure in time of war. Imagine if all the drawbridges around Suzhou were lifted during the night; the moat would really serve to cut off the city from the outside world, and all the people living outside would be isolated from those in the centre. Fortunately, I wasn't alive then, and in fact, when I was very young, the Qi Gate drawbridge was replaced by a medium-sized cement bridge.

But for many years, the locals living near the Qi Gate continued to call the concrete bridge over the moat a drawbridge, out of habit.

When you crossed the drawbridge and walked north along the gravel street, you would see two other bridges. The first one was the South Road Bridge and then, if you carried on walking, the North Road Bridge would come in view. As for the names of these two bridges, I'm following the common designation used by people living outside the Qi Gate. I don't know if they have more elegant formal names but I want to talk about them the way I always have.

These two bridges are regular stone arch bridges like you see everywhere in the south, lying over the same branch of the river. For many years, they have been like a pair of sisters looking at each other from afar. They really are like twins, since both are single-span bridges with enough space underneath to take two boats sailing abreast. There are stone steps down to the water on both sides of the bridge and the people living along the river often washed their clothes there. The stone steps under the bridge were also used by boys playing about in the water. Standing there, you can see a stone tablet with the date of the bridge's construction. I remember that the stone tablet under the North Road Bridge was carved in the reign of the Daoguang Emperor of the Qing Dynasty. I imagine the South Road Bridge would be the same. They were originally twinned in shape and spirit.

It's impossible now to see the North Road Bridge when standing on the South Road Bridge because your line of sight is blocked by another behemoth between the two. That's a steel-gray railway bridge. The famous Beijing-Shanghai railway line crosses the north part of Suzhou, running by the street leading out of the Qi Gate and over the river spanned by two roads. That is why the railway bridge appeared, so the two bridges I've described were cut off from one another. I think it was put in place about sixty years ago. Maybe the railway bridge was built by the Westerners, or the straight steel bridge made people feel a sense of alienation or adoration, but right up until the present day, people on our street still call the railway bridge the 'foreign bridge' or 'foreign railway bridge'.

The railway bridge crosses the street outside the Qi Gate, so the people who live beyond it would have to come back and forth under the foreign bridge pretty much every day. Trains would thunder past right over your head, with a puff of steam, a rattling of coal lumps or the occasional ejection of fruit peel or shells.

For all that they have been separated, the two stone-arch bridges still face each other on the river. Now let me continue to describe these two ancient bridges.

The area west of South Road Bridge is called Xiatang. The houses in Xiatang are bunched up along a narrower street, which forms a T-shape with the South Road Bridge. There are no shops in Xiatang, so the people living there have to walk across the South Road Bridge every day to buy vegetables on the street alongside it. Xiatang residents used to call the street on this side of the bridge 'the street'. It seems that the road running in front of their own houses did not qualify as a street. When Xiatang women meet at the South Road

Bridge and say hello, one will say: Do they have fresh pork on the street? And the other will reply: No, there's nothing on the street.

On the east side of South Road Bridge is the street leading to the Qi Gate. Clustered around this bridge there is a candy shop, a coal briquette shop, a butcher, a long-established herbalist providing Chinese medicines and a vegetable market. Every morning and evening, vegetable farmers out beyond the suburbs would pick fresh produce and spread it out along the street. At such times, the bridge would become very busy and this often caused road congestion, so cyclists in a hurry would get annoyed and complain. If you want to hear how Suzhou people quarrel, the market by the bridge is a good place to go. Moreover, compared to the women from the North Road Bridge area, the women living around the South Road Bridge seem to be much more obstinate. There is no way to explain this. It is my impression that the South Road Bridge was always noisy and full of quarrelsome people.

Maybe it is because my home was closer to the North Road Bridge but I always liked this bridge better. My school was not far from it, so I walked under the North Road Bridge every day. Sometimes when I went to my mother's factory to have lunch or take a bath, I would carry my satchel across the bridge, counting the steps. There were eleven steps in total; always the same, of course. Once over the bridge, there was a clean, short cross-street. This faced the North Road Bridge but the streets outside the Qi Gate were called straight or cross in relation to it, so this was a cross-street. I don't know why I particularly liked this cross-street but I have done so ever since I was a child. Maybe it's because the street was so clean and the houses along it so neat. Maybe it's because my mother walked from here to work in the factory every day. Maybe it's just because the cross-street ran at right angles to the street leading to the Qi Gate, so it really was a cross-street.

There was a teahouse right by the North Road Bridge, a two-storey wooden building with three long windows facing out towards the river, the bridge and the street respectively. In my memory, the teahouse is always full of clouds of steam and a sweet fragrance. Most of the customers are old people from the streets and surrounding suburbs. They would sit around the battered old tables, sharing a pot of green tea between five or six people, talking about this and that, or just keeping silent. Occasionally, there might be a *tanci* performance, or there'd be a few *pingtan* fans in attendance. The teahouse used a tiger stove for boiling water, with rice husks for fuel, which lay in a heap out in front. The old woman in charge of keeping the water boiling was a friend of my mother, and mum told me that she used to own the teashop but not any longer—now it had been collectivised. The teahouse beside the North Road Bridge must have seemed to many people to epitomise the landscape of the south because it was often used as a background for films. However, the cameramen who captured it on film are no doubt unaware of the fact that the teahouse beside the bridge no longer exists. A fire the year before last burned it to the ground. It was one hot July night, and plenty of residents from beyond Qi Gate watched the fire from either side of the river. Apparently the fire in the tiger stove had not been extinguished properly and sparks had flown out. People came rushing over but there was nothing they could do—the flames consumed the teahouse right before their eyes. Of course, the stone bridge next to it was completely undamaged.

Now you walk over the North Road Bridge, the open space on the left side is where the teahouse used to be. Now it has become a place where hawkers sell fish and fruit.

The suburbs north of Suzhou cover a small area and the main street leading out of the Qi Gate is a small place but there are still four bridges there. As any local could tell you, the four bridges starting with the southernmost one are the drawbridge, the South Road Bridge, the foreign railway bridge and the North Road Bridge. If you think about it, these names are quite ordinary but also a little odd, right?

The reason I haven't really mentioned the railway bridge is because it was a scene of much bloodshed and death in my childhood. I have seen the bodies of seven or eight dead people on the foreign railway bridge but I never saw any corpses on the drawbridge, the South Road Bridge or the North Road Bridge.

BOATS

The passenger boat to Changshu sailed past my window every morning. It belonged to the Steamship Navigation Company, so it was painted in blue and white. The white of the cabins and the blue of the hull contrasted sharply, making the whole ship look magnificent. There were countless vessels of one kind or another passing by on the river every day but my favourite was the passenger boat going to Changshu. I used to draw it on my sketchpad and when my art teacher saw what I'd done, they were very surprised and said: I didn't know you were so good at drawing boats.

As a child, everything is easy to explain. Children's graffiti will often unconsciously reveal their favourite things and my love for ships has continued to this day.

In my mind's eye, the waterways and canals of Suzhou run clean and bright. In the 1960s and 1970s, the economy might have been stagnant but the rivers of my hometown flowed every day, carrying with them countless boats sailing for Changshu, Taicang or Kunshan. The most common were fleets of barges. Seven or eight barges would be tied together and pulled by a steamship which would be racing on at the head of the line. I could see clearly two sailors playing chess on board the steamship, and a couple and their children on each of the barges behind. It was the families living on the barges that caught my attention, particularly if they had children my own age. That kind of floating life, forever on the move, was mysteriously attractive to me.

My keen observation of passing ships may also have had a hidden motive, related to a casual joke my mother once made. I don't remember how old I was at that time, nor under what circumstances my mother said this, but she told me, "You aren't my kid. I got you from the boats." This is the kind of pointless joke a mother will often have with her children, and when you grow up, you know it's not true—your mum only wanted to see your look of panic afterwards. But I was too little then and couldn't understand this kind of complicated joke. So what I got from it was another background, even if it were only conjecture. Perhaps my real family *was* out there on a boat somewhere and I too belonged on a barge!

I can't be sure whether or not my interest in ships had some element of self-exploration in it but sometimes I would lie in front of the window near the river and watch the boats passing by in front of my eyes. I would pay close attention to the faces of the family on board and wonder if this is the one? Could it be that family over there? It's always painful to look at the world with a secret deep in your heart. When the river was relatively clean, I would often see a boat fishing for bricks in the river. There were two women on the boat. The mother was extremely thin and had a crippled leg. Although her daughter was strong and tall, her face was covered with freckles and looked ugly. At the time, I felt a kind of terror, thinking: What if I were the child of this family? It was also at this time that I comforted myself: That's impossible… you're just scaring yourself… all this about me and the boat is a lie.

When I was in primary school, a real bargeman's child came to live in my uncle's house next door. My uncle had daughters but no sons, so contacted by friends of friends, this boy's parents agreed to send their child to my uncle's house for possible adoption. He was an honest and dull child with a silver amulet round his neck like so many other boatmen's children. I had a fanatical interest in the boy's background. While laughing at the amulet, I asked him all sorts of questions about why he didn't stay on the boat with his parents. I asked him if it was more fun for him to live at my uncle's house than the boat? The boy just said that he wanted to go to school. He didn't want to talk to me and seemed unwilling to be friends with me, which made me feel a little sad. One day, I heard a racket coming from the river outside my window, so I ran out to have a look. A big wooden boat drew up close to the stone dock by my uncle's house and the couple on the boat were busy trying to make it fast to the shore. A little kid stood at the bow of the boat and waved desperately towards the bank, shouting: Brother! Brother! Brother! Then I saw my aunt holding the boy and standing by the dock. I knew that this must be the boy's boat. The man and woman on board were his parents and the shouting kid was his baby brother. I looked at the scene almost with envy but then I realised that the boy was not happy at all. Looking at that cheerful family, he seemed completely miserable. I decided he didn't know when he was well-off—his mother was really pretty and his father handsome and strong, and they lived on a boat… but he was crying!

The boatman's son lived at my uncle's house for one term before he was taken away by his grandfather. Strangely, as soon as he left, my fantasy about my other life on board a boat also went away.

Maybe it was because I was growing up or because the son of a genuine boatman destroyed my illusions about them. At this point, I became a mere spectator when boats sailed past on the river. At that age I still had other fantasies about ships but they were all related to riding the waves and sailing far away. In the nighttime silence or during the early morning, I would sometimes be awakened by the sound of quarrelling outside the window. Some boatmen liked to scream and shout at each other. One voice would bellow: Where are you going? And then the call came back: We're on our way to Changshu. Tucked up under the blankets I would think Changshu is too near—you should point your boat in the direction of the Yangtze River and head to Nanjing or Wuhan, or maybe even the mountain city of Chongqing... wouldn't that be great!

When I graduated from junior high school, I applied for the Seamen's School in Nanjing but I didn't get the necessary grades. That condemned me to a life without any connections with ships or navigation. Now, I am quite sure I don't have any kind of special affinity for boats—on my one and only sea voyage I was terribly sea-sick the whole time—but I still firmly believe that ships are the world's most lyrical and beautiful means of transportation. If I were still living in a house by the river, if I had a son, I would repeat the same lie to him that my mother told to me, "I got you from the boats. Your real family is on a barge somewhere."

Lies about boats are also wonderful.

TALKING ABOUT THE PAST

Talking about the past, the first thing that comes to mind is a century-old street in the north part of Suzhou. A long limestone-paved road which in July, during the hottest days of summer, seemed to take on a light rust-red colour, while in the depths of winter, covered in ice and snow, it presented a grayish hue. It took about ten minutes to walk from the south end of the street to the north end. There was a bridge at the south end of the street which had at one time been a drawbridge, like so many other cities in Jiangnan, but had now been replaced by a concrete bridge. At the north end there was another bridge which connected the Suzhou to Shanghai highway, while in the middle there was what we called the foreign railway bridge. The railway bridge straddled the street, narrow like all the roads in that northern part of the city. Every day, trains roared past on their north-south journey.

Our houses, shops, schools and factories were jam-packed in between these three bridges, and the locals also spent their time walking back and forward between them, year upon year.

Now I see a boy with a satchel on his back, rolling a hoop down the street. When he walks under the railway bridge, a train is roaring past overhead and the water splashing down from the locomotive falls from the gap between the tracks, and an apple core tossed from a window falls at his feet. The boy may be me, or my brother who was two years older, or the son of one of my neighbours. But anyway, such was the scene of my childhood.

I wouldn't dare to boast about having had a happy childhood because, in fact, my childhood was a little lonely and a little overshadowed. My parents basically had nothing to their name except their four children. My father worked in an office in the city, riding a worn-out bicycle to and fro every day; my mother worked in a cement factory nearby. Although beautiful when she was young, by middle age her face was often swollen, either because she was overtired or because she was sick with one of her many ailments. For many years, my parents supported a family of six on a combined income of about eighty yuan, and from that you ought to be able to imagine just how hard their lives were.

My mother passed away many years ago now but I still remember well how she would carry a basket with her when she went to work at the factory. Inside, there'd be her lunch box and a stack of hand-made quilted cotton soles. Sometimes there'd be rice and leftovers in her lunch box; but sometimes there'd only be the rice and nothing else, while the soles were there to make shoes for us kids. She was a clever and competent woman but she had no spare time, so she'd make soles for our shoes during her breaks.

During the long years of my childhood, I don't remember fairy tales, candy, games or any excessive indulgence from adults. What I remember is hardship. I remember the dim fifteen-watt lightbulb that lit our home, the damp concrete floor and the simple furniture which gave off a musty smell. Four children sat around a square table eating a pot of pork and cabbage soup. The two older sisters gave the scraps of pork to their younger brothers but because there wasn't much meat in the first place, it was gone in a few bites.

Mother once went to the shop that sold soy sauce and cooking oil to buy some salt and lost five yuan. She spent the whole day searching for that five-yuan note. When she realised she was never going to find it, I heard her crying sadly and I said to my mother: Don't cry. When I grow up, I will earn one hundred yuan for you. I was only seven or eight when I said this but I was a precocious and sensitive child. It comforted my mother but it was also quite useless in the straits we found ourselves in.

At that time, Chinese New Year was my favourite thing. During New Year, you could set off firecrackers, get lucky money, wear new clothes and eat peanuts, walnuts, fish, meat, chicken and many other foods you'd never normally so much as see. Just like everyone else, my parents liked to make their children happy for the few days of the New Year holidays.

When the debris from the firecrackers, sweet wrappers and husks from roasted melon seeds had all been cleaned from the streets, our greatest annual pleasure was over. Going to school, returning home afterwards, doing my homework, playing marbles or kicking a discarded cigarette packet about–because of my precocity and lack of a gregarious personality, I rarely participated in the games the other local kids played. As it got dark, the situation at home often became uncomfortably tense and difficult. My parents would quarrel, sometimes at the tops of their voices, sometimes in an undertone, while my sisters would hide behind the door and cry. As I stood under the eaves, looking out at the long street and the passers-by hurrying along, I felt angry about their hurtful behaviour: Why did none of our neighbours quarrel? Why was it my family that was always arguing?

The street where I grew up has often appeared in my novels, though it was disguised as 'Toon Tree Road'. I've ended up recording various of the people I knew and the things that happened to them but because the memories of my childhood are at once very remote and yet very clear, there can be an almost dream-like quality about them.

I began school in the autumn of 1969, which was an era of considerable turbulence. The walls were covered with slogans; if you gave them to a kid to read now they'd be completely absurd and incomprehensible but every child was familiar with them back then. I remember that the first time in my life I wrote a complete sentence, it was something I'd got from a propaganda poster. It was a sentence with a special cadence, "Revolutionary Committees Are Great!" At that time, there was no such thing as preschool education, nor were kids influenced by advertising and television as they are today, but the slogans and propaganda posters put up on the streets taught them to read and even the stupidest child could write such phrases as "Long Live Chairman Mao" and "Attack our Enemies."

The primary school was located in a former church. The nave where the pastor had once preached was now used as the school auditorium. The children often held meetings there, sitting in row upon row of chairs, but our criticism meetings or opening ceremonies were quite different from the religious services of the past. This auditorium with its round windows and stained glass, and a small European-style building behind it which now contained classrooms for the youngest pupils, were the most beautiful buildings for miles around.

My teacher in primary school, surnamed Chen, was a gentle, white-haired woman. Her smile and elegant manner made her a wonderful teacher for any child. Unfortunately, she was getting old and suffered from glaucoma, so when I was in third grade, she went back to live in her hometown in Hunan along with her daughter. Later on, I had many teachers during my time as a pupil but the one I respected most has always been Ms Chen. Perhaps it was because starting school is so precious to children or maybe it was just because she had a kind and gentle smile which was rare in that dark period of our history.

When I was in the second grade of primary school, I had to take time off from school because of a serious illness. I lay in bed, drinking bowl after bowl of traditional Chinese medicine. It was a lonely time and I suffered a great deal. When a group of students came to visit me under the teacher's supervision, I hid behind the door and refused to come out, ashamed to face them when I was sick and getting special treatment. I couldn't go to school which gave me a sense of inferiority and loss, but instead I often dreamed of my school, classroom, the playground and my classmates.

Speaking of my classmates (including those in both primary and secondary schools), we all grew up together, knowing all about each other's families and each individual person's glory and disgrace. Many years later, we've ended up all over the place but occasionally we'll still bump into each other in the streets of our hometown. Chatting about this and that, the memories of our childhood pass lightly. I like to move their stories into novels because they are typical of teenagers in the south. I don't know if any of them have found their shadows in my work—maybe not, because I know that they are married and have children, and are busy living their own lives. They have no time and interest in reading these stories.

Last summer, I went back to Suzhou to stay with my family for a bit. One day, in crossing a stone bridge, I met one of my teachers from middle school. When she saw me, her first sentence was: Did you hear that Mr Song passed away? I was very surprised. Mr Song was a maths teacher: the head teacher at my high school. He can't have been more than forty-five years old at the time, and he was a very strict and dedicated teacher. The woman said to me: He got liver cancer, you know... they said he was tired to death. I don't remember what I said at that time but well recall her parting words, "He was such a good teacher but you all forgot about him. He was in the hospital every day looking forward to having some of his old students come to see him but no one went near him. Just before he died, he said he was very upset about that."

Right there in my hometown, standing on a stone bridge, I received the heaviest emotional blow of recent years. I had to admit, I really had almost forgotten Mr Song. This kind of forgetfulness seems to be in line with the general mentality of modern city people. There are few who will miss their former teachers, classmates and old friends. People lose connection with the past, intentionally or unintentionally, and are totally committed to carving out their own future. For me, people and things from the past are just material for my writing. I feel sad about this and I have begun to wonder whether the past can be so easily set aside. For example, on that summer afternoon, when my teacher asked me on the stone bridge: Did you hear that Mr Song passed away?

Speaking of the past, I always remember my childhood spent in the northern suburbs of Suzhou. I also think of the day twelve years ago, when I left Suzhou and went to Beijing to study—how relaxed and empty was my mood. Through the window, I saw a paper kite floating in the air above one of the villages. I saw birds flying here and there over the fields and trees. Kite and birds: they were the shadows of people's past and future.

THE EVENTS OF MY CHILDHOOD

Our family used to live opposite a chemical plant. The main gate of the chemical plant and my home were pretty much straight across from each other. When I was very young, when I had nothing to do or I didn't know what to do, I often stood at the door of my home to watch the workers of the chemical plant go to work and then again to watch them leave.

The overalls worn by workers at the chemical plants were very strange. They were made from black silk fabric with upturned cuffs on the sleeves and trouser legs, and they were baggy like the pants that martial artists like to wear, making them into 'martial arts' overalls, I guess. As soon as men and women who worked at the chemical plant arrived, they all changed into that kind of clothing. When it was windy, when they walked around the factory area, their clothes would bulge out until they looked like ambulatory lanterns. Even today, I can't imagine what the people who designed the overalls for the chemical plants were thinking. They didn't fit in with the blue work-clothes everyone else was wearing at that time, and made the people wearing them look out of place compared to other working-class people. Many years later, when I saw some fashionable women wearing loose black silk shirts and trousers, I always felt that they looked quite wrong: they looked like workers in a chemical factory.

There was one woman, a nanny in the crèche at the chemical factory—I still remember her face. She pushed a pram to work every day with her own child sitting up in it: a little girl. She was at least seven or eight years old at the time. The girl always sat up in the pram, grinning from side to side. I wondered why she was still using a pram at that age. On one occasion the mother stationed the pram outside the guard room while she went and chatted with the old man inside. I rushed over to inspect the little girl and found that she couldn't stand up... she couldn't even hold up her head properly. I understood vaguely that there was a problem with the girl's bones, probably rickets or something like that. I still remember that there was a pool of saliva next to her mouth, which had flowed there unconsciously.

There was also a man, one of the bachelors who worked at the chemical plant. I am sure that he was a bachelor because I often saw him in the morning munching on a flatbread or a deep-fried dough stick, and he'd be holding a red-bean stuffed bun in his hand as he leisurely turned from the street in through the factory gate. The man was about twenty-seven or twenty-eight years old, and his face was very ruddy. I always thought that his colour was the direct result of what he had for breakfast every day. I got a bowl of boiled rice and a few pieces of dried radish every day, so I always envied him: such a lavish breakfast, and he ate so much—how wonderful! I always paid attention to the man with the red-bean stuffed buns but the only thing I was interested in was what he was getting to eat today. Once, on my way to school, I saw him sitting in a snack bar, eating again. I really wanted to know what he was getting, so I couldn't stop myself from going in and having a good look. I could see two dumplings floating in the bowl and the fat in the clear soup. I was sure he'd been eating meat dumplings and had bought four—I knew that four dumplings cost one *mao* and four *fen*. Generally speaking, people wouldn't buy just two dumplings but four or six, otherwise it just wouldn't be cost-effective. I still remember what I was thinking when I walked out of the dim-sum shop. I thought, this guy eats four dumplings a day: how can he afford it? How much is he earning a month? I could only come up with one explanation for this extravagance; that is, he was a bachelor. An unmarried man could spend every penny on his breakfast and eat whatever he damn well wanted to!

· · ·

I still vaguely remember that the chemical plant produced coal tar derivatives, which were most likely used to make naphthalene: I don't need to explain how I know this because I am sure you can guess. Every day when I was a small child the whole place stank of camphor. It seemed to me that the smell emerged from the chemical plant's chimney. The smell not only got up your nose but also stuck to the clothes that my family or neighbours were drying outside. Somehow we got so used to it we didn't notice it in the air in the street but people from other districts would cover their noses and say, "Oh, what is that stench? It smells terrible!" That kind of person always annoyed me.

I liked to smell the mothball-scent in the air. I didn't care about pollution or the damage that it does to the human body—of course, now that sounds quite idiotic but at the time I didn't know what air pollution was, and it wasn't just me, adults didn't know either. But even if we had known, nothing would have changed. They wouldn't have done anything to the factory over the issue of the smell. Adults sometimes complained about how much they hated the chemical plant but I thought it was just because some of them didn't like the smell of naphthalene.

The building next to my house was the factory dormitory, where two families lived. In fact, the door to their building faced directly onto the front gate of the chemical plant. One family had two sons and a daughter. The two sons were strictly disciplined by their severe father and never came out to play. But since they wouldn't come out to play, I went to their house instead. One of the sons was already pretty much grown up and very fat like his mother; the other was in my older brother's class and very thin—both of them were really quiet. I went to their house uninvited and they didn't throw me out but they ignored me. I saw that the fat big one was writing something. I asked him what it was and he told me that he was writing in Spanish.

It's true; back in about 1973 or 1974 I had a neighbour learning Spanish! I still have no idea what a young worker thought he was doing studying Spanish. To begin with, the house next door was just a temporary home for those two families. By the time I was in middle school, both of them had moved out. The house overlooking the river was removed to make space for the chemical plant's own oil terminal and a large pipe was installed connecting the plant to the building next door, ready to take oil delivered by tankers directly into the factory.

A group of migrant workers came to build the small oil terminal —they came from Yixing. One of them liked to chat with us, and he'd jump into the house from the stone steps next door and come and get some water to drink. One day he did just that but accidentally dropped the glass on the ground and broke it. The migrant worker was very embarrassed. What he said was something that I've always thought very striking, "This glass is really terribly poor quality."

After the oil terminal was up and running, there were often some oil tankers anchored on the river outside the back door of our house. I'd seen the two workers in charge of oil transportation before; of course, they were both wearing those peculiar black overalls and quietly sitting on a bench looking at the pressure gauge. The man was bald and looked kind-hearted, while the woman was even more familiar to me because she was the mother of one of my primary school classmates. I often saw the two of them sitting there watching the oil pump. They seemed to get along perfectly well, which was quite different from the behaviour of a primary school boy and girl when they've been forced to sit together. I never paid much attention to them. After dark, when I ran out of the back door to pee in the river as usual, I wouldn't look at them. I believe they didn't look at me either.

That summer, the woman who watched the oil pump, the mother of my classmate, committed suicide by swallowing a lot of sleeping pills. I was really shocked to hear that because, after all, she'd been sitting next door to my house watching the oil pump all this time. I have a lot of theories about her suicide—many strange guesses—but because they are just guesses, I will not dwell on them here.

Memoires should be true and accurate, and everything else should find its place in a novel.

GOING TO SCHOOL

The first time I went to school was not so that I could learn anything; I went to play or just because there was no one to look after me. I was about five years old at the time. I went to school with my elder sister. Vaguely I remember a row of mud-brick buildings located in a quiet street. An old janitor stood in the playground ringing an iron bell. My elder sister took my hand and walked into the classroom. Imagine a preschooler sitting in the middle of a group of fifth-grade girls, staring timidly at the blackboard and the teacher in front of it! The woman teacher's hairstyle and dress were similar to my own mother's but her clear and loud Mandarin pronunciation made her appear solemn and impressive. At that moment, I admired her more than my mother.

It was a sunny morning. I sat in my elder sister's classroom, making up the numbers, and no one paid the blindest bit of attention to my presence. I may have had a folded paper dart with some political slogan printed on it clutched in my hand as the sunshine of 1967 shone down on me through the glass window. I was completely oblivious to the bloody and wicked elements in the air; so I merely remember the loud voices of the girls reading aloud around me, resounding again and again. In any case, it was the first time that I felt the beautiful order and rhythm of education.

Maybe there is always a false and beautiful aura in our childhood memories. Looking back, these events took place during the very worst period of the Cultural Revolution... so perhaps my older sister's school wasn't so warm and lovely after all.

I started school when I was seven years old. Before I went to school on my first day, my parents took me to a photo studio to have a full-length portrait taken. In the photo, I am wearing a military-style uniform made of yellow cloth, holding a *Little Red Book* up to my chest and grinning happily. This photo later became a souvenir of this early stage of my life.

My primary school used to be a Catholic church. The school gates faced onto the main road and if you looked in over the low perimeter wall, you could see the black brick chapel. This had long ago been transformed into a small auditorium for the school. A fan palm, rare in those parts, grew beside the school gates. From the autumn of 1969, this primary school under the palm tree became my first school.

I remember well the scene of us queuing up in the playground on the first day of school. The first-grade classroom was in the small building where the priest had once lived. In front, there was a blue wooden fence with a red-painted iron placard hanging from it: 'Study Hard and Make Progress Every Day'. This slogan was familiar to all of us. However, there were always things to surprise you at school; for example, the bauhinia tree in front of the building was covered in star-shaped flowers and its round leaves spread out in the palm of your hand made a very loud and crisp report when slapped together. There was also a slide and carousel by the wall: although the wooden frame had almost rotted away, it was rare to find toys of that size for kids to enjoy. The livelier children rushed forward to take possession of them, leaving the more obedient standing around and watching.

That first day was full of excitement and amazement but I also had my moment of unhappiness because, when arranging seating, the teacher put me and a girl surnamed Wang at the same desk in the first row. I hated sitting in the front row because it made people think I was weak and pathetic; I hated sitting at the same desk as that girl because she was so badly dressed and dim-witted. All the other girls were dressed in flowery skirts but she was wearing patched blue trousers and her face was covered with trails of snot. She kept glancing at me with frightened eyes. I noticed that she had a copy of Chairman Mao's *Little Red Book* in an aluminium bowl. The bowl had a handle, so she could carry it with her wherever she went. It seems ridiculous now but her parents must have told her to carry the *Little Red Book* like this.

So on that first day, I sat in the classroom with my face and body averted, furiously indignant about my unsatisfactory placement.

My teacher, Mrs Chen, was about fifty years old at that time and I know virtually nothing about her: just that she came originally from Hunan Province, and after her husband passed away, she and her daughter lived together for many years in the only accommodation available to the school, which was actually upstairs from the first grade classroom. Right up to the present I still remember clearly that Mrs Chen's bobbed hair was already flecked with grey, her cheekbones were quite high and her eyes narrow but bright as a lamp. I remember that she wore a gray coat and black shoes all the year round, with a refined and elegant air. Standing in front of the children entering school for the very first time, it might be that she set a standard that they would apply for the rest of their lives: a teacher should have just such bright eyes and a kind smile, should have this beautiful, strong soprano voice, and her pointer should be placed straight on the textbook, instead of being regularly raised to hit the children's heads.

One plus one is two.

B, P, M, F.

A, O, E, I.

They were the most marvelous sounds I'd heard in my entire life. I remember that Mrs Chen taught me basic arithmetic and Chinese pinyin. How many Chinese characters did I learn in first grade? Two hundred? Three hundred? I can't remember clearly but I do remember that I used those words to write a poster criticising Mrs Chen. It was a trend sweeping schools in those terrible times. Every day on the radio, people were calling on others to open fire on someone-or-other, so another classmate and I 'opened fire' on Mrs Chen. In our wobbly handwriting, we wrote a poster pointing out that Mrs Chen had knocked against the table during class. We thought that was a case of the 'absolute authority of teachers' denounced day after day on the radio.

I think Mrs Chen must have seen our poster up on the wall of the first-grade classroom. How would she react? I remember her smiling as usual in class, passing by me at the end of class, just reaching out and gently touching my head. That gentle touch for me the touchstone for how much we had lost in 1969. Although this wrong resulted from my own childishness and the tenor of the times, I still feel heartache more than twenty years after the event whenever I think of it.

In the third grade, Mrs Chen and her daughter left the school. Her departure came about because she suffered from glaucoma and was almost blind. They all said that it was the result of so many days of staying up late working under her lamp. I remember it was an autumn evening when I was walking along the street and saw a bicycle rickshaw slowly coming by. On it were Mrs Chen and her daughter, squeezed in between two old suitcases and some stacks of books. It seemed that they really were going to go back to their hometown in Hunan. Without thinking, I called Mrs Chen's name but then hid in the doorway of someone else's house. I remember Mrs Chen calling my name and waving to me. I heard her say to me, "It's getting dark, go home quickly." I suddenly remembered that she suffered from an eye disease and could not see clearly that it was me. How could she have known that it was me that had shouted to her in the street? Then I realised that Mrs Chen distinguished her forty or so little pupils by voice. No matter where or when, teachers can usually call each of their students by the right name.

I never saw Mrs Chen again. If she were still alive, she would be very old indeed. Perhaps nobody ever forgets their first teacher. To my mind, Mrs Chen served as a beautiful beacon in a chaotic age. She brought many a wonderful illumination to a child's confused mind which would accompany them on a long and changeable life journey. The arrow of time has shot down the withered branches and leaves of the past but some things have a new green colour year after year, just like my memory of my first teacher, Mrs Chen. My daughter is right at this moment strapping on her rucksack to go to school. Every time I take her to her school in the former Catholic church, I tell my daughter that it is the same place where I went to school when I was a child, and Mrs Chen's voice resounds in my ears from more than twenty years ago. "It's getting dark. Go home quickly."

It's getting dark. Go home quickly.

A BEDRIDDEN CHILD

My first experience of illness came from an old, dilapidated cane chair: the sickbed of a nine-year-old boy.

When I was nine years old, I couldn't understand why I had a strange illness that made me want to pee all the time; and I couldn't understand why my legs were covered in countless red sores. I didn't know just how serious the consequences of leukopenia and thrombocytopenia were. That day, as my father pushed the bicycle, I sat on the rear seat and my mother supported me silently. By the time the three of us left the hospital, it was almost dusk. I felt that my parents' mood was as gloomy as the sky. I knew that I was ill, so it seemed to me that I had the right to demand things of my parents. So in a sweet shop that was going to close, my father bought me a chewy candy in the shape of an orange. The orange was very lifelike and the two green leaves embedded on top were even more realistic. I remember that was the first gift I got when I was ill.

It's fun to get sick. If you get sick, you can eat food you couldn't have before. You can get more attention and care from your family. You can announce proudly to your neighbours' kids: I'm sick, so I won't be going to school tomorrow! But it was just how I felt to begin with; soon the painful features of my condition dispelled all my childish happiness.

The food I was fed once confined to bed was far from being delicious. The doctor said to me: You can't tolerate salt so you mustn't eat any. Under no circumstances whatsoever are you allowed to eat salt. If someone gives you any in secret, it will kill you. Are you going to obey? I said I would—what's so special about not going without salt anyway? And to begin with, I did ignore my need for salt. My mother bought something from the drugstore that tasted like salt but wasn't, and put that in my food. It was a little salty but in a weird kind of way. There was also a special sort of soy sauce, which was brownish-red, but the colour was off. Once I started having to deal with these peculiar foodstuffs, it wasn't long before I began to fear them—I thought how wonderful it would be if I didn't have this illness that meant I couldn't eat salt…. how could there be such a strange illness that meant you couldn't tolerate it? Several times I took a chopstick and hesitantly dipped it in the salt pot, but I still didn't dare go any further because I remember the doctor's warning. I could only comfort myself with the idea that if I wanted to live, I'd have to hold off the salt.

Being ill is not just a matter of sleeping, free from all cares. The doctor put forward the proposal that I should stay home from school for half a year. I remember that I was very happy at that time, fearing only that my parents would object. My parents believed in traditional Chinese medicine (TCM), so they agreed to let me stop going to school because they were hoping that the doctors could cure me with Chinese medicine. At that time, they thought that

Western medicine would just treat the symptoms and that you needed TCM to actually cure the cause. So later, I acquired my painful memories of consuming so many herbal decoctions that we ended up ruining three earthenware pots. For a child's taste buds and stomach, those herbal decoctions were rank poison. I held my nose and drank them for the first few days but, in the midst of all my pain, I came up with a good way to avoid taking medicine—I would go to school! Once, before my mother had even finished pouring out the medicine, I made a rush for the door with my schoolbag. I thought I would rather go to school than drink the medicine, but my mother stopped me before I'd gone more than a few steps. My mother stood by the door with a bowl in her hand. She just looked at me with a stern expression. What I read from it was a wake-up call: Do you want to die? If you don't want to die, come back and take your medicine.

So I went back. A nine-year-old child can also be afraid of death. Now, thinking back on it, it seems very cruel that my fate should be becoming so frightened of death when I was only nine years of age. Was this a trick of fate or the source of my redemption? I still haven't made up my mind on that.

For a nine-year-old child, being confined to bed means that time passes very, very slowly. The southern plum rains fell constantly—drip, drip, drop, drop—and I kept needing to pee with my own plum rains. I hated the rain outside but I hated my own kidneys even more. I hated the earthenware pot on the stove and the bitter smell it exuded. I hated the cane chair creaking and crackling under my body. My experience of illness was that each day was worse than the last.

One day, several kids from my class made an appointment to visit my family. I saw how lively and cheerful they looked and my heart was pricked with jealousy. I left them there and ran into the inner room, slamming the door. I didn't feel like crying but I wanted to save myself from self-pity and the sense of my own inferiority. Face-to-face with them, I suddenly suffered an unspeakable pain. Overhearing them chattering away, I suddenly realised how much I missed my school. I really understood that being sick was not fun at all.

After several months of being bedridden, I was left to heat up and drink my own herbal medicines all alone at home and I followed my doctor's advice strictly. The neighbours and our relatives all said: Such a good boy. My parents would then reply: He hasn't touched a grain of salt in half a year. I don't think they understood how I looked at the matter. In fact, there were only two ideas in my mind: one, I was afraid of dying; two, I wanted to go back to school with all the other pupils who were not sick. That was the sum of my spiritual support.

After six months or so, I recovered and went back to school. I remember it was a sunny day in autumn and I was jumping rope in the playground. I was jumping tirelessly, changing from one kind of fancy step to another until I'd collected quite a crowd and it was only then that I put down the rope. It had served its purpose: I wanted to tell everyone that I was better... Now, I was just the same as everyone else.

At the age of nine, I had left my bed of pain. But from then on, I thought I knew more about health than anyone else.

BORN IN THE 1960S, A LABEL

To be born in the 1960s, as far as I am concerned, is nothing to regret and nothing to celebrate. Strictly speaking, it was my parents' choice. If I had been born ten years earlier, I would have been sent down to the countryside like my sisters and spent my youth in a country village that had nothing to do with me; if I'd been born ten years later, I would have been at a loss to understand terms such as the quotations of Chairman Mao, Criticising Lin Biao and Criticising Confucius, and Counterattacking the Right-Deviationist Reversal-of-Verdicts Trend. But what does this have to do with anything? All history can be learned from history books but you usually can't find your own history there because the only person who can write that is you yourself, regardless of what era you were born. History can always utterly obliterate your own personal life experiences, including the date of your birth.

Being born in the 1960s meant that I escaped the calamities of many political movements, though I have some confused and strange memories of them. At that time, I was still a child and children never make moral judgments about the outside world.

Their interest in violence was partly the result of their education at that time and partly natural. I remember when I was in primary school, I heard that my older brother and sisters in middle school had made one of their teachers climb a 'mountain' made of tables and chairs. Then they yanked a table out from underneath and the teacher tumbled from the 'mountain peak' to the ground. I didn't see this cruel scene with my own eyes but I knew the teacher concerned. Later on, I often saw her when I was in middle school and I want to make it clear that her face was unforgettable because, even after so many years had gone by, she still had black and purple scarring to her face. I would like to say that many of my siblings have records of doing terrible things, which can be excused in many different ways, but the facts are the facts, which cannot be altered. As a child watching from the sidelines, no one can blame me for what happened, not even myself. This is one of the reasons why I, as a person born in 1963, can be more relaxed than they are, and also one of the reasons why I am more complicated than the people born during the 1970s who know nothing about the Cultural Revolution.

Chinese society always used to be a very special society and it is still special today. In ancient times, people my age would have had grandchildren by now but today they are still generally referred to as 'young people'. When these aged 'young people' see real youths wandering around in full health and vigour, they sometimes feel they are just shoddy fakes. When 'young people' see those who lived through stormy times talking about the Cultural Revolution and such-and-such a movement in the newspapers or on TV, they will say to the real young people around them: You don't know about this stuff, do you? I know all about it. But in actual fact, they're outsiders—at best, they're just witnesses and bystanders. These people born in the 1960s belong to the generation that connects the past and the future in Chinese society today, but they are marginalised precisely because of this. Some of these people drift along on the tide of cynicism, and some take an early jump into the mentality of the middle-aged and elderly. The former became the darkest members of the crowd in the 1970s, while the latter became fresh blood in middle-management positions and went their own way. These people never considered the hidden subtext behind their birth in the 1960s. They are now middle-aged, with parents and kids to look after, and their difficult daily grind is quietly eroding the special label they have because of their birth date. This generation has learned to pay homage to real life and to let everything else go.

Of course, a generation can go to make a book but what marks what goes between the covers is not the date of publication but each of the individuals that makes up the story. People who write articles always generalise in this way, struggling to come up with something new to say on the subject but I am willing to set up a fallacy: there is no such thing as group spirit. Just like the babies born at the same time in a maternity hospital, they leave and go their separate ways, and although they may meet again once grown, there is one thing that is almost certain: they won't recognise each other at all.

A SECOND HOMETOWN

Before I left my hometown at the age of 18, the farthest away I had ever been was Nanjing. It was a special trip, not for tourism or visiting relatives. At that time, hundreds of middle-school students from all over the province gathered in the Party School hostel on Jianye Road to participate in a large-scale essay-writing competition. I didn't succeed in winning the competition. I remember that before returning to Suzhou, a group of us were dawdling in the square in front of the railway station and suddenly realised that Xuanwu Lake was right in front of us. I don't remember who was the first to run to the lake but we all followed one after another; I also am not sure who was the first to wash their hands in its waters. A large group of middle-school students lined up on the bank and everyone put their hands into the lake and washed them carefully. I still remember the voices and faces of the young boys and girls squatting by the lake to wash their hands. With the passage of twenty years, the waters of Xuanwu Lake have long gone from our hands, leaving no trace behind, but somehow or other that handful of water ended up changing my life. Of all of those Suzhou middle-school students waiting to go home, maybe I was the only one who was destined to stay beside the Xuanwu Lake.

There are lots of people who love the idea of going to live in Nanjing. They want to live in a city that is neither too big nor too small; they don't want too much bustle and commotion, and they don't want the whole place to be completely dead; they don't want to live cheek-by-jowl with their own parents but neither do they like the idea of being too far away; they can't afford to have their own garden but they'd like picturesque scenery in the city where they live; they see themselves as highly intelligent and superior but want those around them to be simple, honest and generous. I'm probably just this kind of person, so when I was 22 years old, I volunteered to go and live in Nanjing. I've been in Nanjing for more than ten years now, and enjoy it more than ever.

Apart from the universal complaints about the cold in the winter and the heat in the summer, pretty much everyone seems to love Nanjing. There are lots of cities that have made an effort to go green but the canopy of paulownia trees along the streets of Nanjing is really incomparable. (Nanjing people adore these trees and forgive them the fluff that falls from them in spring. You can see many city cyclists coated head-to-foot in fluff in the spring but the expression on their faces makes it quite clear they don't mind a bit). Many cities have one or two scenic spots that the locals are proud of, which are subject to mixed reviews by visitors from other parts of the country. However, Nanjing's Zhongshan Mausoleum is always wonderful. When you climb to the top of Zhongshan Mausoleum, you will find that the beauty of this city is extraordinary. Zijin Mountain and the Yangtze River are no longer natural barriers; they are part of the landscape that has nurtured Nanjing since time immemorial. The forest in the eastern suburbs is a huge green pillow. Every night, it whispers to the Taiping Gate: Go to sleep, Nanjing…. And then Nanjing will sleep. Every morning, it says to the Zhongshan Gate: Wake up, Nanjing… And then Nanjing will wake up.

The sleep of the ancient capital of the Six Dynasties is never too long; Nanjing wakes up. Where once the horses and carriages of emperors rolled past, the bicycles of the local people now hurry by; at the construction sites around Xinjiekou, the pile-driving machines do not care what the ghosts of the princes and princesses buried around the mausoleum of the founder of the Ming dynasty think about the noise, for they are determined to make their deafening cry for the construction of a new Nanjing. In an old alley in the southern part of the city, an old woman carries an old chamber pot across the old Qinhuai River but she can't dump the contents in the river. She has to pour it into the septic tank of one of the public toilets. Although Nanjing has not eliminated the need for chamber pots, even Shanghai hasn't done so yet, so why should we make such a fuss about it?

It is not in the character of Nanjing people to be anxious, though it can seem so when they speak. In recent years, everyone has been wanting to get rich, and that includes Nanjing people, but because they are never in a hurry, many things happened more slowly here than in other places. When Nanjing people joined the gold rush to Haikou or Shenzhen, they discovered these places were already packed to the rafters so they just came back. When Nanjing people discovered that others had made a lot of money by producing fake goods, they realised sadly that they would never get rich like that. So they set out to make a little fortune. They decided to go home and make salted duck. Supposing that the locals couldn't eat enough salted duck, it wouldn't matter if they couldn't sell it, because they could eat it themselves.

Nanjing people fulfill my ideal of how people should be, so I have been very happy living here. One day this summer, I suddenly felt really gung-ho; remembering that even after all these years there were plenty of beauty spots recommended by my friends that I'd never been to, I collected up my wife and daughter and headed out to the eastern suburbs. Not being a holiday, there were very few visitors, and we walked along a little path beyond the library under the shade of ancient trees, all the way to the Linggu Temple. On the way, we did not hear the sound of people's voices, but just listened to the birdsong and the babbling brook. It was a strangely sweet feeling, as if the whole place belonged to us… as if we were showing a treasure to ourselves and we felt very happy and content.

Perhaps it is natural that if a person likes where they live, they will find pleasure in every plant and tree. Many people now live elsewhere, far away from the place where they were born, without homesickness or sorrow, living quite contentedly. The ancient expression about 'finding a second hometown elsewhere' probably originated here.

MY EIGHT HUNDRED METRE HOMETOWN

In my dictionary, a hometown is often reduced; sometimes it contracts down to a narrow street, sometimes it is flattened, it is scattered fragments of memory, flashing cold or warm lights. My dictionary is a writer's dictionary, and all the words I need have already been packed up and rendered easy to carry, including the heavy and huge word: hometown.

Everyone has a hometown but my strongest feeling is that my hometown has been hiding, dodging and even melting away. More importantly, it is a series of question marks: What is home? Where is your hometown? These questions are always open. After so many years, I am still imagining my hometown... discovering my hometown.

In the summer of 1982, after living for more than twenty years on a street called Qimenwai, having seen all four of their children grow up there, my parents moved to a new house. If you walked north for another five hundred metres, along the old road in the northernmost part of Suzhou, crossed the bridge there, and then made your way down a very short and narrow street, on the left was the cement factory where my mother worked, and the factory accommodation on the right was their new home. As the crow flies, they'd moved less than eight hundred metres. At that time I was studying at a university in Beijing, thousands of miles away, and I was full of enthusiastic images of my new home because it was in a newly-built building, up on the third floor... just the height of the new building, with an indoor lavatory, balcony, and so on was already very exciting. I clearly remember that first afternoon when I came home for the summer vacation; I stood on the balcony of our new home looking at the scenery, near and far, with new eyes. In the distance, straight ahead of me was the large white chimney and kiln of the cement plant. Off to one side, you could see the black chimney and factory buildings of the charcoal works. The Beijing to Shanghai railway line ran behind the cement plant but unfortunately the kiln obscured the tracks and trains, so I couldn't see them. In fact, the house I lived in as a child lay eight hundred metres to the southeast, well within the range of my vision, but my view was blocked by other buildings so I couldn't see anything. It was the first time our family had moved in many years; we moved from living opposite a chemical plant to living opposite a cement plant and charcoal works. From air polluted by coal tar derivatives, we fell into the arms of cement dust and charcoal fumes. Air quality wasn't a hindrance to any member of the family; the only problem was the change this brought to the daily round. We were eight hundred metres further away from everything. My father went to the city centre to work: his bicycle journey was now eight hundred metres further. My mother had eight hundred metres less to go when she went to work but if she wanted to visit my grandparents or her brother and his wife then she had to walk a further eight hundred metres. For me, that eight hundred metres was an expansion of my world but the drawback was that the scale was too small. My life had stretched from one street to another but that only amounted to eight hundred metres: I had lost nothing and gained nothing. That summer, I came to understand the meaning of the word 'hometown' for the first time but the hometown I imagined for myself did not exist in this eight-hundred-metre world.

Those eight hundred metres became a symbol, just like a person's journey to find their hometown can be very short and very long at one and the same time. That eight-hundred-metre world was our family's destiny. The only difference was that the relocation in the summer of 1982 separated us from my mother's family by eight hundred metres, which is not far but not very close either. This was a headache for my mother in pickling season since there was nowhere to put her big vat in the new house and, besides which, she had a great deal of faith in her second brother's skills—it was her opinion that the pickles he packed were just the best. Now with no vat to hand and her brother living further away, she had to give up on making pickles. Our move was problematic for me too and this was worse than not being able to make pickles since, in accordance with my mother's instructions, I had to visit all of our relatives every summer vacation or New Year's. At least twice a year, I had to walk eight hundred metres back to our old house to meet my grandmother, my two uncles and their wives: from having been part of the big family living at Number 127, I had become a relative... a guest. This new identity made me feel strange and uncomfortable. Where we used to live (because it was public housing) had now been allocated to a family of strangers, and I looked curiously at our former home, very disappointed to find that it was really not the same because the new residents had painted the walls, changing the layout of the rooms, and they'd also changed my mother's family's way of life. It wasn't just that strangers had intruded upon my family but my relatives had adapted to these outsiders' way of life.

And our family, at least to begin with, had also been strangers in this block. My parents were immigrants to Suzhou from Yangzhong Island in Zhenjiang. Before the 1980s, Yangzhong County was listed as my native place on all my personal documentation but afterwards I was required to change it to Suzhou. This requirement ignored my father's origins and emphasised the importance of my place of birth. Since then, my identity has been inextricably linked with Suzhou.

Our family was a little unusual: thanks to several families coming together and living in a new place, it seemed as though the younger generation would have a new hometown. But the concept of a hometown is not so easily changed. Most of our neighbours were long-time residents of Suzhou and they readily accepted our family long ago. However, the daily life that went on in Number 127 and 125 was not quite the same as everywhere else, and this was particularly obvious from the way we spoke. There was no agreement in our family about what language we spoke: my grandmother could not speak a word of Suzhou dialect; her oldest daughter-in-law couldn't speak Yangzhong dialect; my parents and uncles alternated between the dialect of their hometown and that in Suzhou—they spoke to each other in Yangzhong dialect, while to us kids or to outsiders, they'd speak in fluent Suzhou dialect.

For the longest time, the local dialect spoken by our elders made us children feel afraid—it was kept secret, for fear that outsiders might overhear. Unfortunately, this secret couldn't be hidden forever because our parents never felt ashamed of their hometown. The dialect in use on Yangzhong Island sounds quite similar to that of Subei, and popular attitudes in Suzhou (like those in Shanghai) mean that Subei dialect spoken in northern Jiangsu has always been deeply despised. Regional discrimination was ingrained. My sisters and cousins suffered a lot from this: once they got into a quarrel with other girls, their parents' accent would always be dragged in— it simply did not matter how much they emphasised the fact that

Yangzhong Island is located in the middle of the Yangtze River and is administered by Zhenjiang, and Zhenjiang is south of the Yangtze River, which has nothing to do with Subei. Usually, the answer they'd get was that Zhenjiang is no different from Subei dialect. Regardless of whether your hometown is north or south of the Yangtze River, you aren't from Suzhou, you're from Subei!

We kids defended our parents' hometown, its geographical location and the dialect and accent, partly out of vanity but also out of anger. When you are annoyed by your parents' accent, how can you feel the glory of the word 'hometown'? On the contrary, what the next generation experiences is the difficulty of cutting themselves off from and forgetting their hometown. In the final analysis, children have no hometown, particularly when you are talking about kids like us, whose parents had moved from some godforsaken village to the big city.

To be separated, reunited, and then separated again was the outcome of my mother's family's migration from Yangzhong to Suzhou. A landless family will never be able to escape the separation that is their destiny. A couple of decades of really hard times kept my mother's family together in one place, in a close-knit family circle, but in the end, during an era of rapid development and change, all that vanished. The first, second and third generations of the family finally ended up scattered to the four winds. Five years ago, with the demolition and reconstruction of Qimenwai Street in Suzhou, my uncle and my third aunt were resettled in other residential districts. Likewise, thanks to the inevitable estrangement of relatives, I have never even been to their new homes. I have a lot of cousins in Suzhou but I don't know where they live. Some of their children have come to Nanjing to study and I try to reach out to them, inviting these young college students to my house for a good dinner. After such meals, I would get a phone call from my cousins to say thank you but afterwards we resumed our long estrangement and lost contact. The lively family circle of my childhood has withered away to nothing. For me, my family is now entirely composed of my immediate relatives. Every time I return to Suzhou, my footsteps turn in the direction of my father's house, and where my brothers and sisters live, and even they don't live under the same roof. There is a great distance between their houses, far more than eight hundred metres. For me, once it gets over eight hundred metres, my idea of a hometown starts to become confused, to become erased. In this way, my 'eight-hundred-metre' hometown has disappeared.

That is why I say: after so many years, I am still imagining my hometown... discovering my hometown.

I went to my parents' hometown, Yangzhong, and it was utterly alien to me. Whatever traces were left behind by my parents' generation were long gone and so I returned to Suzhou, to the northern part of the city, my 'eight hundred metre' hometown, but it too had vanished. All that was left behind were the two stone bridges built during the reign of Emperor Tongzhi in the Qing Dynasty, one to the south and one to the north, for people to pay homage to. I found that with the demolition of the ancient houses, the northern part of the city has become very empty but also very small—the space between the two bridges now looks much less than eight hundred metres!

Therefore, I suspect that my 'eight-hundred-metre' hometown is just an illusion. How big a hometown do I actually want? Where is the hometown I need? Do I know? Maybe I don't know. That is why I say: right up until the present time, I am still imagining my hometown... discovering my hometown.

GIRLS FROM TWENTY YEARS AGO

Impressions and feelings about women change year on year. There are basically only two genders, and women are one of them, so of course they will follow the basic laws that entail that things are in a constant state of flux, including men and women. Therefore, everything is in line with both scientific principles and my own conjectures and expectations.

Twenty years ago, I saw the women around me with the eyes of a boy and I still have a clear memory of what they were like. This all happened during those turbulent years—the 1970s—when I often got to hear women shouting in clear, sonorous voices about long live so-and-so or down with such-and-such. This came from live broadcasts of mass meetings from high-pitched loudspeakers out on the street, or what I heard with my own ears at the factories nearby.

Women have amazing voices, which were particularly suitable for the role of shouting slogans for the crowds to repeat, and they made a very deep impression on me at that time.

In the 1970s, women wore blouses in blue, gray, khaki or a discreet floral pattern, and baggy trousers in blue, gray, khaki or black. In the summer, some of them might wear skirts, but only school-age girls wore flowered skirts. Adult women had skirts that were blue, gray or black and they were carefully pleated. The most fashionable girls wore white skirts made of Dacron, but because of what they were made of, it was sometimes possible to make out the colour of their underwear through the fabric. This kind of white skirt attracted unwelcome attention from men and from disapproving older women. In our street, the sort of girls who wore white skirts were usually regarded as borderline delinquents.

Most of the girls over the age of eighteen were sent down to the countryside to work, so the women to be seen out and about were mostly middle-aged and married. They carried baskets as they made their way to the market to buy tofu and vegetables. The women I saw most regularly at that time were those middle-aged women, walking along with their baskets and chatting loudly to one another. There were also a few young girls who'd managed to stay in the city but I didn't know whether one was prettier than the others because I had no idea that women were supposed to be beautiful.

I remember a pale and thin woman of about fifty years old, with her hair done up in an old-fashioned bun, walking down the street every day with an iron placard hanging around her neck. On it were written in black ink the words: 'Counter-Revolutionary Capitalist.' I heard that this woman was actually the concubine of some capitalist or other. What surprised me was that in such an environment she still kept her love of beauty—she had her hair done in such a unique and elegant style. However, her hairstyle caused outrage, and so someone shaved half her head just as they would a man's. People with half their hair shaved off in punishment—the so-called yin-yang style—were everywhere in those days, so to see this woman with half her hair cut off didn't surprise anyone.

At that time, girls dreamed of finding a husband in the army, but only the prettiest girls could hope to marry such a man—the next best thing was to marry a veteran. It seems as though girls and their parents all adored the solemn green military uniforms with badges on their red collars. If a local girl got selected to join the army, her friends might well literally cry with envy.

No girl in those days would be willing to marry the son of a landlord, nor someone classified as from a rich family, counter-revolutionary, a bad element or a rightist, so the latter's marriage partners would be girls from the same kind of background or ones who had something else wrong with them. Many years later, the girls who married such 'bastards' reaped their own reward: government campaigns in the late 1970s to 'restore things to normal' and 'implement effective policies' brought them various economic and housing benefits, not to mention other kinds of compensation. Years later, at a time when they were already middle-aged, they could look back on the sufferings of the past from the perspective of a comfortable present.

Some girls who were sent down to the countryside ended up with village boys as their partners. Such marriages were often publicised in the newspapers of the day as a sign of revolutionary fervour, and these city girls were held up as models for women in the new era that was dawning. Their photos were almost identical: they'd be standing in a paddy field somewhere out in the countryside with short hair, a straw hat and bare feet, holding a sheaf of rice in their hands, with the words, 'In this Vast Realm, We Can Achieve Much', written in red around the brims of their straw hats.

Romantic love and secret affairs still happened in those days—a girl might blush as she came into view of her neighbours, seated behind their boyfriend on the back of their bike. Girls need to be extra careful on evenings like that: they might go to one of the parks which had free entry but if they couldn't resist their boyfriends' impulses and they ended up kissing behind a tree, it was very likely that they would be spotted by an inspector, in which case they might end up being taken to an office somewhere for interrogation and concomitant humiliation. Girls who dared to flirt with their boyfriends in a park sometimes got into all kinds of trouble.

However, women who had an affair were faced with an even

darker prospect. Just like the heroine in Hawthorne's *The Scarlet Letter*, she would bear a heavy scarlet letter, not on her cheek, but in her heart. No one would sympathise with women of this kind; no one was interested in the motives and reasons for her adultery. People would despise this kind of woman—even children of seven or eight years old. I remember when I was in primary school, two of the girls in my class got into a quarrel. One of them said to the other in a cold and mature tone, "Your mother's a whore! She's nothing but a shameless bitch!"

The other responded tit for tat, saying, "It's your mother that's the whore. She got caught with a man; I saw it with my own eyes."

Why is it that no one accuses fathers of committing adultery? That's something that children find really strange. Therefore, it seems that in every human society, at every level, whether you are talking about the elderly or about children, people are most likely to find fault with women, and they demand a much higher standard of morality for women than they do for men.

Reading Simone de Beauvoir's *The Second Sex* a few years ago, I decided that I quite agreed with the key point she made in her book. To my mind, women are also the passive and suffering gender. The strange thing is that this impression was formed when I was young and ignorant in the 1970s, so now I realise that there wasn't much reasoned thought behind it—after all, this was an abnormal era.

Today's women are not at all like those of the 1970s. I am quite sure that any man would agree with this, so it is unnecessary for me to elaborate. What I want to talk about instead is what came to mind when I watched the 'Miss Nanjing' competition on TV not long ago. The girls appearing on the screen were all very beautiful and attractive, and each of them was only about twenty years of age: the loveliest of girls. Any man would agree that they were a gorgeous sight. But I felt sorry for the beautiful girls of the 1970s: are they sad to have been born at the wrong time? They'd all be middle-aged women today. Where are they now?

AN AUTOBIOGRAPHICAL MOMENT

I was born at home in Suzhou on 23 January 1963: it was the night before Chinese New Year's Eve. That evening, my mother had planned to go to the factory to work the night shift, but all of a sudden she gave birth to me, and I landed in a wooden basin. Of course, my mother told me all about this much later on.

I spent my childhood living in an old street in the north suburbs of Suzhou. My memories of the life we lived there has always been very clear and deep. Many of my short stories are based on that period of my life. As many critics have noted, they are 'told from the perspective of a child' and are 'childhood memories'. That must mean that my writings are naïve and immature, for which I can only apologise.

I was an obedient child. I listened to my teachers at school, my parents at home and the leader of the gang we kids had formed. One year I got ill with a very serious nephritic condition. The doctor refused to let me eat salt, so I listened to the doctor: I didn't touch so much as a grain of salt for nearly half a year. Right up to the present day, I am still very obedient; I listen to our political leaders, to my parents, to my wife and to my friends. One friend suggested that I buy a microwave oven, so I did, and then found that I didn't use it. My wife said: if you don't need it, sell it to someone else, maybe just a little cheaper than what you bought it for, so I ended up selling it to someone else at a reduced price.

I have never been rebellious nor a very macho character, which also makes me feel embarrassed sometimes.

My only firm faith has been in literature, which has freed me from many unspeakable sufferings and worries. I love it and feel a deep gratitude for it. I am grateful that such a profession could exist: it has provided me with a livelihood and filled my existence with wonderful things.

When I was a child my family was poor so I had no opportunities for self-cultivation or the pursuit of art. I have two sisters and a brother. My second sister is also interested in literature: she would often borrow books from other people which she then took home to read. She never borrowed things for very long—just three to five days—and she'd finish reading them in one day and then pass them on to me. I read books like Tolstoy's *The Awakening* or Stendhal's *The Red and the Black* in the space of a single afternoon: I would read until my head was all muzzy and confused but I still insisted on carrying on with this ridiculous, unintelligible reading. Perhaps because of these books, I somehow managed to avoid many of the bad habits acquired by other local teenagers. I just stayed quietly at home, cultivating my imagination.

When I was in high school, I started to write fiction, sending out a few manuscripts, which of course came straight back to me. I also wrote poetry. My first poems were written in a plastic-covered notebook and I still have them. I have never read them again but I continue to cherish them.

In 1980, I was admitted to Beijing Normal University. One day in early September, I boarded a northbound train and left the ancient, humid city of Suzhou. After a journey of twenty hours through an alien countryside, I walked out of Beijing station. I remember the bright sunshine that afternoon, the streams of people crossing the square outside, and the sky-blue stop sign for the No. 10 bus. I remember how empty I felt at that time, and how strange.

For me, those four years of study in Beijing were the real beginning to my life. I felt a sense of freedom; I could sense a vibrant culture all around; and I was buffeted by new ideas from all over the world. I have a great nostalgia for that life: after my second class of the morning, I would walk out of the university gates with my bag on my back and take the No. 22 bus to Xisi, and there I would have a bowl of cheap, high-quality Korean cold noodles at a Yanji-style restaurant. Then I'd go to the library, Beihai Park, or to an art museum to see an exhibition, and then walk down Wangfujing Street window-shopping, before taking a bus to Qianmen to watch an old copy of the Japanese film *Muddy River* on show in a small cinema there.

At this time, I wrote a lot of poems and novels, and sent them out to every publisher I could think of, and eventually some of them were published. In 1983, the journals *Youth*, *Young Writers*, *Skyflight*, and *Stars* published my writing for the first time. I was terrified of rejection and I worried about this becoming known to my classmates. Therefore all my correspondence at that time went to one of my classmates in Beijing. She understood me very well, and always encouraged and supported me in her own special way. I remain grateful to her to this day.

When I graduated from university, I chose to work in Nanjing. It was a peculiar decision to make, moving to a strange city. However, it turned out that I had made the right choice. I have always liked the place where I live but I couldn't tell you why that should be. I worked for a year and a half in the Nanjing Art Institute but I was too careless and self-willed to be a good college instructor, and the senior people in the organisation disliked and discriminated against me. This was not in the least surprising and turned out to be a blessing in disguise. Having been recommended by friends, I got a job I loved, becoming an editor at the magazine *Bell Mountain*. At this point, my life took a first step towards stability.

I got married in 1987 and have remained happily married ever since. My wife was a classmate of mine in middle school, and she was trained in Tibetan-style and military dancing. She looked very beautiful when she performed on stage. I told her that I fell in love with her at that time but she didn't believe it. My daughter Tianmi was born in February 1989. I love her so much that I feel embarrassed about it: why in the world should I be the one to have such a wonderful, beautiful daughter? I won't say any more about it but they have divided my life in two and that is the way it should be —there is nothing about my life before them that I am reluctant to give up.

Such an ordinary life.

I am now living in a dilapidated building in Nanjing, reading, writing, greeting the people who come to visit me, playing mahjong with my friends. I have no ambitions, no greed and I don't have affairs. This kind of life is just as it should be. My emotions are calm and my life is calm. That means my writing has also become calm.

What else is there? There's nothing more to say.

MY ALMA MATER

I never realised that the teachers in the primary school who taught me when I was a child would continue to remember me. My nephew is now studying in the same primary school and on one occasion when I went back to my hometown, he said to me: My teacher knows you. She said you're a writer. Are you a writer? I muttered something, and my nephew continued: My teacher said she taught you Chinese, is that right? I kept nodding and said yes, but I was feeling curiously shaken. I imagined how those primary school teachers who witnessed my childhood would talk about me, I wondered what those teachers would be like now, and suddenly realised that a person can have many unlikely people who care about them. They are concerned about you, but you have thrust them into some far corner of your memory.

My memories of my primary school, a former Catholic church, were beautiful and vivid but I never wanted to go back and have a look again because I was afraid of meeting any of the teachers who taught me. My niece also went to the self-same primary school when she was little, and on one occasion I went to pick her up and walked in through the school gate only to catch sight of the familiar auditorium. Many past events seemed to flash before my eyes and I moved forward as if by magic, in a trance. I wanted to continue deeper into the grounds but I didn't get very far before I saw the headmaster coming out of his office. That familiar figure made me flinch and, after hesitating for a few seconds, I ran back to the primary school's gates.

Occasionally, I have mentioned this to my friends and found that they have had similar experiences. I don't know if this is a good thing or not. I think many people have the same idea as me: they are accustomed to keeping some part of their life perfectly preserved and unchanging in their memories.

Twenty years after I left my alma mater, I received an invitation to celebrate its 70th anniversary. I had no idea that my school was so old and now I have discovered this, I feel proud.

At first I didn't want to go back for this occasion, for my time was fully occupied in dealing with all sorts of trivial issues. It was my father's words on the phone that changed my mind. "It'll only take half a day," he said. "Can you really not spare half a day?"

So in the end I went. On the train back to my hometown, I amused myself by guessing the purpose of each passenger's journey. I decided it must be something closely related to the life of each one, whereas I was making this journey for the sake of the child I used to be, for the sake of my memories, and that was surely quite unique.

On a sunny afternoon in autumn, I went back to my primary school. The children played music to welcome all of the guests who attended the ceremony. Just as I walked down the corridor of the teaching building, a teacher who had taught me mathematics quickly moved forward. She called my name and asked: Do you remember me? Of course, I remember her. In fact, I can still remember the name of every teacher who taught me. What made me uncomfortable was that she moved forward to say hello to me so quickly instead of greeting me as a teacher would a student. Later, I met an old teacher who had been terribly kind to me, now long retired. She said that if we met in the street, she wouldn't have recognised me. She said: When you were a child, you were very quiet... as shy as a girl. I am sure that this was the impression I had made on her memory, one of her thousands of recollections of thousands of students. Although this made me feel a little embarrassed, I was moved by it.

Just at that moment, my white-haired old teacher caught tight hold of my hand. Traversing the corridor, we came to another classroom where more teachers who had once taught me could look at me. Or to put this another way, when I held on tight to my teacher's hand, what came to mind at that moment was a spring outing more than twenty years ago, when she'd held me by the hand and walked with me to the front of the bus and said to the driver, "This child's been terribly sick, let him sit next to you."

Everything is so clear.

I forgot to say that my old primary school moved to a new site two years ago. There are no old associations with these classrooms and playgrounds, but I still find myself with strong feelings on the subject. In fact, what I remember is *my* primary school, and I will occasionally turn those dusty pages. I blow the dust off, and the memories are there safe and sound underneath.

THE CAVE

Walking along beside the ditch, I saw the homes of crabs and water snakes. They lived in various rough holes on the narrow sloping bank. The holes made by the crabs were a little larger, perhaps the size of a fist, while the water snakes' holes were surprisingly small: they fitted into a very tiny space indeed. You have to admit that the water snakes can squeeze into the smallest cracks. I bent over and looked closely at the holes but I couldn't help wanting to know whether there was more room inside the hole or not. I wanted to put my hand into the crab hole to have a feel but I didn't know whether the crab was at home. I was afraid of its two big claws and the dark and mysterious world inside the hole. I remember how timid and conservative I was in my childhood. Right then and there, I gave up trying to explore holes in the ground.

I've now seen much bigger, more spectacular holes in the ground. In southern China, there are caves of different sizes in almost every karst mountain and limestone landform. Some caves have been developed and become local tourist attractions, and their underground rivers and stalactites in various forms appear in beautifully printed picture books, crying out to people who are keen on traveling and exploring: we have a unique landscape! Here is a hidden cave! People have the same curiosity about caves as they do about light and darkness. They cross the underground river by boat and look up at the cave roof. With the help of directions from the tour guide, they spot any number of immortals, heroes, demons and ghosts in the weathered rock face. Here is a lovely goddess hanging in midair above a limestone slope; there is a fearsome demon suspended from the roof of the cave—of course, these roles are played by stalagmites and stalactites, assisted by lighting and a bit of paintwork. What is worth pondering is the way people deal with caves in peacetime. Nowadays they look to this secret and dark underground world for entertainment with myths and legends but long ago, during the war years, and more recently during the Cold War, people respected caves. Those were the glory years, at least as far as caves were concerned. People respected them not just as a place to escape the flames of war. If people regarded the earth's embrace in the same way as their mother's, then their feelings for caves were close to children's love for their grandmothers. This is all quite natural, after all, the earth has a mother too, and this would be the cave complexes that I am talking about—just like the village which I visited many years ago deep in the Yan Mountains where the people called the only cave they have there the 'Granny Cave'.

Dark and humid underground spaces have always been ready to save people from the outside world, just like the cellar featured in the film *Underground* by the Yugoslavian director, Emir Kusturica: this magical and vast underground world ends up becoming a safe haven for people in time of war. The joy and freedom that they gain by escaping underground is much richer and more interesting than any above-ground retreat. In this film, the wise director shows us that the cellar—this underground world—has its own mission and responsibility. Its generosity ensures that it will encompass all those who need to escape: officials, civilians, prostitutes and war-profiteers, not to mention creatures like orangutans, tigers and parrots. There is a saying that each day in a cave passes as slowly as one hundred years above—and this expresses a very negative view of life underground. However, in Kusturica's extraordinary vision, he begins by eliminating people's impression that life in the cellar is dark and unbearable. His underground world is full of fun, there are things to buy and beautiful people everywhere, and so there are cross-currents of desire. Although they are deprived of sunshine and moonlight, in every other way, this is paradise.

This film reminded me of the works of three great writers: Kafka, Dostoevsky and Proust. I imagine that Kusturica was at least somewhat influenced by Kafka because, in a sense, this film is an extension of Kafka's short story, *The Burrow*. However, that doesn't matter, what is important is that with the help of this film and the three people mentioned above, my fantasies about underground worlds have become more concrete and profound, and as a result of this, I've become an aficionado of caves. This is a wonderful thing: descriptions of the sunshine leave me cold; descriptions of the earth make me feel dissatisfied; but a film director and three writers have explored the world beneath our feet and I am not just convinced but inexplicably comforted!

I have seen these lost souls lodged in their caves: Kafka, Dostoevsky and Proust. Kafka's cave is undecorated. On a beechwood Biedermeier table lies the crust of the last piece of black bread he ate during his lifetime, for this short-lived civil servant no longer has any need for food. That's a good thing for his famous long-lived beetle—it has been eating this crust of black bread with relish for more than a century. I've seen Dostoevsky's cave, not in Moscow but in Siberia, where he was exiled. This cave was even colder and an icy wind blew in from the birch forest beyond, while snow fountained down from its mouth. There was no stove here and its owner shivered as he waited in despair for his next epilepsy seizure. The slightly warmer cave belongs to Proust and it is quite different from the others. It is elaborately decorated in crimson velvet with fireplaces and candlesticks, and there is a walnut bed. It all looks magnificent but in the final analysis, it is a cave. With his refusal to admit sunlight and fresh air, the noble bourgeois Proust comes to seem like a poor miner suffering from tuberculosis, coughing up blood, telling his servant over and over again about Swann's love, fantasising about the activities of the Baron de Charlus.

I heard the sound of their words penetrating further and further underground, and they repeated a disturbing movement—they were digging caves... even as they proved themselves unfit for manual labour, they insisted on carrying on. How sad to see the pale faces, purple lips and sickly weak bodies of these geniuses! On the other hand, between them they provided the incisive and profound argument for the necessity of digging out these holes. Loneliness made them feel calm but a fear of real life threw them into confusion, so their writings are little short of a miracle: calm but manic. Even during their own lifetimes, their souls had but a limited connection with their bodies, and it was their souls that first made the decision to leave the world and go underground. Go underground! They lived out their short lifespans in subterranean activity, like white asparagus. If the literary world at the beginning of the 20th century mourned the deaths of these three geniuses, it was with the understanding that they had always had one foot in the grave and nobody should be too sad about what had happened to them.

"The best thing about my burrow is its peacefulness." This is one of Kafka's statements about his underground city. But peace is not the only demand of the cave's guardian. What is more shocking is Kafka's method of digging it out. "I can only rely on my forehead to engage in such a kind of work. Therefore, I use my forehead thousands of times, day and night, against the hard soil. If I draw blood, I will be happy, because this is the proof that the walls are strong and everyone will admit that my city wall was built in this way." People who are used to living a healthy life can't bear this kind of confession while other cave lovers will shed tears over it because they are the only ones to sympathise with this strange man: yes, it is not easy for people to make a home, and it must be even more difficult for people to make a burrow.

In fact, it's easy enough. Think about the crabs and the water snakes. They can have burrows, so why not people? As long as the hole is big enough to hold a person, it can be your last home. This is the lesson we have been taught by the three great writers and an excellent director. I think that people will eventually signal their agreement but nevertheless the location of your burrow is key. In the Kusturica film I mentioned earlier, the entrance of the cellar was located in the house of a fraudster, which proves very dangerous and troublesome. If I want to dig a burrow, I would be sure to choose the most secret location, and I would never tell a fraudster where it was, not even my friends—no one.

MEMORIES OF THE WATER TANK

I don't know why but recently I have begun to miss our big water tank.

Our majestic, huge water tank was removed from the house many years previously and it disappeared from my life a long time ago. Suddenly, I find I miss having such a huge and heavy container about the place. Maybe this feeling is related to creativity or perhaps it is merely practical.

When I was a child, having water on tap was not common. Residents in a street shared a tap, so every household had a tank in which to store water. I remember that it was usually my two sisters who had the job of going to a pumping station to fetch water. They filled two tin buckets and then lugged the water home with their shoulders askew. They poured the water into the tank with a kind of furious expression often seen in those engaged in repetitive labour. Naturally, I stood idly by and watched the water level in the tank rise in a twinkling of an eye as the clear waters crept up the brown walls. It was strangely exciting and thinking back on it now, this was because of a classic childhood secret, which centred on the fact that I imagined there was a mussel living right at the bottom of the tank.

Please forgive me for telling this overly naïve story to adults. The story goes that a poor but kind-hearted young man picked up a discarded mussel by the river. He felt sorry for it and took it home, raising it in his only water tank. According to the rules for telling fairy stories, this mussel was no ordinary mussel. Of course there was a fairy living inside! I don't know whether it was to repay the favour or because she fell in love but every day when the young man went out to work, she would jump out of the water tank and transform herself into a capable young woman, cooking a good meal for him and setting it out on the table. Afterwards she would hop back into the tank. So this terribly poor young man, who didn't know where his next meal was coming from, now had enough to eat and warm clothes to wear, so all of a sudden he wasn't poor any more.

I am still shy of analysis but when I was a child, I heard ever so many fantastic fairy tales from adults, so why did I love the one about the mussel so much? If it's not simply a genetic wish to enjoy leisure without any hard work, then it's the common desire to get something for nothing. It was never my job to keep the kettle boiling but I very much enjoyed going and lifting the lid to our family's water tank. When the cover came off, I would lose myself in vain and passionate dreaming: where is the mussel in *our* tank? Where is the mussel fairy? I was ever-hopeful of seeing the mussel at the bottom of the tank open and the fairy coming out of the shell. At first, she'd be about as big as a pearl, then she would rise up through the water, gradually growing bigger. By the time she climbed out, she'd look like a regular fairy. Then I introduced a touching, realistic detail into my fantasy. The fairy would go straight over to our square, eight-seater table and clean it briefly. Then she'd start to move between the table and the tank, bringing out plate after plate of delicious food: chicken, duck, fried pig's liver and a large bowl of braised pork in fragrant savoury sauce. (There was no fish in any of the fairy's dishes, because I didn't like fish when I was a child)!

Obviously, I never saw a fairy-tale appearance in my water tank, the same as when I went to other people's houses to take the lid off their tanks. There'd just be water in there: no mussels and no fairies. Occasionally, my mother bought mussels in the market and cooked them with tofu but I had other ideas about where the mussels should end up. I always thought that we should put the mussels in the tank just to see what would happen. I tried this, but because the musty taste of the mussels affected the water quality, my experiment was soon discovered. The family took the mussels out of the bottom of the tank and threw them away, "Look, the water we've gone to such trouble to haul back is now undrinkable! What a tiresome boy you are... you look so clever but you do such stupid things!"

I never thought that I might be stupid, even in such instances of compulsive childhood behaviour, I stubbornly insist on discounting intelligence entirely and blame it all on curiosity. I read about Fellini's childhood curiosity in his autobiography, when he recalled without the slightest shame the scene of him diving under the dining table to look up the maid's skirts, saying, "It was dark and unapproachable, which was unattractive to me." I believe that his childish exploration of the maid's body was not done out of sexual desire but from curiosity. Curiosity is like a wonderful plant: even if it grows in dark spaces, it may eventually blossom with gorgeous flowers. I saw the flowers of curiosity in Fellini's films, which made me suddenly understand why so many artists have been tirelessly exploring and expressing in their works, but it is only in Fellini's films that the sex is so innocent and so exciting, and the combination of innocence and excitement is really endearing! For other children who were Fellini's contemporaries, the most important influences came from their Fascist families, church and school. For Fellini, the biggest influences on him as a child were sex, the circus, films and spaghetti. Sexual desire offered him self-exploration, the circus was a chance encounter, spaghetti was part of his daily life, and the cinema was the first place to allow him amazement. This is a simple but unexpected fact. In Fellini's opinion, all his curiosity and childish enthusiasm finally come together in 'amazement' and this was his artistic motivation and the source of his productivity.

I miss that water tank; in fact, I miss my curiosity. Children in those days had Mao Zedong Thought and fanatical politics and very little in the way of material goods, but that did not do them any harm. Every family had a water tank, and having that tank was enough for children to learn to dream, their dreams swimming through the tanks like fish. The world that children see needs to be developed just like their bodies; they don't know anything about reality yet, any more than they know what is waiting for them in the future. Just as with stimulating gonads, stimulating imagination, stimulating intelligence, what kind of stimulation is most conducive to children's development? I don't know, but I appreciate everything that the water tank gave me.

And it is not just the water tank, I also appreciate all the other romantic, mysterious or terrible stories that spread through the locale in those days. There are all kinds of ways to tell fairy tales but when nobody is telling you a story, go and listen to what the water tank has to say to you. I have always been convinced that every adult's serious artistic creations are an expression of their childhood curiosity—at least this seems to be true for ordinary adults. Curiosity is like a nebulous cloud in the vast sky: sometimes it shines brightly, sometimes it is dark and gloomy, and sometimes it tears like gossamer. Whether you are talking about people, about animals or about things, the impulses of curiosity are not dissimilar to the movement of clouds. They seem delicate but, in fact, they are unpredictable and uncertain. The remaining shreds of curiosity that adults retain are all directed to concrete, utilitarian ends, and some develop directly into knowledge and technology. Curiosity about human affairs developed into the humanities, such as history and philosophy. The infinite curiosity about things developed into numerous scientific disciplines and led to countless technological innovations. It also led us step by step into material culture; indeed, half of people's curiosity took them over the threshold of culture and art, elevating us further and further, while the other half went astray, heading towards the basest aspects of humankind, leading to vulgar gossip and innuendo. Sometimes we cannot avoid having 'keeping up a good reputation' being used to justify prying and prurient curiosity, and some people keep manically twitching that net curtain: their spying becomes like a black cloud hanging over other people's heads. As for writers, whose curiosity is deliberately retained, they play the luckiest and the strangest role with respect to curiosity. They seem at once to be both fortunate and unlucky. An author's curiosity is encouraged by himself and others because this is relevant to the organisation of the text and the characters' psychology. Their curiosity is all-encompassing and yet slightly vague, because it has no practical value or specific direction. Utilising this vague curiosity, I must make the sharpest dissection and explanation of the real world, so my profession sometimes makes me feel that it is at one and the same time a fate, a challenge and even a miracle.

A miraculous career needs miracles to support it. My childhood yearning for miracles has been maintained through the medium of a water tank. As time went by, I lost my tank and in the process some part of this miracle was also lost. I have never liked to over-aestheticise my childhood, nor do I want to sit in the tree of memories showing off my abundant emotions but I can't bear to lose the memory of my childhood water tank. The tank itself has disappeared from my life but, in fact, for many years I have been repeating the action of opening the water tank in my writing. Who knows whether this is awaiting or pursuing inspiration? You can't see life in a water tank but you can see a mussel. You can't see the fairy emerging from her shell but you can see the light of a miracle.

At the age of 31, the American poet e. e. cummings wrote a poem, almost like a child's scribblings. I love this poem and I don't quite know why. One part reads as follows:

Who knows if the moon's
a balloon, coming out of a keen city
in the sky—filled with pretty people?

The moon is certainly not a balloon. There may be some cities in the sky but they are mirages. Are people in keen cities pretty? I don't think so. No matter how lovely the city, there will always be some vicious and ugly murderers—but it's really wonderful to be able to write a poem like this! I don't have too many rhetorical devices at my command, so I'll just talk about the water tank. Finally, I want to thank the water tank for its complex symbolism; our daily round was enriched by this gigantic tank and even as the water level dropped day by day and it became muddier, we could still be optimistic because of the fairy inside the mussel-shell. Since she could cook, she ought also to be able to provide drinking water or water for domestic use, so we must put our faith in the water tank.

To believe in the water tank is to believe in life.

SINGAPORE'S CHINATOWN, DURIAN AND OTHER THINGS

This must be the closest city to the equator that I have ever visited. Its sultry atmosphere and brutal sunshine do not attack you suddenly: every foreign traveller is prepared for them. Therefore, Singapore can be hot with a clear conscience and, because its conscience is clear, it can get over-hot. I exited the front door of the hotel, only to feel a burning sensation on my skin. Once I calmed down, I realised that it was perfectly natural—it was just the Singaporean midday sun beating down on me.

I headed off to Buffalo Cart River—otherwise known as Singapore's Chinatown. The name somehow excited me and I liked it very much. I told my friend when she came to collect me that I wanted to go to Buffalo Cart River and she shot me a sympathetic glance. That look was probably just commiseration for people like me whose minds have been poisoned by travel agents. Nevertheless, she told me the way to Chinatown and suggested that I take the subway. She said: it's very close to here but it's too sunny to walk. At this time of day, we don't usually go out.

But when I visit a strange country, my favourite thing is going out for a walk around. When I got there, I discovered that Buffalo Cart River had nothing to do with buffalo, carts or rivers. In contrast with the rest of this clean and magnificent garden state, this seems to be the only overgrown flower bed. Buffalo Cart River is just a traditional Chinese area but there weren't many people out and about on the streets. The shops were densely packed and the casually-dressed assistants, with a kind of lazy tropical demeanour, offered their wares to passers-by: electric fans, slippers, shorts, cheap goods, Nanyang safflower oil, eucalyptus oil, *bak kut teh* (pork rib broth), *laksa* curries; here's the Chaozhou guild hall, massage rooms, private clinics and the museum. They all made the same gestures with their hands, neither humble nor proud: everything here is for sale... don't worry, you don't have to buy anything... please have a taste... it doesn't matter if you aren't here to eat...

come on in... you don't need to come in... Yes, I went for a walk and it was fine but it was just too hot, I was sweating so much that the Buffalo Cart River would soon be flowing again. At the same time, I was mulling over a stupid question: why did Buffalo Cart River seem so familiar to me? Maybe it's because it resembles the old parts of Guangzhou and Xiamen, which I've been to many times.

My hotel was located in the Clarke Quay area, with a small bridge leading directly over to the street on the opposite side of the river. At night, the lights in the side streets were carefully illuminated; the plants on the riverbank glowing a beautiful green and the painstaking efforts of gardeners outlined in geometric shapes. The bars and restaurants near the river filled with guests emerging from the pitch-darkness from who knows where—the scenery along the river reminded me, as the pop star Na Ying does, that the day does not understand the darkness of night. This is the darkness to be found beneath the lights and so this is a cheerful darkness, a rich and peaceful blackness. For tourists like me who come and go in such a hurry, it's easy to remember the hot and silent streets in Singapore during the day, and we are just as easily attracted by the crisscross of cups and plates under the riverside lights. I asked friends to go there, drank some beer and ate some absolutely delicious black pepper crab. Suddenly, I was confused. Which one represents Singapore's mood: day or night?

Many years ago, I travelled around Malaysia, from Kuala Lumpur to Malacca, from Penang to the Genting Highlands. That country reminded me from time to time of the word 'Nanyang' with its forests of coconut palms and rubber trees, and many times, right before my eyes, there were pictures of workers from Fujian and Guangdong going out at the crack of dawn to tap the rubber. In Singapore, I just went from the hotel to Chinatown, my explorations only reaching as far as the Merlion sculpture out by the water's edge. The size of this country means that travellers like me, who have a vulgar ambition to experience every kind of landscape in a single trip, are left dissatisfied—particularly since this city-state's Nanyang style can make it seem like a mini theme park. Travelling from one end of Singapore to the other, in a flash, your journey is over; nevertheless, it so happened that this small country reminded me for the very first time during my travels of yet another, even more distant country.

On the last night before leaving Singapore, a painter friend took a few of us off to eat durian. It was not a common eating experience but a little adventure. We drove to a durian stall that the painter was familiar with for a bite: this was our durian main course. Then the painter friend said that he would take us somewhere else to eat a durian midnight snack. The car drove along a pitch-black road and then suddenly a tiny flash of light appeared in the darkness, hanging in the midst of a forest. Under the lamp was a durian stall. A man stood majestically beneath the lamp, waiting for his customers in the dark.

I was frankly amazed at how brisk the business was at this stall in the middle of the night but the painter explained that the durian here were picked at high elevation on a mountain in Malaysia—these were no ordinary fruit. I suddenly thought of my vague memories of the landscape in Malaysia. I thought of the first time I ate durian by the side of the road outside Penang many years ago. It was also under some trees but we ate surrounded by tropical sunshine mixed with road dust. The fruit were sold by an old woman dressed in black with a straw hat on her head. I wondered if there are durian in Indonesia... whether countries along the equator in South America have durian too. Finally, I thought about the coconut groves and coconuts of Hainan Island. I was too embarrassed to mention these passing thoughts to my companions but there is one thing I would like to tell my Singaporean friends which seems polite and appropriate to the occasion: Singapore makes me realise just how big this world is.

BEIJU IN SUZHOU

Beiju: the name of this place alone is shot through with an inexplicable sense of trouble, which makes people feel they dare not ignore any story that comes to fruition there. But I don't seem to be the sort of writer who is good at telling stories about days gone by, so what I am going to tell you is a tale of my own experiences in Beiju.

Suzhou people all know that the so-called Beiju is a small plaza located behind the famous Guanqian Street: a square with no defining characteristics, which is perhaps a little bit dull and uninteresting. Of course, this square has been in existence for quite some years. I don't know what Beiju was like in the past, but for as long as I can remember, it has been the centre of Suzhou in my mind. I have lived away from Suzhou for many years but when I think of my hometown, what comes to mind is, of course, Beiju—I remember the market in Beiju, the Enlightenment, Great Light and Yan'an cinemas, and the Suzhou Bookstore which I actually never set foot inside. I even remember my panicked attempt to find my father's bike among the heaps of bicycles in the square—once I'd learned to ride a bike, I often rode my father's beloved bicycle to Beiju. I don't remember what I went there to do; I just remember that having wasted half a day there, it was almost dark and I needed to hurry home because it was getting late but I couldn't find the right bicycle.

My memories of Beiju begin with the popularity of model operas towards the end of the Cultural Revolution. When I was in primary school, the school often organised that we children would be taken to see *The Legend of the Red Lantern* and *Shajiabang* when they were shown yet again in the cinema. A group of us primary school pupils living in the northern part of Suzhou City lined up, sang revolutionary songs and walked about three kilometres through the streets and alleys to Beiju. Sometimes we went to the Long March Cinema (now renamed the Great Light), and sometimes to the Yan'an (which retains its original name), to watch a film that was already familiar to us but our hearts would be filled with the happiness that comes from gaining a holiday. I have to say that even in an era which advocated hard work and plain living, children still showed a great appetite for fun. All of us kids hoped to be taken to the Yan'an to watch the movie there and there was a very simple reason for this preference—it was because the seats were upholstered. All the seats in the Long March Cinema diagonally opposite were hard benches.

Now I still can't explain why I cycled to Beiju over and over again as a teenager. The reason may be very simple, because there was nothing on the street I lived on except a few shops selling soy sauce and vinegar, and people there had long been so familiar as to be boring. When I came to Beiju, I was in the centre of Suzhou—it was important for me to see a lively place, full of people coming and going. When I heard some of the people in the crowd speaking in a Northeastern accent or in the tones of Shanghai or Beijing, I felt that Suzhou was in China, China was on the earth, and the earth was very big. This kind of association excited me, so when I looked around, I was looking forward to my future and fantasising over and over about what would happen to me.

I don't remember that much ever happened under the Beiju paulownia tree. When my wife and I first fell in love, we were already working somewhere else—we'd become strangers to Suzhou. Occasionally, we went to the Western restaurant downstairs at the Enlightenment Theatre, and we'd take my wife's younger sister (then still in middle school) with us—this was not at all the common situation of a young Suzhou couple meeting in a park. Nowadays, what I recall most clearly is a young bespectacled kid called Liu; this is twenty years ago, so I don't really remember what he looked like—he was a middle school student at a different school, very intelligent and silent. We met in a summer camp for children with literary talent. At camp, I was the youngest child present and with my peculiar nature, I found it difficult to get along with the others: I didn't expect to make friends. But Liu didn't dislike me and always walked with me (maybe he thought it was appropriate for us to become friends). At the end of summer camp, he lent me his copy of *How the Steel Was Tempered* to read and we agreed that I'd give it back to him three days later. We were to meet at the small park in Beiju. I remember how we met in the park three days later. He emerged from the alley next to the bookstore with a stiff smile on his face. I probably wore much the same expression. I handed the book back but I didn't even know how to thank him. I didn't say a word. We stood in the middle of the park and looked at each other for a minute. Then he said, "I'll be off then."

"Me too," I replied. Then we went our different ways.

I guess I lost a friend that day in Beiju. A person with my kind of character finally found someone who could possibly become a friend but now I watched him disappear from Beiju, walking out of my life forever—I never saw Liu again. It's something that has always made me sad to think about: it makes me feel a bit of a fool.

Later on, and more than once, I found myself wondering about young Liu—particularly the occasion when we met in Beiju—and I ask myself: you're just standing there, look at you… look at him! If you aren't going to talk to him, why did you bother coming?

Actually, I can't describe my mood back then; I just remember Beiju. A person's life can leave its traces in many places: life itself removes some but retains others—you must remember the ones that remain.

THE SOUL OF THE CITY

One summer evening a few years ago, I was walking with a friend from the north around the mausoleum of the founder of the Ming Dynasty, when I suddenly felt that something unexpected was happening. This accident was due to the receptiveness of our senses to the special atmosphere of a place. On that roasting hot day, when we touched the stone walls of the mausoleum, we felt a kind of moist, cold feeling. Under its covering layer of moss, the stone walls were dreaming a grey dream with the Fengyang Flower Drum Song as its background music, and starring an emperor named Zhu Yuanzhang. There was a strong smell of decaying grass or leaves pricking our nostrils, which usually can't be smelled until autumn. However, at the Ming Dynasty Xiaoling Mausoleum, the season of decay comes at the height of summer.

Therefore I can say that I suddenly encountered the soul of Nanjing on that day at the mausoleum.

Before I left my hometown at the age of eighteen, the furthest I'd ever been was on a trip to Nanjing. It was a special journey: at that time, hundreds of middle school students from all over Jiangsu Province gathered at the guest house attached to the CPC's school on Jianye Road in order to participate in a large-scale essay-writing competition. It was three days in total: a one-day competition plus a one-day tour of the city and then the award ceremony on the final day. By now, I've forgotten most of the details of what we got up to during those three days since I wasn't one of the talented young winners to be made much of, so what I recall most clearly is the hot weather when we left Nanjing, how the Chaotian Palace gradually slipped past the windows of the train, how the big umbrella-like paulownia trees on the Baixia Road and Taiping South Road shaded the handful of pedestrians and the deserted shops—this was a tree-lined city. It made a very good impression on me. Later, a large group of us were waiting in the square in front of the railway station and suddenly realised that the large area of water next to the square was Xuanwu Lake. I don't know who first picked up their feet and ran down to the lake to wash their hands but everyone followed suit: a group of middle school students lined up by Xuanwu Lake and washed their hands. At that time, the sky in Nanjing was bluer than it is now and the water in Xuanwu Lake was also clearer than it is today. I remember the sound of splashing water as a dozen of my friends washed their hands and their smiling faces, whether naïve or mature-looking. More than twenty years later, all the water drops on our hands have vanished leaving no trace behind, but as for me, though I did not know it at the time, my future was already inextricably linked with the waters of that lake. Apart from myself, I don't imagine any of those other middle school students later came to live in Nanjing.

This is a legendary city—the home of emperors—but also a weak and miserable city; and the glory and shame of this city go hand-in-hand, its glory days as crystal-bright and short-lived as dewdrops. Having been loved and favoured for a short time it finds itself abandoned, and that condition endures for ages. In the history of China, this city, as the centre of political power, as the capital of the country, appears just as unexpectedly as the blooming of flowers—and before you know it, it has lapsed into obscurity again. This city is an open tome and on every page the tattered banners of the former capital of the Six Dynasties flutters. It is a book read by writers and poets, and by the remarkable heroes of Jianghu. Everyone senses the city's noble qualities but before you come here, you cannot understand its tragic heartbeat. Eight hundred years ago, Zhu Yuanzhang, a beggar and monk from Fengyang in Anhui Province, chose Yingtian as the capital of the Ming Dynasty after many years of struggle as a Jianghu outlaw. After centuries of neglect, Nanjing—the Southern Capital—enjoyed a period of unique lavishness and splendour. Unfortunately, it was not the fate of the city to retain this too long. Soon the Ming Dynasty moved the capital to Beijing, leaving the infrastructure of the city unfinished, so that all Nanjing retained were the tombs of its princes and nobility. More than one hundred years ago, Hong Xiuquan, a deranged Christian belonging to the 'Society of God Worshippers' in Guangdong Province, suddenly collected a large group of followers and went on the rampage all the way to Nanjing. He had a fatalistic view of this city as the predestined capital of his Heavenly Kingdom of Great Peace. However, if there was to be peace in this place it was without the Heavenly Kingdom; if the Heavenly Kingdom was here, there would be no peace. Zeng Guofan, a native of Hunan Province, mobilised an army of local people against him and conquered Nanjing, crushing Hong Xiuquan's dream of crowning himself emperor of China.

Superstitious people in later generations might sometimes feel grateful for the Ming Dynasty. Even if the ghost of the Jianwen Emperor cursed his uncle, Zhu Di, for his wicked cruelty, at the same time we should also be grateful for Zhu Di's decision to move the capital. Perhaps this move extended the history of the Ming Dynasty by one or even two hundred years.

Many imperial dreams have ended in Nanjing. This is a city full of traps. It has never belonged to opportunists. Whenever one of them has fallen under the spell of this land of emperors, the results have been disastrous for them. It seems hard to say who the city likes to belong to, but it is quite clear who it will never favour.

I have now lived in Nanjing for many years. It is standard for some people to want to reside in Nanjing. They are drawn here by the aura that this city possesses of brilliant cultural achievements—this aura can render special even the most boring of everyday lives. In so many corners of the city, you can open any north-facing window to see mountains and rivers, while looking south gives you a vista of historical remains. Since you are not planning to ever make yourself an emperor, it doesn't matter that this is not the capital city—it's a nice manageable size: throughout its history, it has been possible to traverse the metropolis on foot. The kind of people who come here are not enamoured of bustling and noisy cities but they don't want somewhere completely dead and boring either; if they can't have their own gardens, at least they can hope for a picturesque park not far away. These people observe those around them in silence, and then compare them with themselves, to conclude that they are of superior intelligence but nevertheless they are simple, kind and easy to get along with. Supposing that they were fish, they would find that the city is nothing but a gently flowing river. Undoubtedly, I am one of these people. I have many friends here, almost all of them working in relaxed, self-centred professions, writing, painting, and so on—they live very contentedly here. It does seem as though they have managed to get something for nothing. The city that emperors had no choice but to give up has become a paradise for such people.

Except for the widespread complaints about the climate in winter and summer, those who come here from other parts of the country can hardly bear to hurt the calm, peaceful heart of this city by saying anything critical at all. The Zhongshan Mausoleum is always the principal attraction for tourists. When you climb up the hundreds of steps and look out into the distance, a vast forest stretches out before you in every shade of green for miles around. You have to admit that the officials who took care of Sun Yat-sen's funeral really did do a good job. This is the perfect place for a great soul to be laid to rest. In an age of peace, the Purple Mountain and the Yangtze River do not have to function as natural barriers against the enemy, therefore they are in a happy mood and try their best to nurture the city around them, creating an auspicious atmosphere that envelops the whole of Nanjing. After revolution and struggle, the city manages to look very restful while the forest in the eastern suburbs is like a pillow. The city leans on this pillow and takes an afternoon nap through the four seasons with a contented, self-satisfied air.

After their afternoon nap, in the streets and alleys of Nanjing, some strange ovens begin to belch smoke as they are lit. Countless small shop owners and ducks start a battle which is waged all over the city. They use iron hooks to get the ducks into the ovens. In the afternoon, you can smell them roasting on almost every street. At dusk, when housewives are cycling home from work to prepare dinner for their families, a vast array of different members of the duck family await them in the windows of each shop—whole glistening roast ducks, pre-prepared salted duck, gizzards and heads and feet. I can't even begin to imagine how many ducks and geese Nanjing people eat a year.

I remember that I came to Nanjing in early 1984 to work in a college. Behind my dormitory there was a side road leading from Hexi to the west of the city. Every morning, I could hear the quacking of ducks coming to Nanjing. Year after year, so many ducks came to Nanjing every dawn to sacrifice themselves to the unchanging appetites of the city. This is part of a unique tradition— a tradition that pertains to ducks, and also to the people of Nanjing. I have never had any intention of exploring its origins but by chance I read an Italian novel about an aristocratic family down on their luck holding a banquet for an important guest. The first dish the host thought of was duck. I can't help laughing when I think about it. It seems that ducks are not friends with this city by chance. Whether this relationship is accidental or not, it is true that food can offer you important clues about culture.

With the rapid advancement of globalisation at the end of the twentieth century, daily life everywhere tends to be similar. But sometimes a duck can serve to remind you that a city has its own nostalgia and dreams.

Even now, there are lots of beauty spots around Nanjing that my friends tell me about but which I have never been to; however, if a person likes where they live, they will patiently discover the charms of each tree and blade of grass. In the past, when I was still young, I would go swimming with my friends at Zixia or Qianhu Lake every summer. From the first of these lakes, you can see the city wall by the Zhongshan Gate; while the other faces Purple Mountain. I remember that night, swimming in Zixia Lake at the end of August, when a group of friends came on their bikes to join me. We floated about in the cool waters and when we raised our eyes, we could see the blue-black night sky with a million stars sparkling in it. Apart from the lapping waters, we could hear the trees rustling in the breeze. You could hear the sound of your own breathing and it almost seemed as though you could also hear the grass and tree-leaves breathing beside the lake. My youthful heart was suddenly moved by this city: what a beautiful place, what a peaceful place… how lucky I am to live here!

This feeling has not been erased by the passing of the years, so I have no regrets about choosing to live in an abandoned capital whose glorious past is inscribed in history books: I have enjoyed the simple yet wonderful life of an ordinary inhabitant of this city. I'm still obsessed with discovering the city—but as everyone will understand, the city doesn't have to meet me halfway.

WHAT IS THE SOUTH?

One afternoon many years ago, I was in a third-floor workshop about the size of a matchbox, looking out at a narrow, dilapidated side street: it was one of the poor lanes and alleys that I was only too familiar with, overlooked in spite of so many years of municipal reconstruction. There was no need for any building work here—at one end, it led to a stone-arched bridge built during the reign of the Tongzhi Emperor in the Qing Dynasty and at the other end, it debouched onto farmland and a certain brigade's threshing ground (1960s and 1970s), or to a new ring road and an industrial area comprising both state-owned and village enterprises (1980s). When I was looking down at the street in the afternoon sun, I suddenly remembered how I used to walk along it to have lunch at the canteen of the factory where my mother worked. I remembered the public toilets under the bridge; and the housewives and children of my age from one end of the street to the other… I recalled how they would sit at table and eat their lunch under the gaze of anyone passing by. What makes me sad is that after so many years have passed, the public toilets are still there and although the gravel surface has now been replaced by cement, the roadway is still so narrow and damp. Nevertheless people still enjoy the convenience the narrowness of the road brings: it is easy enough to lean your bamboo pole for drying clothes against the roof of the house opposite. People walking and cycling down this street still find themselves passing underneath sheets, jumpers, suits, trousers and even underwear. Such is the streetscape I am most familiar with. The disordered and messy visual impression it makes is nevertheless redolent with freshness and liveliness. Some of the old people I knew must have died by now but most of them are still alive. Most of them have raised their children or even their grandchildren on this street. Everything in the daily round of a small street is still the same, just like an old-fashioned clock. No matter how turbulent the time it ticks steadily onwards, marking out the dates on the calendar and the events in the news reports. Its pendulum moves slowly but at its own pace. This serves to correct a prejudice I have long held in my mind in favour of speed and change: slow does not mean that it is inaccurate; unchanging doesn't mean that it is dead.

That afternoon, I was startled to hear a public service announcement being broadcast on that little southern street. Because of its striking simplicity and because of its profundity, I was moved by its strange power:

I have never felt sufficiently affectionate towards the place to be able to describe Toon Street, where I was born, in eulogistic terms. It consisted of an unattractive pale stone road, two rows of old-fashioned houses without beginning or end, the atmosphere stank of mold and the dark windows were haunted by our neighbours with their pinched, wretched faces. I grew up in the south, dropped there like a grass seed from the beak of a flying goose—I was subject to forces beyond my control. I have hated life in the South for a long time. This is the eternal stain that Toon Street has left on me.

This is the beginning of a novella I wrote that summer: *The Fall of the South*. Now I should explain it, but I find myself in a dilemma and I find a kind of hostility in my writing towards what is at once a fictional and a real place: the South. What is the South? What does the South represent? And what does the hostility towards the South mean?

Perhaps, first of all, it comes from my hostility to memory itself. People usually prescribe their own emotional response to their memories, for better or worse, whether they are trying to whitewash themselves or not, or they will adopt a calm and objective perspective as they strive to record history as they saw it. But it so happens I have chosen to adopt a certain ruthlessness towards my recollections. There is a kind of paranoid, unexplained hostility to them. My so-called southern life only comes from a mechanical connection being made between the fact of my existence and a certain geographical location. My South is a street that runs through my recollections of the 1960s and 1970s, and I was a child at the time. A child's understanding of the world around him is vague and also can be quite uncertain. If people's hostility towards something comes from its potential or obvious harm to you, I cannot accurately describe the details of this harm any more, so I suspect that my hostility may be unfounded.

All descriptions based on memories are unreliable and therefore untrustworthy. For example, I mentioned one of my primary-school teachers in one of my writings. I always thought that my memories of her were crystal clear. I thought I was restoring a figure from the past but my other primary-school teachers later on proved to me that I'd even got her native place and family background wrong. The only thing I got right was my description of her physical appearance. Sometimes the facts make you panic: reliable things exist in reality but not in memory, so I have to doubt my hostility, which is also unreliable. I also have to suspect my idea of the South —where is it? Have I ever had a hometown in the South?

The much-admired Argentinian writer Borges wrote a wonderful short story called: *The South*. "Everyone knows that beyond Ribadavia is where the South begins." In this short story, the South gradually begins to extend its meaning beyond just being a place while the crippled and sick hero Juan Dahlmann forms a powerful triangular relationship with his copy of Weil's *Arabian Nights* and *The South*, which governs all the ideological space the writer wants to express. Juan Dahlmann comes south and in the end the *Arabian Nights* can no longer serve to conceal a cruel and cold reality. In a grocery store, someone throws a small ball of breadcrumbs at the sick Dahlmann, so one of the people in this world least fit to engage in a duel ends up having to withstand an underhand attack.

The meaning of *The South* may be a symbolic expression of this situation.

But where is my South? How much do I know about 'The South'?

At the north end of the street where I grew up, there was a teahouse. The teahouse was an old two-storey wooden building which faces the river on one side, the bridge on the other, and the third towards the street. For the longest time, just like any film director who is good at choosing his locations, I thought it a suitable 'southern' landmark. I have struggled to call to mind the people who used to live there: to begin with there was an old woman who manned the stove but eventually she got too old for the work and a new member of staff—also a woman—arrived. She was much younger but the expression that each of them bore when shovelling rice husks into the belly of the stove was surprisingly similar. They frowned in just the same way, constantly muttering swear words. They seemed to complain about life but, at the same time, to enjoy life. The faces they made as they worked was the basis of the expressions of southern women I described later on in my writings. The more important extras in this scene were the people sitting around and talking; they would sit around the greasy octagonal table and drink tea from cheap Yixing pottery. I used to consider them typical residents of the South: they were leisurely, laid-back, talkative and sociable, very much interested in politics and national affairs but when they discussed such things they proved to be unbelievably ignorant and short-sighted. They might chat casually about food and drink but here they would show their unique personal tastes and profound knowledge of the subject. They would sit there, relaxing and indulging themselves less than a kilometre from home and they would quarrel loudly, killing time in pointless arguments without anyone really opposing them, speaking a peculiar, discursive language. This was a game they played with themselves and they enjoyed it enormously. This style of aimless teahouse conversation was later something that I appropriated for use as the narrative rhythm in marking the progress of my story.

But reality is often even more dramatic than fiction, as can be seen from the teahouse mentioned above. As with the key sets of so many irresponsible movies and novels, the teahouse ended up burning down. In the spring of 1990, a few months before I wrote *The Fall of the South*, the teahouse suddenly went up in flames and was wrecked beyond any hope of repair. When I returned to my hometown, I saw the ruins. When I walked around the remains of the teahouse, I felt a curious sense of loss but this feeling was not induced by the destruction of the teahouse, rather from the sudden death of a blueprint for my writing. My mourning is not so much the sadness we feel at the loss of something familiar but rather the mourning of a writer for a symbol or an image.

If that teahouse represented 'The South', then the South is undoubtedly highly combustible. It is so fragile that it has proved even more short-lived than I have myself, which makes people feel they cannot put their trust in it. I wonder: What is my South? Where is the South?

How much do I actually know about a small southern street that I have so often described? Can my stubborn memory of it continue, as time goes by, to touch any part of the reality of the South?

What flashed into my mind was a scene associated with the street ahead. I'm afraid I'm going to have to talk about another public toilet. The history of this toilet is very short: I remember when I was a child, it didn't exist. The place where it was built was then just an open space and the people living behind it had been planting green onions and cockscomb plants there for years. One day, the toilet appeared. Like all such basic public toilets in the South, it was built in a hurry. The concrete floor inside was not even smoothed when it was put into use. It was intended to be of benefit to local residents but no one looked after it, so it became very filthy and smelly. This was a special toilet, giving users a real frisson of danger, because it faced a nearby residential area. From the high-rise buildings there, you could clearly see the faces of users and even their posture. Therefore, for both users and any residents of the high-rise buildings happening to be out on their balconies, it was doubly embarrassing. As a writer, when I looked out at the street from the balcony of my home, I couldn't ignore the existence of the toilet—my eyes seemed destined to rove there. An ambiguous and unclean sight led to a more difficult-to-express disgust and hostility. The disgust and hostility were not only physical but the public toilet also functioned as an obstacle to me being able to faithfully record this street scene. Fortunately, it was doomed; unlike the fire at the teahouse, this unwanted public lavatory was knocked down and afterwards a house was built on the site. Later on, a young couple lived in that house. Sometimes when I passed by, I could see them through the window, sitting inside watching TV. I am very happy; this is pretty much the biggest change in the street in many years. This has a special significance for me because as I walked there, thinking about the changes to this open space over time, I suddenly realised this was just like the triangular relationship recorded in Borges' short story: the green onions and cockscomb plants, the public toilet and the young couple's home. This is a triangle worked out in my memories of one small street from which I can vaguely make out the details of the story of the South I need.

But is this the South? I am just as skeptical as you are. The South I seek may be a dark and empty place, or perhaps it is just a literary theme. For many years, the South has been there in the South, and the residents of the South have lived in the South; still the theme of *The South* floats through time and space. All efforts to write about the South sometimes prove empty—there is nothing there—so the mysterious legend of 'The South' resides more in text than in any geographical location.

I have walked down that street countless times now. After all these years, I am still filled with awe for this street. This is the same awe as the flying goose feels for the woods, for they are just passing by. When it comes to 'The South', who is not just passing by? When I cross this street, I feel exhausted; I miss my memories but I can't help seeing 'The South' as I remember it—a world battered yet still strong. As in *Remembrance of Things Past*, when Guermantes takes his last walk through Combray, "How vast the world is under the bright lights but how small in the eyes of memory." The experience of a writer lost in 'The South' is much like that of Proust lost in the theme of eternity and time.

Walter Benjamin put it well, "None of us has time to live the true dramas of the life that we are destined for. This is what ages us—this and nothing else. The wrinkles and creases on our faces are the registration of the great passions, vices and insights that called on us; but we, the masters, were not home..."

Yes, my writing and I both dwell in the South, but I often feel that I am not at home.

THE USES OF CHILDHOOD

The French writer André Malraux described his childhood impressions in his *Anti-Memoirs*, "Most of the writers I know loved their childhood but I hated mine." For some reason, this concise retrospective of his life as a child aroused my sympathy and my disgust.

I don't know whether Malraux's near-legendary life wandering around Indochina was a compensation for his lonely childhood. I don't know whether his exotic writing such as *Man's Fate* or *The Royal Way* allowed an overabundant imagination to fill in the blanks. But I think that regardless of whether he loved and hated it, his childhood memories are the heaviest element in a writer's box of tricks. Whether these memories are dark or bright, we must bear with them and cherish them: we have no other choice.

Now I think of my own closed and lonely childhood with both love and hatred. I remember a winter afternoon many years ago, when I was skipping rope on the street outside the front door, dressed in a bulky cotton-padded coat and trousers. I saw some adults come running through the streets of northern Suzhou. This was probably during the Cultural Revolution in the late 1960s. If I were to describe the fanatical expressions and empty eyes of passers-by at that time, I would be writing fiction—this is not something I remember. I cannot describe what was going on outside but I do recall that I was skipping rope on that cold winter afternoon and I was jumping away. This is a memory from my childhood—how simple and how vivid! This memory is useful to me. I can also recall a dangerous game that my friends and I played on the railway in this era of toy shortage. We would all find some copper wire at home, wind it in a circle and then put it on the rails. Then we would wait for the train to arrive, wait for the wheels of the train to roll over our respective copper wire rings and, as the train speeded away, we saw that the copper wire rings crushed by the wheels were now flattened and enlarged. These deformed—or perhaps transformed—objects were important for our popular nailing-copper game. I would say that copper wire is also part of my childhood. A few years ago, I saw one such copper wire circle in my father's drawer. The associations it aroused were just the fragments of childhood. But now I have to give it some emotional colour: should it be love or hatred? Either would be fine; whatever I need.

In fact, our childhood continues and even grows in us. How many nights a person has to face in their life when darkness is blackest in children's eyes; how many days a person has to welcome when the sun means nothing to children. In this sense, childhood is worth describing. James Joyce's *Dubliners* depicts this kind of intense darkness and meaningless sunshine; just like the boy in *Araby*, in order to buy a gift for his beloved, he takes the train at night to the bazaar but what happens when he gets to the market? The last lights are being extinguished!

A fruitless childhood is waiting for the future but where is it waiting? It's in a huge, deep pit. Roland Barthes once truly described such a situation. In his autobiographical writing, he recalled, "We were playing in a big pit and then all the other children climbed out but I couldn't; they laughed at me from above: if he can't get out, he's the only one! He's not one of us! According to Barthes, it was his mother who rescued him from the pit.

Children don't realise that their games foreshadow their future plight. Loneliness is almost everyone's destiny while fear and resistance will become their most important mission. Writers will often sensitively capture the details of the fears and struggles that began in their teenaged years. In Yu Hua's early novel *Setting Out At Aged Eighteen*, the eighteen-year-old protagonist begins his escape from fear and starts his resistance by leaving his hometown on a long journey. However, the road leading away is continuously undulating, "As if stuck to the waves, I walked this mountain road and I was like a boat." In fact, the image of the road is still a symbol of fear. The youth in the novel can't see any cars on the road and, in fact, the only car he encounters ruthlessly rejects his request for a ride. This reminds us of the boy standing in the darkened market in *Araby*; it also reminds us of Roland Barthes in his childhood, trapped in the pit and unable to climb out but on this occasion his mother is not present. I feel that Yu Hua's novel describes a prolonged, resolute and independent childhood. Coincidentally, Mo Yan's unconventional novel *Joy* describes a young mother, also predestined to struggle with her fears, but whereas mothers are usually imagined to symbolise warmth and shelter, in the eyes of this young man, she is covered with fleas!

Mo Yan wrote, "Fleas were crawling all over Mum's purplish stomach! Crawling in her dirt-encrusted navel! Crawling over her breasts that hung down like deflated balloons!" Here, the image of a mother that is revolting to readers can stimulate your thinking. The mother is always present: this filthy and frail woman has raised her son and will as surely destroy him. Of course, this is the fear of the main protagonist in the novel once he has grown up. This terrible reality was concealed during his childhood but it will eventually be cruelly revealed. In this process of revelation, authors have found a certain underlying theme: perhaps a common strand in humanity. Therefore, when a mother covered in fleas appears, his childhood has been beautifully used by a writer.

Maybe we will all use childhood to record some of our most mature ideas. Why not use it? Listen to Leo Tolstoy. He said, "When a writer writes, he will eventually return to his childhood."

A DIARY OF SEVEN DAYS IN LEIPZIG

ONE: LEIPZIG'S FACE

Leipzig's face, which has been covered for many years by giant posters advertising international expositions, is a little pale and itchy. People who come to Leipzig every year may see only the city's body and not her face.

As merchants from around the world left the city with their exhibits, Leipzig completed her annual mission to clean up the battlefield of trade and send away customers' orders and checkbooks. She turned around and began to take care of herself. This season is Leipzig's very own: leisurely, a little cold but much as it is in spring and the city's breathing is natural and smooth, its face is now fully exposed to the sun and the wind, its seriousness and its beauty revealed a little more each day. The seriousness is due to the city's history and culture, and people's memories—those are awe-inspiring. The beauty is also the result of civilisation, so it is not publicised but neither is it shy: it is the beauty of self-confidence. No matter what angle you look at it from, it is amazing.

The two overlapping M's symbolise the city of Leipzig, and they can be seen all over the place. Someone might tell me that this is Leipzig's face but I always have trouble remembering the sign. However, I have no problem calling to mind the building where the sign is affixed or maybe a tree next to it. For a city of flesh and blood, all such signs are pointless. The face of the city needs you to cuddle up with her. Only when you are snuggled together can you feel her temperature and begin to take a sketch of her. As for myself, what I want to capture is not only the city's face; not just lines but also expressions. The city's expressions will obviously be profound. According to my tourist brochures, Leipzig has its own glory and pride, as well as suffering humiliation and trauma. My personal vision, ultimately, is my own record of the city. It does not have to take account of anything else since all that matters is what I myself have seen.

I brought a Samsung camera on this trip to Leipzig. It's a good camera but bulky. What I most regret is that I didn't bring the smaller one from home. The smaller ones are more convenient to carry about; right now, I take this big beast out and snap here and there—it makes it too serious, like I'm some kind of third-rate photographer.

But there are so many places worth taking pictures of and surprises are everywhere.

This is the hotel that I happened to pass by the day before yesterday: the 'Hotel am Bayerischen Platz'. Because I thought the building was very beautiful, I went over to get a closer look. There was a sign on the wall: Karl Marx stayed here in this hotel!

Two: Leipzig's trams

Nowadays, we live in an era of wandering between heaven and hell. Language and words are also shifting but they are even more confused than the times, because no one knows where the heaven of words or the hell of language is. There are more and more scientific and technological words in the dictionary: many of these form a vocabulary that I do not understand. When I read the instructions for new electronic products, I end up in a muck sweat. However, in the end, I have learned something. This is my secret and my biggest nightmare as a writer.

Nowadays, a lot of words have been tortured out of existence. 'Simple' has become a style of furniture and a porcelain plate design; 'nostalgic' stands in with a group of similar made-up words; while 'lyrical' is almost reduced to being a sign of some sort of mental illness. These words are remote from you but suddenly, at a certain moment, they all appear at the same time, like three missing children—they run towards you with an attractive power and all of this comes about thanks to the trams in Leipzig.

The day before yesterday, it was cloudy and rainy in the morning. I walked along the Strasse des 18 Oktober towards the old railway station. I saw a tram forging through the continuous drizzle and, coming from the direction of the new city hall, I heard the sound of another sliding on the wet track. Right at that moment I was inexplicably moved. I saw the tram coming towards me with those three words: simple, nostalgic and lyrical. It suddenly occurred to me that when I was a child, I went to Shanghai with my father and that was also in the rain. On a rainy morning, I saw a tram in Shanghai. I was standing outside the fence surrounding the railway station construction site, and all of a sudden I called to mind my first childhood trip and I thought about my father who nowadays lives alone in Suzhou and who has never set foot outside China in his whole life. I don't know why I like trams so much. This affection has nothing to do with environmentalism. I just make an immediate subjective judgment that a city that has retained its trams has also retained its poetic spirit, and all kinds of other beautiful memories. Perhaps not surprisingly, good things do not only have their romantic side but must also be practical.

In recent years I have been all over the place, and some other cities have also preserved their trams but for the most part they are reduced to being relics of the past: carefully maintained as an old-fashioned means of transportation—they are as much for show as they are a way of getting from A to B. However, the trams in Leipzig are still running boldly, like a classic warhorse, and they run around the city all day long. Almost every day I took the No. 2 or No. 16 tram to Leipzig city centre. They were my steeds and a wonderful gift from Leipzig.

It so happened that today I took the tram to city hall. In Gabriele Goldfus' office, I bumped into two of her visitors who happened to be from the tram company. I don't speak German so after saying hello, I had no idea how to praise their trams, how to say they're a classic warhorse. This is a fact, not a compliment. So I decided it would be better to begin with literature. I don't know how many romantic poets there are to be found in Leipzig's coffee shops, whether they ever read aloud their works or not, but there are poetic voices to be heard all the time echoing through the skies over Leipzig. In my opinion, whether today or in the future, Leipzig's trams will definitely become the last romantic poets in the city.

THREE: THE ST. THOMAS CHURCH

Among my friends, I number many fans of classical music. Those who love classical music are to a certain extent anchored to reality but they do not breathe the same mundane air as the rest of us. They take in a different kind of oxygen. In my opinion, there is no big mystery to this. All classical music can be regarded as a kind of blast from the past; and things that science has failed to preserve for us can nevertheless survive in music.

Some people's faces are extremely ruddy; some people's faces are strangely haggard—this is not merely the result of endocrine function and blood circulation. A person who breathes classical air is maybe more serious than ordinary people and perhaps they are also more romantic: it is hard to say. However, most of these people have transformed themselves into a stave; they have their own tunes and melodies when they speak or are silent. People who love classical music are not looking for comfort and sustenance from it, but for a simple and beautiful way of life. What they are looking for is a wider sky in which to fly or perhaps not to fly at all but just to be still.

Music may create happiness but it can also give rise to pain. The best music can often ignore people's feelings: that is its right. People's feelings are instantaneous and physical, so feelings are just feelings. Great music always escapes from the flesh, soaring upward, ever upward, obstinately and arrogantly upward. I personally know little about classical music; classical music was initially closely related to religion and it retains that connection. For some people, especially atheists, their love for music has become a kind of belief in itself. All my friends have finally become converted to J. S. Bach.

The writer Yu Hua said that the structure of his *Chronicle of a Blood Merchant* was influenced by the *St Matthew Passion*, with its repetition, gyrations and sublimations. Regardless of whether this is credible or not, it left a deep impression on me, as deep as the impression made by the story of Xu Sanguan selling his blood to support his family. I'd like to say something about this—perhaps this is something that Yu Hua already knows but I would still like to put it on record here. The *St. Matthew Passion* was composed by Bach for the St. Thomas Church in Leipzig. At no stage in his life did Bach suffer for music's sake but he was always tired of life. In the long years he spent at the St. Thomas Church, he rushed between funerals, elections to the bishopric, choir and church, hurrying to each and every one of the occasions when music was required: he might as well have been selling blood for a living!

Music runs in Leipzig's blood. This is the city where Wagner was born, the city where Mendelssohn conducted the Gewandhaus orchestra, the city where Schumann and Clara lived together. This has become a city that classical music fans all yearn to visit. But above and beyond that, it is the city of Bach: how glorious and proud! Bach spent the busiest period of his busy life at the St. Thomas Church. The ruins beside the church mark the site of the school where Bach's children went to be educated and where his house stood. The St. Thomas Church's boys' choir, which he devoted himself to cultivating, used to be famous—indeed it is still famous today. In the past they sang in the church; now they don't just sing in the church but all over the world. No matter whether you have listened to any of Bach's music or not, just as a matter of common knowledge, you should know that Bach's brilliance has travelled through time and space, becoming brighter and brighter.

I didn't come to Leipzig because of Bach and the St. Thomas Church but when I leave, I will remember the glory Bach brought to this city, the glory of the St. Thomas Church. Some of my friends, perhaps everyone who hopes to make out Bach's footprints, will come here sooner or later, because this is where Bach's last traces finally disappeared.

Bach's tomb is right here in the St. Thomas Church.

. . .

Four: Coffee Cantata

Although the city is quiet and a bit deserted, there are always tourists in front of the St. Thomas Church. Classical music fans from all over the world go to Leipzig, searching for this famous landmark on their maps. It doesn't matter that you don't know any German; it's easy enough to find it. The city is very small, so the map is not complicated.

I can see tourists massed in front of the St. Thomas Church every time I go past but how many of them come to pay homage to Bach and how many are here for the fast food, I would not like to say. Some people with digital cameras in their hands, behave suspiciously like me: they are determined to take something of the St. Thomas Church away with them. Bach is already in his grave so we can't shake hands with him but at least we can take a picture of his statue. Take a picture of Bach's statue, take a picture of his famous big nose. Go back and kiss the picture.

I cannot imagine how harassed by cameras and lights the statue of Bach in front of the church door must feel every day and I wonder if Bach is aware of this as he looks down from heaven: is this a sign of his glory or a worry to him? Will he feel a little uneasy about it all? Will he confide to his admirers: my music is just music, composing and conducting is my business, and deciding whether that music is great or not, sacred or not, is up to you. Will he lament that it's all too late? Where were you in the eighteenth century? If you'd come then you could have put some money in my pocket, bought milk for my boys' choir, or better yet new clothes for all of my children…

My friend here tells me that Bach's statue appears so life-like and natural because actually the sculptor was representing his situation at that time. The second button of his coat is unbuttoned because he had to play the organ and conduct the chorus, so he had to use one hand more often. Occasionally, he had to take music scores out of his coat, so he left it unbuttoned so as not to waste time. His left pocket is turned inside out in a silent protest about money. Tell the bishop and the church's kind benefactors that I love music but I also want to eat. I have nothing left. Give me some money!

I believe in my friend's interpretation of the statue. All great men go unappreciated until almost a hundred years after their deaths, and they have to convince the great men of another era first, just as Bach convinced Mendelssohn and then the world. In my opinion, if Bach were alive now, he should be in exactly the same position. If he were here today, would anyone put money in his pocket? This is a serious question. The good thing about the statue is that it speaks both to the past and the present.

I am just a visitor to Leipzig: one of the key features for getting to know Leipzig is getting to know Bach; or likewise, in getting to know Bach, you need to know more about Leipzig. Nowadays, one of the most practical ways to get to know Bach is to spend money in his name. At the Bach Cafe next to St. Thomas Church, every day of the week there are people sitting reverently, sipping their drinks and admiring the statue opposite. I've had a drink there, too. I didn't know what Bach's 'Coffee Cantata' was but I'd agreed to meet a friend from Leipzig that day and she'd said "Old St. Peter's Church" but somehow or other I'd misheard that as the St. Thomas Church. I walked there happily through the rain but the weather was getting worse, so I sat down in front of the Bach Café and ordered a cup of regular coffee, waiting for my friend. My phone rang and I quickly realised my mistake; however, it was too late to do anything about it. She had to come by bike as fast as she could through the pouring rain. I felt bad about this and started to look around me—raising my head I spotted a reference to a special coffee on the menu board: a 'Cantata coffee'. When my friend arrived, I asked her what 'Cantata' meant and when she explained I suddenly understood—in German, it means 'peaceful' or 'beautiful'.

What a perfect answer. The answer itself is peaceful and beautiful.

Five: Leipzig railway station

When it comes to Leipzig, the railway station is an eternal topic of conversation. When I went to Leipzig, I talked to the local people about trivial matters in their everyday lives. Someone always said sooner or later, in a positive 'can-do' tone of voice: go to the station; they have everything there and it is always open.

Leipzig's railway station is really special. I've asked people what 'promenaden' means in German but unfortunately I've forgotten the answer. Maybe the original meaning doesn't matter; I like to think it means 'considerate'. I have no intention of changing the name of a famous railway station but every time I enter it, I do not have the vague anxiety and sense of urgency I normally feel before a journey. I always feel that the station here has two hands; one is waving to you: please sit down... Why don't you have a cup of coffee...? Have a glass of beer and then go... Another warm hand is holding onto your luggage, gently tugging at you: don't worry... there's no hurry... there's nothing to fuss about... the train isn't going anywhere...

Trains never wait but Leipzig railway station gives people the wonderful illusion that it'll wait for you, it's not going anywhere.

For one person to stop another from leaving requires a warm and sexy embrace; for a railway station to stop a passenger from departing, it needs to let them forget the time, it needs something unrelated to travel to ease their tension.

In fact, it is also a huge mall. There are three floors above and below ground. There are cafés, restaurants, small bookstores, shops, supermarkets, banks and anything else you can think of. According to the Chinese concept of leisure, the only thing lacking is a big bath house. Many people go there without any intention of catching a train: they are there to go shopping or eat. Every Sunday or late at night, when other places are closed, the railway station is still full of light. Half of the lights in the railway station are for the travellers, and the other half for the people who are going nowhere.

On Sundays in Europe, people give over the entire day to the church, their families and their dining tables. But there are some people who don't go to church, some who don't have families and some who don't cook. They feel particularly lonely on Sundays. Leipzig railway station is given over to just such lonely people. Liu Jiaqi, a Chinese student I know, told me that the reason she didn't want to leave Leipzig was that she didn't want to leave the railway station. It watches over Leipzig, and when she was most lonely, she had a place to go.

I'm lonely, too. Of course, I have other ways to relieve my loneliness. Leipzig railway station has not subsumed my soul, but it has certainly taken over my body, especially my purse. At Leipzig railway station, I left a lot of records of my consumption. Here are the records I can think of now. Please forgive me, but I want to list them here.

I bought a phone card at the O2 store—I have continued to use it to keep in touch with my friends here.

I bought a shirt in a clothing store: my favourite brand of casual wear, and they gave me a fifty per cent discount. A few days later, I decided that I needed a thin sweater. I went there but they didn't give me a discount. It turned out that when the adverts said things were discounted for a week, they meant one week only, and it was now past. I felt everything was too expensive without the discount, so I didn't buy it.

I bought a box of shredded pipe tobacco in the tobacconists. On the one hand, because I had not brought enough Chinese cigarettes with me, I was smoking a pipe instead. On the other hand, because the owners of the tobacconists were resisting the pressure of a global anti-tobacco movement, everyone who smokes should pay homage to them with practical actions.

After eating pizza at a Pizza Hut once, I also ate pizza from other stores. Pizza is pizza, which is not bad, but it has nothing to do with fine dining.

When I saw a family selling Chinese food, I came closer and saw that it was the food made by Vietnamese migrants. In fact, it was not Chinese food at all and I don't know why they had to call it that. When I looked at the food piled up in their big iron tiffin-box, I felt very worried about the future of Chinese food in Leipzig, as well as a little angry. They won't let you sell knock-off brands in Germany, so why are they allowing knock-off Chinese food? Why is nobody doing anything about it? Of course, this time, I didn't buy anything.

My most urgent shopping was done on a Sunday. I wanted to go to a friend's house and I changed trams at the railway station. It suddenly occurred to me that it's impolite to go to other people's houses empty-handed but it was impossible to buy anything anywhere else on a Sunday. Fortunately, I was standing right opposite the railway station, so I crossed the road, ran into the railway station and bought a bottle of red wine at Rossmann's shop. With that bottle of wine in hand, I felt relieved straightaway.

It's a considerate gesture but what made it unforgettable is that my purchase came from a railway station.

For many years, I have been travelling almost all the time. In my experience, passing through a railway station is almost like moving through a human sweat gland: cramped, confined, and with all sorts of peculiar smells. How unpleasant it is when a group of people in a panic rush headlong into others who are running. But at Leipzig railway station, everything is topsy-turvy. There is a new order of travel reminding you to slow down, to take your time, it's shameful to be rushing around like that. I am an obedient person, so I deliberately slow down and tell myself that travel, no matter how far you go, is just a walk.

Six: Dear garbage

Maybe all the cities in Germany are very clean. I went to Germany for the first time in 1993, to Berlin, to attend a literary festival; I shared an apartment with Liu Zhenyun and Zhang Yiling. I still remember the name of the street: translated into Chinese it would be called Garden Street. Every day, the three of us went out in the morning and came back in the evening, so the only views we got of that street were either too early in the morning or too late at night. In the morning, the road was very wet, with a glossy faintly blue shine, and the pavement was dotted with dog shit. At night, the street looked blue in the light of the street lamps but the dog shit had either been cleaned up or it was swallowed up in the darkness and invisible. Dog shit is not such a terrible nuisance; so having decided that I didn't hold this against Berlin's dogs, I would say that the impression the city made on me was that it was pretty clean.

Later, I heard German friends say that it was bad luck I had to go to Berlin, all the dogs there have diarrhoea. But in Germany, not all dog owners let them leave their shit on the street.

It's funny that I have started to talk about dog shit all of a sudden. It's not that I have strong feelings on the subject. But in Leipzig these days, except for when I went for a walk in the nearby forest with a few friends one day and I nearly stepped in some on the path, I hardly saw any dog shit. Of course, I'm not particularly looking out for the stuff, and I certainly don't stare at my feet when I walk. But in Leipzig, whether it's dog shit or anything else, garbage is collected very carefully.

On my first day in Leipzig, Marit Schulz, who was in charge of looking after me, solemnly handed me a magnetic card, which had nothing to do with banks, transportation or shopping: it was to allow me to throw away unsorted rubbish. Clearly this was the most important thing on her mind. I couldn't understand the relationship between garbage and a magnetic card, and I didn't know that dustbins now also come equipped with advanced electronic equipment. The next day, I ran downstairs with a bag of rubbish to discover that the two rows of garbage cans were in the classical and modernist schools, either open or with electronic locks. They were sternly waiting for me. I was eyeing the dustbin nervously when a neighbour came up to teach me how to use a magnetic card. She was speaking German, which I don't understand, so she very kindly demonstrated to me so that I could understand. I am ashamed to say that here I am in my forties and I had to have someone teach me how to take out the garbage with hand gestures.

In Leipzig, there are no garbage dumps; subway projects are being built everywhere in the city, there are many construction sites and yet there is no construction waste. It seems that the attitude of the people here towards garbage is either too kind or too strict. They take all their rubbish back to their own homes—where it lands in garbage cans and then in landfill—and never let it show its face abroad. On one occasion, Gabriele Goldfus and I drove past a green hill beyond the Leipzig suburbs. We found that the scenery was most peculiar, so we took a look at the hill that seemed to rise from the flat ground with strange abruptness. Without waiting for me to ask anything, she told me that the hill was actually a landfill site but it had been afforested.

People deserve to be buried properly when they die; there should be pines, cypresses and chrysanthemums planted around their graves. Garbage also deserves to be buried properly, planted over with trees and shrubs, not only for the sake of beauty but also to commemorate their contributions to mankind. This is only fair.

It's uncomfortable to ponder people's fate, so I put this subject aside. Instead, I think about the fate of garbage, which is funny. Environmentalists are right: the earth is not so very big and the future of garbage is closely related to the future of people. All of a sudden I remembered a TV report that I'd seen in China about a merchant ship that had illegally transported rubbish from some First World country to a port in China, having been paid off by both sides. As the TV camera panned across the scene, they focused on a pile of oil-stained lunch boxes—paper products—which had been sorted into different categories. The good citizens who so carefully categorised their garbage can have had no idea that one part of their rubbish would end up going on a long ocean voyage.

The TV report was later pushed to the back of my mind by other, more important stories, and there was no follow-up. I still don't know where the foreign garbage came from and which Chinese factory it would be transported to. From the technical point of view, in modern industry, there is nothing to be surprised at. Many things are made out of recycled garbage, which has nothing to do with dignity and honour, but is purely a matter of production costs. My confusion arises from the fact that while I understand the commercial secrets behind all this, why should I still be so worried about it? I don't criticise those who secretly make money out of rubbish and I have no objections to the rubbish itself. I just bewail the way in which garbage has joined the tide of globalisation. I can vaguely make out the sound of garbage singing on its ocean-going ships. From West to East, it sings its marching songs, it sings an anthem to globalisation.

Dear Leipzig rubbish, I know you are innocent. You can't have been on that ship.

Seven: Made in Leipzig

'Made in Leipzig' is an exhibition of works by a group of different artists; I saw the brochure advertising it in many offices. The cover featured a gas station, painted in a rough, abstract style and there was a faint figure present, which I guess was an attendant. It was interesting that the contents of this exhibition also seemed to be a bit vague because the city mentioned and the actual site of the exhibition were not the same. The exhibition was not being held in Leipzig at all, but in another little town a couple of dozen kilometres away: Torgau.

We went to Torgau with a driver provided by the municipal government at the wheel. She drove and talked with equal bravery. When we left Leipzig, it was raining. Along the way, the rain gradually lessened and by the time we arrived at our destination, it was sunny. In Germany, there are such quiet and beautiful small towns everywhere. When we arrived, there were still traces of rain on Torgau's cobbled roads and there was an inexplicable smell of grass in the air: it seemed particularly fresh and delightful. There were not many pedestrians in the place and those that were would have been tourists. Martin Luther lived in Torgau for a long time and his wife is buried in St. Mary's Church.

People admire historic sites, as they do literature, music or painting. People trust the past and are suspicious of the present. For many contemporary artists, living is the only thing they have to regret.

When we got to the exhibition hall for 'Made in Leipzig', we were the only visitors. Because it was just us, we were free to wander around. We could discuss the art in the exhibition hall without restriction. One of our number had a doctorate in art history. She didn't talk about it casually but I felt relaxed enough to say what I thought. Maybe I know nothing about art, maybe I know a little, but none of that matters—the important thing is describing how you feel. I have always been of the opinion that when you stand in front of a work of art and have a strong reaction to it, you ought to say: I like it. Or perhaps: I like it very much.

So when I saw Tilo Baumgärtel's work, that's what I said: I like it very much. Speaking of which, the measure of how much I like a painting is nothing to do with the standards applied to works of art but to literature. When I see a good story in a picture and this story is full of wonderful metaphors and allusions, I like it. I will blurt out just this self-righteous assessment.

Tilo Baumgärtel is a storyteller. I didn't examine his painting materials very closely—whether he used charcoal or something else —but he is very wary of colours, being fixated upon black and white. There were two of his works in the exhibition, both completely devoid of colour; one was a group of animals relaxing in a living room and the most impressive aspect for me was that one of the cats seemed to be taking a book down from the bookcase:

certainly this was intended ironically. There were great metaphors hidden in this painting, as well as ridicule and irony; the target was not animals but the spiritual life of human beings.

His other painting was more abstract and depicted a person facing a strange wall, the person's back suggested that they were thinking, perhaps pondering how to break through, perhaps wondering how to escape, and so that wall provokes rich associations in people: it is connected with time, with society, with others and with oneself, or simply with the whole world. According to my usual self-righteous way of understanding things, I use the standards of literature to classify other forms of art. I think Tilo Baumgärtel deals with the big questions. Some painters use their brushes to write essays, poems, or reportage, but Tilo Baumgärtel's works are more ambitious. Clearly, he is a painter of novels, and he writes novels that are strictly realistic.

PART 2

Southern Jiangsu Street Scenes

translated by
Nicky Harman

江南市井

- Diners
- Snails
- Pot Stews
- Fish Heads
- Silk
- Dimsum Snacks
- The Galvanised Iron Shop
- The Barbers Shop
- The Butchers
- Selling Medicine
- Teahouse Shop

The women neighbours watched Mrs Hong sitting at the table, a toothpick in her hand. But she mostly didn't use it, relying instead on her sucking skills. Suck-spit-suck-spit… gradually the bowl filled with snails emptied while the bowl for the shells filled up.

DINERS

It is fair to say that he had reached a venerable age. His hair was a snowy white all over, with not a black hair to be seen. Strangely, though, his complexion was very youthful; his skin was as smooth and rosy as a new-born baby. His eyes were unclouded and didn't weep in the wind like so many old folks' eyes do. He'd lost none of his eyelashes and didn't have eye boogers either. He'd lived through seventy hard years and yet his eyes were as bright and clear as water, and as innocent as a youth's. What was his secret? The old man was in no doubt: it was eating that kept him young.

Not that he got a lot of respect from the neighbours. Everyone, young and old, called him Little Buddha. Obviously, this was a kid's nickname. Have you ever heard an old man called Little Buddha by all the local urchins? But this was what Little Buddha had to put up with. His grandson had just learned to talk and he used to babble to his grandfather, "Little Buddha… cuddle… cuddle!" But Little Buddha was not interested in cuddles, he was only interested in food. It was all he talked about, as he stood at the door chatting to the passers-by: eating. Once, he criticised the frozen pork sold at the butcher's either for having too much thick skin or no skin at all. Either way, it didn't taste good. If you were making shredded pork it didn't taste fresh, and if you braised it, it didn't taste savoury no matter how you cooked it. Everyone else said you had to put up with it, pork was so scarce, you counted yourself lucky to get any pork at all. But Little Buddha stood there with an enigmatic smile on his face and shook his head. "There are places you can buy fresh farm pork," he said, "You just don't know." Naturally everyone wanted to know where that was but Little Buddha wasn't telling. Instead, he changed the subject, "Did you know there are boats from Yixing at the dock selling bamboo shoots?" he said. "They're very tender, delicious in a stew!"

So by now you'll all see why a man of such a venerable age was nicknamed Little Buddha.

Little Buddha's old lady was a frugal housekeeper. You'd think she might have picked up her husband's food obsession from living so close to him but although she was always sticking her nose into her neighbours' shopping baskets and advising on what they should or shouldn't eat, she only ate enough to keep herself alive. She had always disapproved of her husband's eating habits. She had nothing against fine food. What bugged her was that he spent so much money on buying it. They should have been putting it by. Everyone knew that although Little Buddha's family were well-off, he had five sons, three of them still bachelors. "It's going to cost us a pretty penny to marry them off," she used to nag. "Why can't you eat a bit less so we can save? Then Four and Five can get married next year! How can someone get to your age and still be so irresponsible?" The old woman used to give Little Buddha a talking-to as if he was a kid.

For an instant, his clear eyes would cloud over with confusion, until he thought of a solution, "Chairman Mao said, self-reliance is the key. Our sons need to be self-reliant!"

Little Buddha was obsessed with eating. Every morning, he went to the city centre. He told his wife he was going to the park to do taichi, but in fact he was having breakfast at Huang Tianyuan's, an old-established eatery. One time, a neighbour saw him sitting there with a bowl of shredded chicken wontons, a fried pork dumpling and a slab of iced cake, all laid out in front of him. Little Buddha looked flustered at having been caught. He wiped the oil from the corner of his mouth with one hand and begged the neighbour, "Please, whatever you do, don't tell my old lady!"

The neighbour kept his secret for him but, unfortunately, he was rumbled when it became clear that their savings and the cash in the drawer were going down. That was the year when, the day before National Day, his fourth and fifth son boxed his ears. No prizes for guessing why. Little Buddha held his face between his hands and fled to the neighbour's, the tears streaming down. The neighbour had heard a lot of arguing in the family but didn't know how to comfort Little Buddha. It didn't take long, however, for Little Buddha to comfort himself. "If you can't eat well at a time like this," the neighbour heard, "what's the point of being alive?"

SNAILS

When young Mrs Hong arrived on the street as a new bride, she was very thin and wore her hair in plaits. The plaits were thin too, as if she was malnourished. Her husband, Hong the Third, was a stocky man who'd spent years as a metalworker, with well developed muscles from all the sandcasting he'd done. He may have been a tough guy but he felt the heat. In summer, he rolled his sleeves up to his shoulders and his trouser legs to his knees. In polite circles, a physique like that was admired but the folks of Toon Tree Street, who knew nothing of polite society, just figured a muscleman was a brute. When Hong and Mrs Hong were just married, his co-workers and the neighbours used to make dirty jokes about him crushing her in bed.

Mrs Hong was always busy at the stove, stirring something crunchy in the wok. It sounded appetising but it wasn't nice at all, it was snails. Hard to imagine why anyone would cook snails, day in, day out. Her jaw must have got tired from chewing them, maybe that was why she didn't like to talk.

Preparing snails is a bother. You have to cut the heads off so you can get the body meat out. Everyone knows that. But strangely enough, no one ever saw Mrs Hong doing that bit of the work. Then we found out that she bought the snails on the way to work, beheaded the snails while she was at work, then cooked them when she got home. It was all very organised. The women neighbours watched Mrs Hong sitting at the table, a toothpick in her hand. But she mostly didn't use it, relying instead on her sucking skills. Suck-spit-suck-spit… gradually the bowl filled with snails emptied while the bowl for the shells filled up.

The Hongs' married life was decidedly rocky. They were heard rowing in the middle of the night, though they kept their voices low, probably because it was about something indecent. But the rowing didn't seem to solve things and then Hong would beat his wife. He was a brute, more used to working with metal, so no doubt he laid it on thick. Mrs Hong used to scream her head off. Then the neighbours pricked up their ears, in the hopes of hearing her scream abuse. But they were disappointed. Young Mrs Hong had her pride; she just cried out and never said anything coarse.

The day after a quarrel, Mrs Hong never said anything at all but we all saw the hatred in her eyes. She wouldn't cook dinner for Hong, just fried even more snails for herself. You could hear her anger as she sucked and spat, sucked and spat, ferociously. One day, she threw down the toothpick and stopped eating. The neighbours wondered what was going on. They heard her mutter, "What am I eating snails for? I should be eating good stuff, shrimp, crab and duck. That's the way to get it off my chest!"

Mrs Hong was as good as her word. Every time the young couple quarrelled after that, she would spend the next day at home stuffing her face. Although contrary to what she said, it wasn't always expensive stuff. After all, Hong wasn't well off. But she certainly had strange tastes. How could such a skinny woman put away so much soy-sauce duck, fried shrimps and white-cut chicken? The way she took her revenge on her husband, her appetite and her personality – they were all a mystery.

Hong didn't get anything to eat on those days. His wife used to put the leftovers in the food cupboard and lock it. Hong had to break the lock if he wanted to eat it. But the man had his pride too. He wasn't going to give the neighbours a chance to laugh at him, so he often went to a snack bar and filled up on Yangchun noodles instead of dinner.

Hong didn't seem to get any thinner, so the Yangchun noodles must have had some nutritional value. And Mrs Hong got fatter by the day. Everyone on the street could see that. She had a naturally oval face but now it grew into a pumpkin face, with a double chin too. The jokers used to tell Hong that the couple were well matched now. There was no cause for one to be afraid of the other because if the east wind didn't blow the west wind out, then the west wind would blow out the east wind!

POT STEWS

In the 1970s, there was a restaurant selling pot stews on our street. It was state-owned, with two employees, one, the grandmother of a young lad called Tang, was on the verge of an honourable retirement, while the other, Gao Feng, had just been sent there. The young man and the old woman had very different aims and ways of going about things. Gao Feng was slovenly and noticeably careless about hygiene. Whenever he went out to the toilet, he refused to wash his hands when he got back, no matter how much old Mrs Tang nagged him. "Leave it out, all right?" he used to grumble. "No one knew I just went to the toilet. Now look what's happened! You shoot your mouth off and we've got no customers for the pot stews. Don't blame me, it's your fault for shouting."

Gao Feng's arrival coincided with a sharp drop in pot stew sales, which must have had something to do with his personal hygiene. He used to stand behind the counter, picking his nose, so no one wanted to buy food from his hands. A mass of braised pig's heads and tongues and braised pork meat floated, untouched and unappreciated, in their pots. What could Gao Feng and Granny Tang do? The weather was hot and they didn't have a refrigerator like the big places did. Granny Tang sniffed the stews before she closed up and went home. "They're off," she said. 'I'll have to buy them and take them home to eat." Of course, she got them cut-price. Gao Feng seethed inwardly. *You always take advantage*, he thought to himself, but he was too embarrassed to argue with the old woman. He just stared as she went home laden with bags of pot stews.

Not that it mattered much. After all, their stall was state-owned so they got the same wages, no matter how much or little they sold. Granny Tang had been an 'advanced worker' when she was young but now she was about to retire, she'd let her principles slip a bit. She didn't mind ripping off the state here and there. Gao Feng put up with it at first but finally he got fed up and told her, "I want some too, you leave me the pig's head, my friends love it."

"My grandson loves it too," Granny Tang objected.

"If that kid Tang eats any more pig's head, he'll turn into a pig's head himself," Gao Feng said spitefully.

After that, every afternoon at three or four o'clock, a gang of Gao Feng's friends turned up, ready to use their connections with Gao Feng and buy a load of cut-price pig's head. They counted on Granny Tang not minding. They played cards as they ate it and whoever lost had to eat pig's head while the winners counted how long it took. But Granny Tang did get upset when she saw them wasting the pig's head supplies. "I won't ask them to send us any more supplies tomorrow!" she insisted.

But Gao Feng shot back, "Fine! Don't get in any more. We can't sell it anyway."

Granny Tang knew that Gao Feng was having a dig at what she'd been doing, so she gave up and went home early saying her old back was killing her, and left the young men messing around in the shop.

Gao Feng and his friends carried on with the pig's head game for about a month, until one day it was Gao Feng who lost. He had to wolf down three bowls of pig's head stew as the winners counted down. He ended up full to bursting and with a terrible bellyache but there was nothing surprising about that, it always happened to the losers, so Gao Feng insisted on carrying on with the game of poker. Until he had a sudden attack of diarrhoea and had to run for the toilet as quick as he could. He knew that it must be because the meat was off, so he shut up shop and hunkered down by the toilet. And that was the end of the pig's head stew game.

There had never been a problem with the meat the depot supplied before and Gao Feng wondered how it happened to him. A long time passed and old Mrs Tang retired. One day, Gao Feng decided on a whim to clean the counter and found half a bottle of detergent the old woman had left. Light suddenly dawned. No wonder the old woman had said so furiously before she left that day that they'd suffer for it if they carried on wasting pork like that! It was her who'd made them suffer for it. Gao Feng was taken aback. Fancy the old bitch doing that! She was a bad egg and he hadn't been able to see it.

Still, the lads deserved it, everyone knew that. If it hadn't been for Granny Tang being bad, who knows how many state-owned pig's heads would have been wasted!

FISH HEADS

Every Chinese New Year, Ju Desheng and his wife were very busy. We often saw them, seeing their guests to the door in the evenings. Sometimes it was her, sometimes him. Or if the guests were more important, then they'd be there together. Although Ju Desheng was only a section-level cadre, he had style. He'd rest one hand on his hip, stick out his beer belly and wave with the other hand, rather in the manner of Chairman Mao. His wife was warm and friendly: she'd invite her guests to come back for a meal without fail!

She had good reason to be friendly, of course. Her guests had just delivered the New Year stock. Most of it was fish: black carp, grass carp and snakeheads, all fresh from the fish pond, and some are still alive and wriggling. As soon as the guests had left, the couple set to work. There was so much fish that their home looked like a fishmongers. Snakehead was the most popular. You could keep it alive in a tank for quite a few days. The trouble was there was too much of the other kinds. They had to work hard, one scraping the scales and the other cutting and filleting. Then they quickly hung the fish on a line to dry in the fresh air. After that, they could relax. Dried fish lasted, and could be eaten any time.

They pressed all their jars, pots and pans into service but still they didn't have enough. The wife went next door to the Wangs to borrow a jar, saying she was going to pickle some potherb mustard. The woman grinned, "Pull the other one! That fish of yours is stinking the street out. Can't you see how many cats you've attracted?" Ju Desheng's wife was embarrassed at being caught out.

"It's the old man's friends," she said. "They only ever give us fish. We've got fish coming out of our ears! I feel sick when I see fish these days."

"You may be sick of fish, but I'm not," said the neighbour. "If you can't eat it all, pass some my way and we'll eat it."

Ju Desheng's wife hesitated, "Do you eat fish heads?" she asked. "Of course we do! If you don't eat them, give me all of them. I love fish heads!"

Of course, it was important to keep in good with the neighbours, so Ju Desheng's wife gave them the fish heads. The Wangs had a lot of children and their elderly parents were still alive back in the village, so they were quite hard up. At New Year, when other folks brought loads of fish and meat home, the Wangs had to be content with a pig's head and a few frozen ribbonfish. So the Jus' fish heads went a long way to improving the Wangs' menu. Old man Wang was clever and had taught himself to cook. He put the carp heads in a pot and braised them with soy sauce and some chili. They were delicious. The kids couldn't get enough of them – they even guzzled the fish eyes.

The Wangs were so hard up, they were always short of food. They couldn't do like folks usually did, and take a bowl of some special dish they'd cooked next door for the neighbours to try. So for a long time, no one knew that old man Wang could cook braised fish heads. Even the Jus, who had provided the fish heads in the first place, never got to taste it.

In this world, you never know what's around the next corner. The poverty of the 1970s was finally behind us, just like any other era in history. In the 1980s, the winds of change blew in Toon Tree Street and shops opened up. Wang opened a restaurant. Who knows what put it into his head but the speciality was braised fish head. He soon had a lot of very satisfied customers. They said they never knew that the black carp heads and grass carp heads tasted so good braised, let alone that they were even better when they were stewed together!

It didn't take long for the Jus to hear about the Wang Restaurant fish heads. The news left Ju Desheng with a bad taste in his mouth. For the past few years, things had not been going well for him and he got quite abusive. He grumbled that Wang was a man without a conscience. He'd got rich on the back of the fish heads the Jus had given him. When Wang heard about Ju Desheng's grumbles, he tried to placate him by sending over a pot of braised fish heads but the Jus couldn't bring themselves to eat them. His wife thought and thought and then heaved a sigh. "I felt sorry for them back then," she said. "I can't even remember how many fish heads I gave them!"

SILK

The first shop on the right hand side of the bridge was Chengji Silks. In the 1970s, the shop, along with all its competitors, changed its name. It was now the Aimin ('Love the People') Silk Shop. However, there were still older women who couldn't be bothered to learn the new name. They'd get chatting in the street and ask each other, "Hey, d'you know if the Chengji has any new remnants in, stuff you can get without coupons? Why don't we go and see?"

Compared to the other shops on our street, the Chengji/Aimin was spacious. The cabinets holding the bolts of fabric were left over from the old days. They lined three of the walls, their rolls of cotton, poplin, nylon, corduroy and viscose in drab colours seeming to eyeball the women customers. Not that they were much to look at. They were dressed in blue, gray or black, as dowdy as could be. Of course, even a clever housewife can't cook without rice. How could they have beautiful clothes without nice fabric? The bolts of cloths had to take some responsibility.

The till was inside a small glass booth, where the girl cashier sat, looking as if she was reviewing the troops. Three overhead wires connected her booth to each of the counters, a bit like a flyover nowadays. It was all very handy. The counter assistant took the customer's money and their clothing coupon, and clipped it to the wire. The clip was just like a tiny plane. It took off and flew down the wire with a whoosh, and landed in the booth.

For some reason, perhaps because they dealt with fabric every day, the sales assistants, male or female, were all as soft and gentle as their cloth. They completely lacked the aggression and belligerence of assistants in other shops. In particular, there was 'Mrs Shen' as the women used to call her respectfully. She always had a smile on her face. No matter whether you are a good or a bad person, as long as you had coupons and followed her advice in choosing your fabric and its length, she smiled contentedly. She would take the cloth out, roll it over the glass counter – swish, swish, swish – revealing its pattern and texture as she spread it, and let you take a good look. The designs were unadventurous and hard to make out, and the cloth didn't have a lot of substance to it. Maybe its unsatisfactory quality was one reason why it didn't seem to distress Mrs Shen to sell it. Her familiar smile held a hint of an apology. She was placating you, you could see that. The subtext was, I know it's not good material but cotton is so scarce nowadays, you can't get anything as good as before. Just make the best of it and sew some clothes from it.

This Mrs Shen used to own Chengji Silks in the days before it turned into a public-private partnership in the 1950s. I don't know if it was good luck or bad but her career as an owner had scarcely started before it was over. After that, when it was re-named the Aimin, she used to work there cutting out the cloth. She cut and she cut, until all her hair went white. She never lost her smile, the smile that said she served the people, and she was always popular. As time passed, however, some of the female customers began to mutter that she was not as enthusiastic as before. If you asked her something, she seemed distracted. Even more surprising, though she'd been cutting cloth for a lifetime, her hands had begun to tremble. Sometimes, her customers got home and took the cloth out of the paper bag to find that the edge had been cut crooked.

The news got around that Mrs Shen was ill. She had a mental illness with a weird name, which her daughter could pronounce, but which no one else could remember. Everyone was sorry that such a good person was sick in the head. Why couldn't this weird disease pick on some of the foul-mouthed women and brutal men in the neighbourhood instead? Mrs Shen left the shop by the bridge and spent her days sitting in her doorway in the sun with a cushion resting on her knees. She still smiled at people but you could tell she was sick. Her eyes fixed on whatever the passers-by were wearing, her white head shaking from side to side, as if she was saying to them: Ugly, ugly, you dress ugly.

DIMSUM SNACKS

Every morning and lunchtime, the dimsum shop in the market was crammed with customers. There were two sales assistants: one was a fat woman who sold the tokens. She was about forty years old, with freckles and a florid complexion. She looked quite robust as she sat behind the counter. It was only when the morning market was over and she came out to clear the bowls away, that you could see that she had a gammy leg, which she dragged behind her good one as she walked. The other person was a trained dimsum chef, a lad in his early twenties. He was good-looking but he had a terrible stutter. Luckily, he was always busy cooking. If you were face to face with him, it wasn't because you were having a chat, it was because he was ladling out your noodles, soup dumplings or wontons, so his stuttering didn't bother anyone.

He was an expert at dimsum. His small wontons were especially good. He couldn't simmer them in real chicken stock like the fancy Lüyang Wontons Restaurant did but he took the trouble to use pork lard and bones, so when the lunch market opened at two o'clock in the afternoon, he always had queues of ravenous customers, men, women and children, including the young women workers from the nearby textile factories. They ate their wontons and drank the broth, and felt like their spoons didn't want to say goodbye to their bowls. "Come and have another bowl tomorrow," the spoons seemed to be saying, knocking on the edge of the bowl.

It was odd (though people didn't put two and two together till afterwards) that whenever the textile workers came clattering and chattering through the door, the fat woman's face would darken and she was very impatient with them. So after the girls finished and left, they would start to grumble, "What's going on with her? She acts like we're eating her family's wontons. Why does she scowl at us like that? We've paid our seven cents haven't we?" But they liked the young man at the cooker. Perhaps he was shy because of his stutter but, whatever the reason, he didn't talk to the textile girls very much. Still, his slotted ladle expressed his friendly feelings; he always gave the girls an extra wonton or two, and the prettiest and most talkative got almost half a bowl more of wontons!

One springtime, rumours suddenly spread that someone had been caught committing a public morals offence. Fingers were pointed at the dimsum shop. The woman involved turned out to be the fat woman, not surprising when you remember that her neighbours used to say that even though she had a gammy leg it didn't dampen her appetites. According to them, she used to yawl at night like a cat, and her husband was so sallow and thin because she'd worn him out. What was unbelievable was that her man turned out to be the young cook in the dimsum shop. They were sneaking away to do it in a cauliflower field on the edge of the town. An honest farmer caught them in the act and marched them to the police station.

Honestly. That's no word of a lie. The dimsum shop was closed for stock-taking for a few days and then reopened. When everyone crammed through the doors for their dimsum, there was the fat woman sitting at the counter selling tokens, as calm as you please, pretending she didn't see the nasty looks the customers were sneaking at her. Instead, she took out her annoyance on her son, who was sitting eating noodles. 'Eat up!' she snapped at him. 'What are you gawping at? Eat your food instead of eyeballing other people!' And at the cooker, the customers saw a different cook, an older, bald man. The handsome young man with the stutter was gone.

The shop was called Dimsum for the Masses so, of course, the masses had every right to carry on eating dimsum there. But the textile factory girls relinquished their rights. They never went to the dimsum shop for their wontons ever again, after that spring. Some of them said, quite reasonably, that the wontons weren't as good any more, and that was why they didn't want them, but one girl was more forthright: after what had happened, she said, who would fancy going in there again? The food would be dirty, wouldn't it, after the dirty things they did! It was enough to make you sick!

Well, young girls are impetuous and they get emotional about things. The older male customers took a more tolerant view. Just you try it, they said to the girls, if you lean two rocks against each other day after day, sooner or later they'll roll into each other! Besides, they weren't rocks, they were two people, a man and a woman!

THE GALVANISED IRON SHOP

Galvanised iron buckets and pots often needed repairing, and that's where the tinsmith came in. He touted his trade through the streets, banging on a pot and shouting, "Broken pots! Broken pans! Bring 'em all out!" When people heard him coming, they used to run out of the house and throw a leaky-bottomed pot or blackened pan down in front of the tinsmith.

"You only put a new bottom on this pot last year, why's it leaking already?" they'd complain. "If you don't fix it properly this time, I'm throwing it away and getting a new one!" It was obviously a threat that if the tinsmith couldn't do a decent job, he'd soon be out of business.

At some point, I don't remember what year it was, a tinsmith's shop appeared out of the blue. There were two rooms facing the street, in which five men sat. Some were middle-aged, others were getting quite old and wore reading glasses. Some covered their knees with a bit of sacking as they sat in a semicircle, banging away at a pot or a pan. Our once-peaceful street suddenly become quite noisy. It was all a bit annoying.

If you looked closely at the tinsmiths, you could see that

whoever had set it up had given it some thought. There was only one genuine tinsmith, old Sun. The rest were all fakes. When the locals realised, they couldn't stop laughing: the other four men were all rogues dragged in off the street.

One wizened old man called Tang was quite a local celebrity. His life story would have been funny if it hadn't been so shameful. He'd been a soldier, a soldier who kept deserting. First, he was in the Kuomintang army, until he did a runner, understandably enough. Then he was captured and conscripted into the PLA. Joining the revolution was a golden opportunity but he didn't appreciate it and did a runner again. All this running away gave him black marks on his personal file. He certainly was an out-and-out rogue.

Tang then got a job with a group of women, recycling cardboard boxes. He was like a fish in water. At every opportunity, he'd be schmoozing up to this one, pinching that one's bum and making them all feel thoroughly uncomfortable. So now he'd been assigned to the tinsmiths, Tang was annoyed but didn't dare complain. The other layabouts had properly reformed, so he had to knuckle down like them. He watched what the real tinsmith Sun did and took up his hammer, and banged away loudly. The trouble was, he had no idea what he was doing. He was all bangs and no technique. He'd put a new bottom on a leaky pot or pan but you only had to hold the pot upside down and press with your thumbs and the new bottom would pop out. The thrifty women of our street used to fly into a fury at his sloppy work. He'd look hurt and puzzled, and turn to the other ne'er-do-wells to ask, "Who mended this pot? Paper glue is stronger than this." The others were angry at getting the blame and got their own back by marking every pot Tang had worked on with his name in ink underneath.

Tang's reputation went from bad to worse. When the kids brought in pots and pans to be fixed, there was often a condition attached. "My mum said that Tang's not allowed to touch our family's pots!"

The shop could put up with attacks on one of its members but eventually something else made Tang pull his socks up: old Sun, the group leader, came back from a district meeting one day looking very worried – he had some news for Tang, "Your work's too sloppy. Some of our customers have reported to the higher-ups that you're harming our drive to grasp the revolution and promote production. The higher-ups say if you carry on like this, they'll hold a struggle meeting against you and you'll get a beating!"

Old Tang was not a brave man. When he was young, he could do a runner. Now that he was old, his legs were not good. Besides, the Communists had coloured every corner of the motherland red, so he had nowhere to run to. So he made up his mind to learn his craft. "Take me on as your apprentice," he humbly begged old Sun the tinsmith. "You teach me good and proper, and I'll learn good and proper. Otherwise, when I'm dragged onto that stage for a struggle session, the rest of you'll be up there with me."

And in time, Tang became a good tinsmith. In our house, we had a large galvanised iron pot that we used for cooking *zongzi* dumplings, one that Tang had fixed in his later years. It lasted till the 1990s and the bottom never fell off. Whenever it was the Dragon Boat Festival and my mum made *zongzi* in the pot, she always used to say, "It was old Tang who fixed the bottom of the pot, all those years ago."

We still had the pot, long after old Tang had departed.

THE BARBERS SHOP

The barbers at the north end of the street was next to the market, so there were people coming and going every day. Some went in for a haircut for themselves, others took the baby in for its first month hair-shave. Or they just went in and stood behind the barber, watching the customer having their hair cut, exchanging the odd word with the barber (or the other customers). Strangely enough, a lot of people seemed to treat the barbers as a tea shop.

All year round, water was kept boiling on the stove and in winter, the stove and the steam kept the barbers shop nicely warm. In summer, the stove made the shop too hot and the barbers moved it outside. You had to keep it lit. There were no water heaters back then, so the barbers needed the stove. They would fill a pot with boiling water, take it to where a customer sat on a stool, and carefully pour it into a homemade earthenware basin with a tap in the side. Then they'd wash your hair. There was no temperature control. It all depended on how experienced the barber was.

Sometimes the water was scalding, sometimes it was tepid, but no one complained.

Then, out of the blue, a girl was assigned to work in the barbers shop. A female hairdresser, with a round face and her hair cut in a short bob. That took a bit of getting used to. The regular customers found it strange because they were used to talking about anything that came into their heads when they came in and sat on the big swivel chair. Now there was a girl standing next to them, they had to mind their language. They became very serious. But it wasn't only them, the barbers had a hard time getting used to her too. Their work was boring without the usual banter that made the time fly by. With this girl around, everyone picked their words carefully and the barbers shop seemed a lot quieter all of a sudden. Only the buzzing of the electric clippers and the scratching of the razor broke the silence.

The girl wasn't happy either. Although she had her white coat on and tried to show the customers to the swivel chair, no one would go near her. The men had no faith that the girl could do a proper shave, and everyone would laugh at them if they left the shop with a badly-shaved head, 'toilet-lid style'. Then there were the women customers who came in for a cut and blow dry. They didn't trust the girl either, even though they were women themselves. They wanted one of the male barbers they were used to, Wang or Li, and if they were busy, no matter, they'd sit and wait.

Luckily, the girl didn't take it personally when she was cold-shouldered. If the adults don't want her cutting their hair, she would do the kids. She almost forced them into the chair and tied the white bib tightly around their necks. "What are you looking at?" she demanded. "Look in the mirror, keep your head still ....lower!" The clippers whirred decisively, and in no time at all, a circle of hair had fallen to the floor. Now you couldn't run even if you wanted to.

There were exceptions to everything, however, and the older Tang boy was one of them. He walked into the barbers one day and sat down in front of the girl without a moment's hesitation. Everyone watched as he went a bit pink in the face and pointed to his head, "My hair's too long, shave it for me." The young hairdresser was caught on the hop, and hesitated.

"Do you want to…?" she began and she looked at the other

barbers but they looked vague. *We're leaving you to it*, was what they meant. *You go right ahead and shave his head. Whatever you do, he asked for it. It's nothing to do with us.*

The Tang boy had ulterior motives, however, as everyone found out afterwards. This guy may have looked a bit dull and slow but in fact he was a schemer. The other guys were frantically running after the girls but he didn't bother. He simply went to the barbers a few times and picked the girl up.

His young brother, Tang of the pig's heads, now had a sister-in-law, Ms Chen, as the hairdresser was called. Fortunately, the young couple seemed pretty well matched and happy together. If she'd had any complaints, we would all have thought her a fool.

THE BUTCHERS

The butchers shop was a sight for sore eyes, at least for those kids with a big appetite but no money. If their mother went to the butchers with a basket in the morning, their lunch or dinner would be pure joy on a plate, the appetising smell of braised pork wafting from it. Some kid on the street actually wrote that in class: happiness is braised pork. That got him thrown out of the school gate on his ear by the Chinese teacher. "Go home and eat braised pork!" the teacher yelled at him. The kid was as brainless as his parents and was still focused on the business of the pork.

He slammed his schoolbag against the wall over and over, yelling at the angry teacher's retreating back, "Our family never have braised pork. I ate it once at Chinese New Year and never ate it again!"

In fact, you could buy pork, so long as you were willing to go and queue up outside the butchers before dawn every Tuesday, Thursday and Saturday, and so long as you kept in good with the sales assistants, you could buy up to a half a pound of fresh ribs or rump or pork streaky or liver, lungs or large intestines – whatever you could afford.

So why did some of the locals put off going to the butchers until seven o'clock, when the sun was high in the sky, and still go home carrying steaming-hot fresh pork? And why could some get hold of a pig's head wrapped in newspaper when it wasn't even a public holiday? They'd stew it or brine it and the ears were so big and so fat, there would be a big pot of it, all bought for a tiny amount of money. How did they do it, when others had to save up for a whole year for meat?

It's time to talk about the square-faced woman who worked in the butcher shop. Even though this woman spent her days handling pork and a butcher's cleaver, she was an imposing character. A big shot, as we'd say nowadays. Her status and popularity hereabouts would make female government ministers in Beijing jealous. She never talked openly to friends and acquaintances at work but she let her eyes do the talking. They said, "Don't try pulling any strings with me in the shop, I'll see you right, don't worry." Her axe had sharp eyes too. It awarded no favours to anyone. Fat meat and lean was apportioned strictly according to shop rules. If you bought three ounces of meat, that was what you got, not a smidgin more. But then there were those who had been on very good terms with her for many years. They used to hurry to the butchers with a heart-stopping secret. I don't know how much the square-faced woman had given them over the years but their faces looked rosier than anyone else's, and their bodies were chubbier. They thought they just looked after themselves well but what they didn't realise was that good health was inseparable from good nutrition which came, of course, from the square-faced butcher.

Somehow, the square-faced woman picked up hepatitis. Hepatitis was contagious and the Revolutionary Committee of the Food Services Corporation took a decision to let her go. So she left the butcher shop but where was she to go? (People infected with hepatitis could not work anywhere in the food industry.) She was assigned a job selling charcoal briquettes. As we all know, you needed coupons to buy briquettes too then, so the briquettes shop assistants had power over fuel. Although the square-faced woman was disappointed, she did as she was told and went to her new job, where she worked with Bing's mum.

They soon fell out. When Square-face was a butcher, Bing's mum used to barter briquettes with her for meat. Now the power was equally balanced and neither needed the other. Their friendship broke down over something quite trivial. When women quarrel, they like to show up their opponent's shortcomings, and it wasn't long before some old secrets were let out of the bag. "You're such a stickler for the rules now," Square-face accused Bing's mum. "When I bought briquettes before, I'd give you a coupon for fifty pounds and you weighed me out eighty!"

Bing's mum wasn't going down without a fight, and let an even more shocking cat out of the bag, "You're the stickler nowadays! I used to pay you one yuan for three ounces of pork and you gave me half a pound, and two yuan in 'change'!"

SELLING MEDICINE

The Chinese medicinal ingredients store on our street had been there a long time. I remember it when I was very young. It was staffed by some old codgers who stood behind the high counter in its dim interior. They had the air of having seen it all as they gazed out into the street. It was good that they had little to do. If they'd had to get busy working in somewhere like the grain store, the health of the common people would have suffered. Then their shop shut for a few years, its doors blocked by wooden shelves from the soy products shop that were stacked up against it. Those clumsy wooden shelves seemed to be deliberately blocking the way in, as if to say that the medicines market had been 'revolutionised' and people no longer needed Chinese herbal medicine. Of course, this was a biased view, put about by the proponents of Western medicine. Then one day the medicine store suddenly reopened, and word quickly got around among those locals who were not in good health.

The old codgers had gone and the shop was staffed now by a couple of girls. One was very young and the other a bit older, but still a girl. The shop was brightly-lit with newly-installed fluorescent tubes so you could see their faces very clearly. You could read the numbers on the tiers of little medicine drawers behind them, too, but that was not necessarily a good thing. People still believed in Chinese medicine but they didn't always take their prescription to the store on our street. The business of getting your prescription needed careful thought. The revolution needed the energy of young generals but youth and energy are not essential attributes for pharmacists. What if they gave you the wrong medicine?

So the medicinal store was very quiet. The occasional customer came in to buy something like red syrup or liquorice root or wolfberry. The two girls gesticulated a lot and, if you looked carefully, you could see that one of the girls was a mute.

The mute girl was clearly more enthusiastic about her work than the other one. She stood behind the counter from morning till night, looking out at the passers-by with the bright eyes of a deaf-mute, as if to say, Bring me your prescription, let me serve you! But people don't change their prejudices that easily. Even if they did go in to get a prescription for headaches or fever, they would always give the prescription to the talking girl, Ma.

But just the way gold always shines, there are exceptions to every rule. The mute must have believed this, because she didn't look resentful as she stood around with nothing to do. One summer, Luo Ping's sister hung around in front of the store for several days, sneaking glances through the door. The mute waved and beckoned to her enthusiastically, and eventually Luo Ping's sister went in and asked Ma, "Do you sell antacid syrup?"

The girl shook her head and said, "What's antacid syrup? We only have purple and red syrups here." The customer had ignored the mute but she had been lip-reading and now she gestured to Ma. It turned out she knew where the antacid syrup was and she grabbed it off the shelf straightaway.

Luo Ping's sister picked up the bottle and said to Ma, "I've got indigestion and the doctor told me to buy three bottles." Now that she knew where the antacid syrup lived, it wasn't any trouble for Ma to get two more bottles for their customer. Such a rare opportunity for the pair to 'serve the people' and sell three bottles of syrup all at once should surely have made them happy. So the other two were startled when the mute suddenly gave a loud cry. More than that, she grabbed two of the bottles and whisked them away. Luo Ping's sister frantically tried to grab them back but the mute was quick-witted. She got the pen and a scrap of paper, and wrote one word, Death. Then she scrunched the paper, put it in Luo Ping's sister's hand and retreated.

Luo Ping's sister didn't show Ma the message, she kept it secret. But the secret somehow led to her making friends with the mute. There was gossip that summer about Luo Ping's sister: she was pregnant and she wasn't married. There was also terrible news from the city hospital about antacid syrup. Apparently, some young women overdosed on antacid syrup, having heard that it caused abortions, and died.

The mute was very knowledgeable about Chinese herbal medicine. Ma took this for granted because she knew that her colleague was the granddaughter of Liang Wenru, the store owner. But now she was surprised.

"How come you know so much about antacid syrup, it's a Western medicine?" she asked. The mute girl was silent.

Then she burst into tears and said in sign language, "My mum overdosed on three bottles of antacid syrup and died. She was depressed and had had enough of life."

TEAHOUSE SHOP

A teahouse shop is a teahouse. I don't know why the locals added 'shop' to the name. It was making a simple public place sound unnecessarily complicated. If you think about it, people are going to ask, Well, what is it then? Is it a restaurant or a shop? Or they might ask, So, what's the difference between a restaurant and a shop? If you call it restaurant and shop, does that mean that besides serving tea, you can also buy tea leaves there? Our Wu dialect is sometimes clumsy and bothersome, to my mind, so why don't we just skip the bother and call it a teahouse!

The teahouse on our street was a two-storey wooden structure, located by the bridge. From a distance, you would think that it was someone's house. The brown-red paint on the railings had been peeling off for years and no one had repainted it. There was a row of upstairs windows and some were open but others were rusted shut. When you crossed the bridge, you could look right in through the windows to rows of old heads and gray hair, some with their backs to you, some sideways on, motionless, as if they were too lazy to turn around. If you leaned over the bridge railings and looked down, you could see the kitchen, the steam rising from the big range, the flames and a big pile of rice husks they used for fuel. And you could see Deming's granny standing grim-faced in front of the cooker, a filthy apron around her waist, pouring pot after pot of boiling water from a bucket into thermoses. If it was summer, she used to yell, "This heat is killing me!"

With such a hubbub, it had to be a teahouse. Too bad that the customers were all elderly men. Occasionally, you'd hear a woman's voice, elderly as well. That would be Deming's granny protesting that a customer had only paid ten cents but had opened the box of tea leaves and made themselves a fresh cup of tea.

The only reason for a kid to go to the teahouse would be if they were sent to buy boiled water. They'd go in carrying two thermos flasks and drop two cents into a bowl on the stove, which would bring Deming's granny over. As the old woman poured the boiling water into the kid's thermoses, she'd carp at them, "Don't you have a stove at home? Can't you even boil your own water?" She'd pull a face and address her comments to the diners at the few tables, "This kid's a hard worker but the grown-ups in that family are lazy as hell!"

No kid liked our local teahouse. I didn't like it either. But I remember one winter's day when I was on the way to school, my collar tucked up around my neck against the biting north wind. It felt like a mad doctor, stabbing me with needles all over. As I passed the teahouse, warm air gusted invitingly through the door curtain. After I'd taken shelter there for a little while, something made me change my mind about the place. Inside, someone was singing *pingtan* ballads, with someone else strumming along on the *yueqin*. Through the window, the heads of the old folks loomed out of the steam and it suddenly occurred to me that it wasn't so bad being an old man. You didn't have to go to school and freeze your butt off. You could sit in the warm in a teahouse, drinking tea, chatting, and singing *pingtan*. What a great way to pass the winter. I'd be happy to live all my winters like this.

PART 3

The Glorious Gamut of Social Behaviour

translated by
James Trapp

斑

斕

世

態

- Regional Accents
- The Taciturn Man
- Tipsy
- Talking Tea
- Paper Beauties
- Milk Baths and Golden Beds
- TV and Religion
- Stay Cool
- Fascist Advertisements
- Useless Things
- Selling Knock-Offs
- A Master Sexologist
- The Tourist's Point of View
- A Time Tunnel
- Ladies and Gentlemen, Where Are You From?
- Fixed Price
- More Than His Fair Share
- Not Bothered with Trifles
- A Discussion of the Phrase *Chujia*
- Doggy Paddle
- Face to Face
- Ghost Stories
- People Frightening People
- The Spendthrift
- Chatterbox
- Imitating So-and-so
- Paternal Love
- Cement Relics
- Verbal Corruption
- Self-Preservation
- HIV Positive
- Groupies
- Love in Old Age
- The Fate of the Boulevard
- Independent Travel
- A Day in the Desert
- How to Welcome the New Century
- Why Are You Disappointed in Me?

Impetuosity has become a common failing of our times, and I think that people like those two friends of mine are hard to find. I have no time for the wave after wave of trendy slang that comes our way, but I have the utmost respect for this piece of advice, simple as a whisper in your ear:

"Stay cool."

REGIONAL ACCENTS

At the start of the 1980s, I was pursuing my studies in Beijing and it was my first taste of living away from my parents. Many of the problems I had anticipated turned out not to be problems at all, and the only thing that caused me any real grief was the fun my classmates from the northeast had with my Mandarin. I suddenly discovered how clumsy my speech was.

When I came back to university after our first winter vacation, as a kind gesture to my classmates, I brought them back some of the local mandarin oranges that we call *juezi*. One of the northeastern students asked, with a crafty expression, "What's this you want us to eat? *Juezi*?"

"What's the matter?" I asked. "Don't you like oranges?"

The fellow began to laugh uproariously, "You might like to eat *juezi*, but these are *juzi*!"

I blushed crimson to the tips of my ears when one of the others explained to me that in the dialect of some parts of the northeast, *juezi* meant 'shit'. I gave an embarrassed laugh, and from then on began to feel pained by my own speech.

After that, I really strove to copy the Beijing accent. To begin with, I rather struggled with what to do with my tongue, but I gradually got the hang of it, and after a while, found that I couldn't even speak if I didn't have my tongue curled back in my mouth. There was a classmate from Shanghai who I hung around with quite a lot, and I was always criticising his speech for being too labiodental, with no retroflex tongue. Of course, he didn't accept this, and said that my retroflex was random and all over the place. We asked one of the students from Beijing to adjudicate. I remember he looked at the two of us southerners pityingly, heaved a deep sigh, and said, "You don't talk too badly, but you sound as if one of your tongues is too long and the other too short!"

Of course, it was my tongue that was too short. I continued to talk in my short-tongued way for several years, until I graduated and left Beijing. As some of my friends remember it, when I first got back to Nanjing my speech was pure Beijing. I was pretty sure this was not meant as a compliment; the unspoken implication was that it was not normal for someone who had lived in Nanjing for so long, to go away and come back speaking Mandarin so differently. I didn't agree. I thought that I could control it quite easily; but my self-confidence was misplaced. A university classmate I hadn't seen for ten years or more telephoned me one day and, after we had been chatting for a while, he exclaimed, "What's the matter with your tongue?"

Startled, I replied, "What do you mean, what's the matter with my tongue?"

"Why have you gone back to pouting and lisping like a southern hick?"

This phone conversation stirred up all sorts of emotions in me. I felt that my tongue was causing me problems again and that there was nothing I was ever going to be able to do about it. After all the years of trials and tribulations it had gone through, it had reverted to type. Knowing the way things in my mouth worked, I was clear that I was now stuck with a mouthful of unregulated Nanjing Mandarin laced with Suzhou dialect.

Perhaps this is not something to despair over, but a sign of intelligence. In the end, it is the same for everyone: we all change the way we speak to match the circumstances we meet as we drift through life. We are smarter than parrots and that's why we have the regional accents we so like to talk about.

THE TACITURN MAN

At a friend's party quite a few years ago, I heard a girl evaluating one of my more taciturn friends, "He understands how to be silent." There was an appreciative gleam in her eyes as she said this, which clearly indicated her admiration and appreciation of this quality. This is a very useful tip for young lads. Men pay particular attention to any tips or hints that come their way from the opposite sex and adjust their behaviour accordingly. I am just the same. I always considered myself a shy and uncommunicative person, but from the time of that party onwards, I no longer reproached myself for this trait but felt free to live my life according to my own inclinations. If it was possible to get away with not speaking, I didn't speak; if I could cut down on conversation, I did so. From the midst of my taciturnity, I would survey other people, and I observed many garrulous sorts, inarticulate sorts, overenthusiastic sorts, and many people who let their tongues get carried away in a flood of their own passions. I rejoiced in these discoveries and celebrated the fact that I myself was a taciturn man. If I was not inclined to speak, then I didn't just open my mouth for the sake of it; if I wanted to economise on speech, I chose my words carefully.

The ancients tell us that "too many words bring trouble", and this adage had a profound effect on my youthful years. A long time ago, when I was still at primary school, I saw one of the teachers stamping furiously on a rubber ball in the playground. I was really attached to that ball, so I yelled at the teacher like a furious old woman in the marketplace, "You're a nutjob! It's a good little ball! Why are you stamping it to pieces?"

The teacher erupted with anger and scolded me as he took me by the hand and led me to the school office, "How dare you? How dare you call a teacher a nutjob?"

As I was being made to stand to attention in the office, of course, I regretted what I had said, but it was too late for regrets. I hadn't really thought the teacher was a nutjob, but the word had come tumbling out of my mouth, and there was no taking it back. All I could do was silently swear to myself that even if someone stamped on all the rubber balls in the world and they disintegrated, I would just ignore them.

On many occasions, I kept careful tally of my words, like the miser Grandet in Balzac's novel, counting the coins in his strongbox, giving many people a taste of the full power of taciturnity. To tell the truth, not many consider such silence particularly charming, and many more, when confronted with a taciturn man, consider him tedious and rude. Sometimes, when a taciturn person visits a friend of similar inclinations, the resultant meeting is like a 1930s silent movie. To be perfectly frank, I myself have often acted out such scenes in the homes of friends with completely the opposite temperament. When it is time to say goodbye, unbidden and without any coordination, the same expression of relief flits across the faces of both parties, as much as to say that they both feel the afternoon or evening has been a complete waste of time.

But the passage of time and life can change a man, and over the last few years, I have undergone just such an involuntary alteration. Perhaps the process began with the advent of domestic life, or under the influence of some of my more garrulous friends, but whatever the cause, I have now started to talk more volubly. This increased volubility originally stemmed from necessity: my wife wanted to discuss household and national affairs and all sorts of other things, both relevant and irrelevant; my daughter wanted me to tell her fairy stories I had to make up for her, and explain to her the advertisements she saw on the street, and the hidden meanings of shop signs; and friends intent on dissecting every topic under the sun required my participation. I couldn't stay aloof and indifferent, and even if it was just a foolish laugh or nod of agreement, I always had to demonstrate my involvement. Gradually, necessity became habit and, no matter who it was I was talking to, I always found myself striving to be the more talkative party.

The strange thing was I found a kind of unexpected pleasure in my garrulousness. It was a pleasure I had never experienced before; it was a hazy, indistinct sort of feeling, a bit like water spurting out of a tap that has just been turned on, and a bit like a deaf mute suddenly busting into song. Sometimes, talkativeness can turn into a bit of a joke. I have a garrulous friend who once asked, "What day is it tomorrow?"

"It's Sunday tomorrow," he was told.

"Yes, but what day of the week is Sunday?" my friend persisted, and everyone there just stared at him in incomprehension. Even though the joke was on him, I have always felt it makes my friend seem rather endearing. Up to this point, talkativeness is something enjoyable for both parties and even the most taciturn of people may be touched by this pleasure and give a muted laugh.

From one point of view, learning to talk is learning to live. I remember, years ago, I had a visitor from somewhere a long way away and I had felt very on edge making conversation with him. As he was about to leave, he said to me, "You're such a good conversationalist."

I was quite taken aback at first but afterwards I was delighted. It was the kind of delight that a fledgling bird must feel when it first takes wing. Yes, that's it, just as a bird has to fly, a healthy person has to talk: that's what life is.

Of course, life isn't only about talking, it also encompasses silence. Sometimes I can look back with sadness and frustration on the silence of my childhood and adolescence, and reflect on the reasons for so many people's taciturnity. In my opinion, some people are silent because they don't want to talk, for others, it is because they are not good at talking, and for others still it is because they don't know how to talk. For taciturn people, silence is a way of approaching life, but silence is a lock, and having a key to open that lock is what life is all about.

TIPSY

The first time I got drunk was when I was at university and we had all been sent into the mountain region of Hebei to work on the land planting trees. There was one day when we were all ravenously hungry and we went together to a little restaurant in the county town to treat ourselves to a feast. Someone said, "Let's get a bottle of wine; it's wine that makes a good meal." So we ordered a bottle of wine.

The wine that came was a *gaoliang* liquor distilled from sorghum made by a small local producer, but it called itself brandy. It was the first time I had drunk alcohol but when I caught its rich mellow flavour, I exclaimed, "This is good stuff!"

My fellow students all agreed. On top of this, our classical literature professor's sonorous recitation in teaching us Li Qingzhao's poem *Tipsy* had left a lasting impression on me, so I drank rather too much and quickly became a little tipsy myself. What caused people amusement was that I was definitely a little drunk when I left the restaurant and was walking as though I was treading on cotton wool. I was in an incomparably spritely mood and began to shout out, "I'm tipsy! I'm tipsy!"

It came as a surprise that after I went out into society and started drinking frequently and copiously at big banquets, not only did I lose any pleasure in getting tipsy, I actually began to be afraid of alcohol. Even now I don't know where the problem started but I do know I have a dread of drinking culture and of the peer pressure that accompanies it. What do I mean by peer pressure? Not to beat about the bush, it is the social norm and common practice of encouraging you to drink until you throw up.

Once I went with a group on a tour of northern Jiangsu. There were six stops on the tour and the welcome extended to visitors in that part of the country is warm in the extreme. We stayed two days in each place and found ourselves drinking wine twice a day. The drinking culture in that neck of the woods was very prevalent, and the element of peer pressure was also very much in evidence. At each meal, you had to propose at least three toasts, and each toast consisted of three successive cups of wine. So, if you were someone who respected his host and were a stickler for propriety, you would have to down nine cups of wine, and that was just for starters. With peer-pressure culture in full swing, you weren't going to get away with just nine cups: you had to drink three cups with anyone who had the same surname as you, three cups with anyone from the same home town, three cups with anyone the same age as you. In fact, it pretty much came down to drinking three cups with anyone who was the same male gender. I clearly remember how these circumstances quite banished any semblance of Dutch courage, and all I could do was surrender myself to the warm embrace of drinking culture and accept its challenge. In the end there was a limit to my capacity and, with a dozen or more cups sloshing around inside me, I had to make a dash for the toilet, clutching my churning stomach. Thoroughly plastered, blissful oblivion was in sight but unattainable, and the best I could do was to find some respite in vomiting it all up.

So, gradually, I have developed a fear of alcohol. The fear is quite normal, but what is not normal is that sometimes I crave a drink, and when I happen to take a cup, there is nothing the least poetic about it; the real wonder for me is how Li Bai managed to compose a hundred poems after drinking ten litres of wine. If I happen to remember the brandy I drank in the little restaurant in that provincial town, it is with a certain fond reminiscence, but I know that the tipsiness of that time is no longer part of me. After continuous years of drinking, the taste of the wine is no longer the same.

TALKING TEA

When I was little, whenever my mother went to buy tea, she always came back with cheap tea dust. I followed the example of my elders and didn't take tea very seriously. Because of this, for a long time I thought that tea only came as dust, and whenever you drank it, you always had to puff out your cheeks and blow the particles out of your cup. The only piece of general wisdom about tea I knew was the single sentence: tea is a faintly bitter, yellow-coloured infusion whose principle property is to aid relaxation.

As far as drinking tea was concerned, I could take it or leave it, and that is how my ill-informed attitude continued for many years. Then, out of the blue, a tea-loving friend said one day, when he came to visit, "This year's new tea is on the market, what delights have you got for me to try?"

I duly took a packet of tea out of a drawer and said, pointing at the price sticker, "This is a good tea; see how expensive it is."

To my surprise, an embarrassed look came over my friend's face as he took a mouthful, and he asked, "Are you sure you didn't put some mothballs in with this tea?" He looked at me with a disappointed and reproving expression, and went on, "This isn't good tea, it's old and stale."

These few words from my friend shattered my pre-conceptions about tea and from then on, I began to understand the differences between good and bad, old and new. Of course, I also learned the practical lesson that tea and mothballs should not be stored together! I gradually came to understand what my friends were on about when they discussed tea amongst themselves, talking about Anhui tea, Biluochun and Longjing. That is to say, I knew what they were talking about but I still moaned to myself about how unnecessarily mysterious they made it all sound: it was all tea after all, and all green, so what was all the fuss about?

I can't remember the exact year but one Spring evening I brewed some new harvest tea just to quench my thirst and in the first mouthful had a moment of quasi-spiritual enlightenment about the true beauties of tea. I couldn't help but recall Chairman Mao Zedong's famous saying about real knowledge coming from experience. The incomparable green colour of tea and its unrivalled fragrance can only be appreciated when it is there in your hand and there in your mouth. From then on, I was never without a cup of pure green tea in my hand.

I am not a tea merchant, nor am I writing here as a propagandist for the trade, but I have been drinking tea for a long time and I have absorbed more than just its taste. When I think about modern life in the concrete jungle, how full of understanding those little green shreds seem in their metal cannister; how much those green buds swirling in a tea glass remind us there are still fields and mountains out there, where there are mist and sunshine and rain. They remind us that there still remains a world where things are green. If you have the wit to see it, you will know that preserving the trees that line our streets and our parks and gardens is nothing compared to the preservation of tea-drinking: no one buys the leaves from those trees and you can't sell the green of the gardens. So, no matter how much we extol the greenery and protect the trees, nothing is guaranteed survival. But people finding the money to drink tea is the most secure of guarantees as, in that way, at least we can be sure there will always be people conscientiously tending tea plantations. Of course, there may be some tea consumers who are not so self-aware, so let me remind you well-intentioned, environmentally-conscious folk to keep on drinking tea. Of course, to drink well, does not necessarily mean you have to buy expensive tea. You are doing a genuine public service just by drinking tea at all, for that means there will be people producing it. If there are people producing tea, then they are preserving a patch of green for the world. What a fine thing it is to combine pleasure with a beneficial act! We should all thank you for it. And of course, I thank myself too.

PAPER BEAUTIES

What do I mean here by a 'paper beauty'? I mean much the same as an 'armchair general' in that it is all theoretical and I have no abnormal desires or improper ideas regarding beautiful women. I have never seen these beautiful women I am talking about in the flesh, only on paper; I have never heard them speak (neither mispronunciation nor profanity) and I have never smelled their fragrance (neither perfume nor body odour), so I can believe that they are special: specially, completely, stupefyingly beautiful.

Beautiful women, whether they are old and faded or in their prime, live in black-and-white and coloured photographs of all sizes, full of smiles and charm. If it happens that such women step out from their photographs, then they are peerless beauties wearing a fur coat or something fashionable by Chanel. They are fully aware of the power of the image and fend off the lenses of the paparazzi, saying, "Be off with you! No sneak photos allowed!" But there are other photographers, ones who have a way with women, and they have the knack of capturing this power. It is then that in photo albums, newspapers and glamour magazines, we see this cavalcade of extraordinarily beautiful women.

These photographic beauties, whether they are coy and bashful or fiery and passionate, are all offering us their beauty for sale. And we are all their loyal customers, spending our money, be it a few cents or a handful of *yuan*, to buy a reproduction beauty. But true beauty cannot be reproduced; fake beauty is not beauty; so once we have enjoyed the magazine with its parade of beautiful women, we cast it aside and end up selling it to the rag-and-bone man. He in turn sells it on to the firework factory for firecrackers. What a heart-rending journey that is, for so much beauty to end up exploding in the atmosphere into a shower of smoke and shards of paper!

The real beauty is hiding behind the photographs and it needs someone to capture it and envisage it. With Zhou Xuan and Marilyn Monroe their beauty didn't rely on the camera to be realised. Rather, it was quite simply their beauty that brought completion to a photograph, to a photographer, to a record of beauty.

Beauty is a kind of luck and it has no communality. This is why we have no expectation of a photograph of Marilyn or Zhou Xuan. With their deaths, their beauty departed from the world. Beauty is individual and unique; it can't be passed on. All we can do now is cherish its memory in the photographs that remain to us.

When people seek beauty from paper, it is probably because of its therapeutic effect. It can soothe their injured eyes, and if it cannot cure the ugliness of reality, it can calm the nerves and refresh the mind. For men who crave riches and power, beauty is as precious a commodity as silver and gold. It creates an imperative and desire for ownership and that triggers pursuit, competition, bloodshed and countless stories of furious fights over beautiful women. Looked at this way, beauty can also become a deadly poison.

But that is not what I am on about. What I want to talk about is those photographs, and considered as a source of peace and stability, they are a good thing. There is no way photographs can provoke calamities and in them, the woman's peerless beauty is safely contained. This can only be a great blessing for men and for society. And since 'look but don't touch' is a recognised public norm, none of us can have any complaint.

MILK BATHS AND GOLD BEDS

All of a sudden, we find ourselves living in a world where great poverty and great wealth co-exist independently. So, when stories emerge in the newspapers about a new fad for bathing in milk, many people are flabbergasted and tongues are set wagging about it, but I think there are also many people like me who don't see anything particularly exceptional in it. What is there to be surprised about? I have heard that someone somewhere in Guangdong is manufacturing beds made out of solid gold. Bathing in milk is small fry in the luxury stakes compared to that.

I can, however, be pretty sure that there will be quite a few who go pale at the thought of people bathing in milk and many like me will be put off drinking the stuff for a while.

We didn't have cow's milk to drink when we were little and if someone had told us then that somewhere there were people who bathed in it, we would certainly have assumed they were talking about some queen or empress far removed from the life of ordinary people. When we were little, we used Guangrong-brand soap to wash. If someone had come along and told us there was someone who washed with milk, we would have laughed ourselves hoarse. We thought that using sandalwood-scented soap was the height of luxury, so washing with milk wasn't just crazy talk, it was the stuff of dreams.

So, when we learn that milk baths are the coming thing, we are both startled and indignant. For one thing, we think of milk as a luxury foodstuff, a highly nutritious drink that we couldn't lay our hands on. When we think of the bathhouse attendants pouring bucket after bucket of it into the public bath and of all those bodies with their reek of sweat and body odour (maybe even carrying syphilis and genital warts) soaking in the milk, and of it finally draining out through the plughole contaminated by all those bodies, how can we not feel saddened and disgusted? We have no choice but to concede that the age of using honey locust pods and hard scrubbing to wash are over, and even Empress Dowager Cixi's vanilla-scented baths now seem crude and unimaginative; so now, bewildered as we are by it, we must welcome in the age of the milk bath. We have no option: we are living in a time of materialistic excess, and we few remaining reactionary cliques only appear narrow-minded and pernickety.

This fussiness is demonstrated by the fact that we can't bring ourselves to pay a fat sum of money to go and bathe in milk, by the way we turn on the gas boiler to heat water, use Lux soap to wash our bodies and Rejoice shampoo to wash our hair, falsely believing these to be indications of modest affluence. But this illusion has been shown up for what it is by the advent of milk baths, and we little folk clinging to our petit-bourgeois ways of washing, can no longer feel the least bit complacent.

Our perniketiness stems either from our classical sense of propriety or from our stubborn belief in communality of resources. We might ask, "Why dump so much milk in a bathtub when you could be sending it to feed starving children and old people in the poorest parts of the country?"

But the people behind milk baths might reply, "That is a matter for Project Hope and disaster or famine relief; it has nothing at all to do with our milk baths. Yours are the words of infinite righteousness and support; ours are the works of never-ending investment and profit."

Moreover, the purveyors of milk baths have said in a news conference that the kind of milk they use in their baths is only good for bodies and skin; it has little nutritional value if drunk. I do not know if this type of milk actually exists, nor whether this kind of talk is just the new style of commercial spiel and business propaganda. I really want to believe it is true because if it is, and I can tell myself that the milk is neither tasty nor nutritious, I will feel a little more comfortable in myself.

But whether I feel comfortable or not, is of no consequence; milk baths are already on the market, and there is no knowing whether they may not enjoy the same kind of fad as saunas and whirlpool baths. I can't bring myself to try a milk bath myself but there are always going to be novelty lovers eager to plunge into them; there will also always be plenty of pungent milk to splash on the ground but just make sure it doesn't splash on your body, let alone into your mouth.

I also find myself thinking about those gold beds in Guangdong. I don't know if the people who buy gold beds are also interested in milk baths but I reckon that getting into a gold bed after bathing in milk might be considered the whole package.

I do know that although people like you and me may stamp our feet in disapproval but still try a milk bath, we are never going to sleep in a solid gold bed.

TV AND RELIGION

Once, when I was chatting with friends, the conversation turned to the building of churches. Someone observed that places of worship are now so big they have become tourist destinations in their own right. People don't go into them to pray or seek absolution but to gape and stare. Everyone present bemoaned the fact that people's faith today is flagging. The television in the room was turned on at the time and some pop star or other, heavily made-up and dressed to the nines, was leaping about enthusiastically grasping the hands of her audience with her own slim, lily-white fingers. The young audience was screeching in ecstasy, and I almost blurted out, "Look! There's today's religion!"

But my friends were all intelligent, well-educated people and I didn't dare be too hasty. In particular, I didn't want to profane such a solemn word as 'religion'.

There are many churches in the West and temples in the East but their prayers and chanting are being swamped by the same rhythms of pop music. Religious life has been superseded in the hearts of some devoted disciples and in those of many more ordinary people, and there doesn't seem to be any hope of it making a serious comeback. So perhaps we should ask what it is that has superseded it. My choice of answer is: television.

I can't say that everybody now watches television. I have a friend who didn't. He said he hated it but he does love football, and every time the world cup came round, he used to go running off to someone else's house to watch it. But he didn't feel comfortable with this freeloading, thinking he would be better off watching his own set, so he bought one. I haven't asked if he still hates television but I don't think he can say this, as he can't claim he is watching the football but not watching the television. The power and magic of television is that it puts so many things within your grasp: politics, sport, history, documentaries, international and local news. And, of course, there is also the host of young pop singers, actors and actresses in costume dramas and soap operas who are all drawn effortlessly into your broad embrace.

With so many people intimately associated with the television all their lives, following its voice and trusting completely in its instructions, it is just like the Middle Ages and the connection between devout believers and the church. Although the church of the television set is contained in 21 or 24 inches, when you compare it to a priest or a pastor, its reach is all-encompassing. Moreover, it is endlessly eloquent and hard-working, and doesn't wear black robes. Its seductive colours turn you into a gormless idiot, staring at it, wide-eyed and mouth agape, its devoted disciple. This is why I feel that the television set is the worldwide, universal church. The only difference is that the mood of this church is constantly changing, now serious, now inappropriately flippant and, of course, the result for its viewers is that its overall message is too confused to quantify.

I know I am shooting my mouth off and I recognise that my wild talk may offend some of the remaining believers in the true church but I still contend that there are some people who regard the television as their only saviour. As an illustration of this, I recently saw a report on the television about an incredibly obese person in a certain country who, all-year-long, was unable to get out of their house and ended up dying beside their television set. At the time, I thought to myself that the television had been the only respite from their suffering, so what did that make television? It made it their guardian angel!

I'm not being too insistent on this idea, as all the examples I have used come from the television, as do all my conclusions, and it is quite possible that religion has nothing at all to do with it.

STAY COOL

Many years ago there was a terrible road accident on our street; the young man who died in it had only just become a father. Apparently, the baby's cloth nappies had run out and because the weather was cold and damp, the ones that had been washed from the day before were all drying in the factory boiler room. The mother had told the father to go over and get some of them to save the situation. The lack of fresh nappies was a cause of great anxiety to the new parents, so the young man was pedalling his bike as fast as he could, resulting in him crashing into a truck. Afterwards, the eyewitnesses all said that he was travelling too fast and was in too much of a rush altogether.

I remembered this tragic story because of the sudden recent popularity of the expression, "Stay cool!" The first time I heard it was at the card table. I am by no means impassive when I am playing cards. If I have a big loss, I make a lot of fuss about it, whereas my friend is the complete opposite: the more he loses, the more relaxed he appears and the more sparkling his wit. He never loses his cool and is the very image of the consummate card player. Once, he said as much to himself as to the rest of us, "Stay cool!" The sound of his voice immediately quietened the raucous profanities of the card table, and he went on to say, "That phrase has become very popular recently. It's a good one."

It is indeed a good phrase and unusual for a popular saying in being universally effective. I don't know why but it also makes me think of another card-playing friend. There was an occasion when his child was running a high fever and his wife was completely flustered. She rushed out of the house barefoot, carrying the child off to the hospital. Unperturbed, my friend carefully got dressed and followed on behind them. Afterwards, when his wife reprimanded him, he said, "No matter how urgent something is, I've never been so flustered I've gone out of the house without shoes."

His wife was temporarily lost for a reply.

I think that a person's temperament takes them so far but life presents an even wider landscape. My two friends' way of handling fraught situations stems from their natural disposition and is, indeed, indicative of an overall approach to life. They are not willing to give in to the pressure of urgency, and bring reason to bear on every detail of life. In this way, emergencies become just another part of everyday life.

"Stay cool!" is priceless advice for the majority of people but not so easy to follow. Impetuosity is not a virtue, even if it does seem to be a universal way of thinking and acting. It is always an automatic reaction to something: like when your baby needs a nappy change but disposable nappies haven't been invented yet; or when you have just lost big at cards but don't have any more chips in your pocket; or when your child is running a fever over forty degrees and you don't know why. You have good reason to act impetuously but it is all too easy to forget the common-sense question, "What's the use of rushing?"

Impetuosity has become a common failing of our times and I think that people like those two friends of mine are hard to find. I have no time for the wave after wave of trendy slang that comes our way but I have the utmost respect for this piece of advice, as simple as a whisper in your ear, "Stay cool." If they remember this phrase, perhaps those friends of mine who are thwarted in their climb up the corporate ladder might be a little less downcast; those whose dreams of making their fortunes are shattered might stop cursing Heaven and blaming others; and those who live their lives in a state of permanent discontent might learn to cultivate a little patience.

"Stay cool!" How wise that is. We can act impetuously all our lives but what is going to happen is going to happen, and what isn't going to happen won't happen, so what has that impetuosity achieved? Once we give in to it, who is to say we won't end up dying for the sake of a nappy, as that unfortunate young father did? I am no admirer of homespun philosophy but I would say that whilst sacrificing your life to save another is a worthwhile act, sacrificing your life for the sake of a nappy is a crying shame.

FASCIST ADVERTISEMENTS

Survivors of Auschwitz concentration camp may not approve of the title of my essay and, in these times, there are also bound to be accusations that I am clutching at straws in making comparisons between fascism and advertising. I once read a memoir of a Jewish victim of the camp, recalling how much he had longed to read even a tiny bit of a newspaper when he was in Auschwitz. On the one hand, I was deeply moved but, at the same time, I couldn't stop an unforgivable thought floating across my brain: supposing he had got hold of part of a newspaper but that part was the advertisements page? How would the poor man have felt about that, thirsting as he was for prose and for information?

There is violence in every period of history but our forebears would never have believed that, in a time of peace, there could be the kind of violence that emanates from our news media; or, to be more accurate, that emanates from the ubiquitous, menacing advertising in our news media. I don't care whether you believe me or not, and I don't need you to believe me either. These advertisements either use flattery or harness your anxieties; they use the language of violence to make you buy this and buy that. If you are not interested, you don't have to look at them, but it is not so easy to shake free of them. Just like the Jewish people back then wanting to escape the evil clutches of the fascists, it is not something that just happens because you want it to. Suppose you go home, clutching your fluttering heart (and clutching your wallet in your pocket at the same time), you may well see a young fellow coming downstairs from your neighbour's apartment. He smiles at you and says that he works for some insurance company or other and wants to discuss your joining some scheme of theirs; he is as respectful and polite as such uninvited guests always are. Sometimes, an urgent knock on the door will make you wonder what might have happened. You open the door and see a grey-faced fellow standing there, a brand new, shiny-edged kitchen knife in his hand. You are frightened out of your wits, until the man opens his mouth and you realise that he is not an assassin but just wants to sell you a new kitchen knife.

Our ancestors who toiled in the fields would never have believed that their descendants could be laid siege to by surplus consumer commodities; our ancestors hardened by military campaigns would never have believed that their descendants could be left with nowhere to hide under a constant hail of advertising. I was chatting to some friends once about television advertising, and each one had a story about the advertisement they dreaded the most. My pet hate is one for a certain soft drink, in which there is a chap clutching two cans of the stuff in his hands, saying, "Two cans! You just can't resist them!"

I don't know why but I always make a subconscious association with some ruthless bandit, "Two guns! You just can't resist them!" But beneath my alarm, I am also puzzled: isn't the advertisement getting ahead of itself. Surely it would be better to buy just one can, to see what it is like; why are they so insistent on people buying two?

There is another advertisement, quite low-key, which employs a common and familiar method of engaging your emotions. It features a male singer standing in the background, plaintively serenading a bottle of mineral water. The words of the song are to the effect that on buying this mineral water, everybody will find true joy and the realisation of all their dreams. Although he is singing to himself, the implication of his words is quite infuriating, that we ordinary people are so devoid of purpose and ambition that a bottle of mineral water can bring us true joy and the realisation of all our dreams. In addition, there is some problem with the singer's enunciation so that "pure joy" sounds like "poor joy" and "your dreams" sounds like "war dreams", which strikes a very inauspicious note.

I have heard that a television channel once conducted an opinion poll, asking its viewers whether they liked advertisements or not, and zero per cent said they liked them. But even though that television station continues to air its advertisements, there is always a simple way to avoid them: just switch channels. Some advertisements, however, are ubiquitous and inescapable, and we are a captive audience for them. I mean things like the small ads on the staircase of my building for local drain clearing services and floor polishers. They are printed in a certain type of permanent black ink on the stairs of the staircase and, on every flight from the ground floor to my apartment on the sixth floor, there are their endlessly insistent telephone numbers. There is an air of self-deprecation in them letting you step on them, and I feel they are lined up waiting to greet me. I am not the least bit grateful to them and every time I see those telephone numbers with their feigned humility, I want to shake my fists at them and tell them: "I know you've come to arrest me! You're just a bunch of fascists! A bunch of fascists!"

USELESS THINGS

In Seattle, America in 1993, I once saw a young fellow playing a sort of improvised musical instrument. I am the kind of person who likes a bit of noise and bustle, so I pushed my way into the crowd of people who were watching and listening. The young chap had his hair in a ponytail and was wearing a black tank top and black trousers in the style of a rock singer, but the unknown instrument he was playing was clearly meant for classical music. At a glance, it was a bit like a harp and a number of French horns welded together but when I looked more closely I could see that, in fact, it wasn't actually like anything else at all, and was some invention quite out of the ordinary run of instruments. The friends I was with couldn't work it out either and just kept saying, "Interesting! Interesting!"

We stood listening for a while and decided that the sound of the instrument was just as unusual as its appearance. It was quite weak and soft but it had a tinkling, melodious quality, and there was a look of some excitement on its inventor's face as he played it; perhaps it was its first performance. A rather self-serving thought leapt into my head: supposing this instrument became popular in musical circles, I would be one of the first people ever to have heard it. I hurriedly took some photographs of the young fellow and his instrument.

Several years later, I was leafing through my photographs and realised that my hopes on that street in Seattle had completely failed to be realised. Of course, that young man was still an unrecognised talent and over the years I hadn't heard any news of so-and-so discovering a new musical instrument that was now being played in such-and-such an orchestra. It seemed that the whole affair hadn't attracted any attention at all. I let my train of thought continue and realised how puerile my reaction had been back then and how eccentric that young man was. In the 1990s when everyone was trying to patent some new technological invention or other, who was going to be interested in developing and promoting a useless musical instrument that could only produce a few jingles and tinkles? It wasn't the time of Bach and Beethoven, and mankind's inventions were focused on the moon and ecology, and on the atmosphere and the ozone layer. We wanted an effective vaccine against AIDS. We wanted a new house or a new car, a new wife or a new husband. Who was going to waste their precious resources on a new kind of musical instrument? Nobody wanted something that had no practical use.

Nevertheless, I still retained my foolish fancy about that young American's invention and I once asked a friend, who was a composer, "When you're composing, do you ever feel there aren't enough instruments? Do you hope that maybe a new kind will come along that can really convey what your music is trying to say?"

In reply to this layman's question, my friend gave a broad grin and said, "Why would I need one? We have quite enough instruments already."

We have too much of everything, even in music, and this truth made me sad for that young American,

"Haven't you heard, bro'? If people don't want it, there's no point in busting a gut over it!"

I am more clear-headed now, and have made a mental note to myself, thick-skinned and hardened as I am, that taking credit for being the first person to hear a new musical instrument that has no chance of success is no kind of useful credit at all. There is no point in wanting something useless and if I were that young American, I might as well dismantle the instrument to get some scrap metal out of it which I could take to the recycling centre and exchange for some hard cash.

SELLING KNOCK OFFS

I live right by the main street of my town and I just have to step out of my door to be in the heart of the boom economy. Shopping is really convenient and as I walk along the street I feel that many of the shops are winking and flicking their hair flirtatiously at me, as much as to say, "Come and get me!" The huge variety of knock-off goods in the hands of street pedlars are not going to let themselves be left out either. Although they belong on the lowest tier of merchandise, some of them have some courage and self-esteem, and seductively flaunt their elegant forms as they stand or lie on their plastic display cloths.

The ones I really can't forget are a dozen or so bottles of counterfeit shampoo, Soft & Gentle, Pantene, Head and Shoulders, that appear on the kerb every weekend. As I come out of the door of the bicycle shop, I can see them standing on their long wooden table, greeting the passers-by. The three women selling them, all in their thirties or forties, are not very polite or well behaved, and chat amongst themselves as they look after their stall, sometimes kicking up quite a rumpus. Every time, I notice how carefree and self-possessed they are. One of them has a red sash across her shoulder with the words 'Direct from the Factory' printed on it; she stands there looking more official than the others, but she never hawks her wares, making it clear she is ready to meet you on equal terms, as much as to say, "It's up to you if you want it or not! People are really crafty today and their ability to spot knock-off goods is much better than it used to be. They don't have to look too closely at what you are selling; they can tell it's fake and they don't buy. So that's why I have this attitude: I'm not going to try to persuade you; I'm not even going to look at you."

Three years those three women have been standing there, unflinchingly selling their knock-off goods. At first I felt a sort of *schadenfreude* as I watched their desolate business, but quite recently I was in a really good mood as I passed through the district, and when I saw those familiar figures in the distance, my feelings for the three women underwent a subtle change. I began to have a whole new degree of respect as I asked myself: do you have that kind of perseverance? No, you don't! I felt I was looking at the most determined women on the planet and found myself believing the old proverb, "sincerity can split open metal and rock". I really wanted to go up to them and console them, "One day you are going to sell some of those bottles, even though they are knock-offs."

To my surprise, as I was hesitating over this thought, the three women caught my body language, exchanged glances and immediately split up. The one with the red sash stayed where she was, looking even more dignified, while the other two suddenly turned into customers. Standing around the bottles of shampoo, one of them said, "They're really cheap. I'm going to buy a bottle!"

And the other said, "They're over forty *yuan* in the big shops. What a bargain! I'm going to buy a bottle too."

I was completely taken aback that the three of them could suddenly transform themselves into shrewd businesswomen, and all I could think to do was turn and walk away. I felt some remorse and recognised, when it came down to it, my own lack of charitable instincts. The truth is I don't despise knock-offs, as we need the inferior qualities of the fake to appreciate the worth of the genuine. They also contribute to the prosperity of the economy. But passing off fakes as the genuine article is not a fun thing and that's why I decided not to play their little game.

A MASTER SEXOLOGIST

The best profession for a bookworm is to be a librarian, and a drunkard should be a wine-taster. Some people spend their whole lives suffering the torture of their own lustful desires; some live dull lives resolutely suppressing those burning desires; and some indulge themselves, and if they go too far in so doing, become sex offenders. The majority of these people will never have considered whether there is a way they can quite appropriately immerse themselves in the joy of sex, without anyone trying to stop them. There is, however, one such road they can travel, but to do so requires favourable circumstances, dedication, investment and the ability to turn an interest into an academic discipline. This is the route the famous sex researcher Alfred Kinsey took to become a Master Sexologist.

I am not mocking Kinsey in writing this, quite the opposite, in fact. I am full of admiration for this now deceased American. It is just that after I recently finished reading a biography of him, on the one hand, I felt sorry for the hardships he endured during his life whilst, on the other, I couldn't help thinking what a lucky man he was. Dr Kinsey lived in a puritanical age in America and wanted to be a Puritan himself; but from an early age he was tormented by peculiar and excessive sexual desire. If he had not had his research into sexology to occupy him, it is common for men such as him to end up dying from depression. But Kinsey was lucky; the exuberance of his sexual passions, his acquired learning and education, and the fact that he was in the right place at the right time, all propelled him to the heart of sexological studies. And what he studied were the kind of things other people really want to snoop into, such as foreplay, orgasm, intercourse and homosexuality. In conducting research, you have to get personally involved with your field of study, and Dr Kinsey didn't just research the female body, he was even more enthralled with the male. Nevertheless, the police did not arrest him and his own wife made no objections. Indeed, that woman, in dedicating herself to her husband's work, to the extent of committing her own body to it, provided Dr Kinsey with a lot of valuable scientific data.

Dr Kinsey's great good fortune was that he was able to liberate himself in the course of conducting his research and the great strength of his studies lies in the completeness of their data. It is all first-hand and completely reliable; it is personal and experiential, and doesn't include irrelevant material from secondary sources. Because of all this, Dr Kinsey's sexological research caused a sensation at the time and proved enormously successful. It can also be said of Dr Kinsey's success that, if it hadn't been him undertaking the research, but some clean-minded, clean-living Puritan, the result would not have been the milestone volumes we now have; not *Sexual Behaviour in the Human Male* and *Sexual Behaviour in the Human Female*, but maybe even *How Humans Can Avoid Sexual Behaviour*, which we certainly would not have found very interesting.

You could say that Dr Kinsey's great stature speaks for itself, but there are some people who denigrate him, saying that he really was scraping the bottom of the barrel. Although this is being petty and mean-spirited, it does not necessarily do him an injustice.

THE TOURIST'S POINT OF VIEW

When friends ask me where I am from, I reply confidently, "Suzhou".

Mostly they respond as I expect and may exclaim in admiration, "Ah, Suzhou is nice. It's a lovely place."

At this point, I say deprecatingly, "It's alright, but it's a bit ramshackle."

My interlocutors then shake their heads and say, sincerely, "That's alright, all interesting old historical towns and cities have a bit of a battered air to them!"

I know that what I am encountering is the tourist's point of view, which I too share when I am in historical cities like Xi'an, Kaifeng or Luoyang. I regret that they have not been able to keep their original form from the Tang Dynasty so that, when I go out sightseeing, I could get some inkling of what it was like when Yang Guifei bathed there or Wu Zetian watered her peony trees. But where Suzhou is concerned, I object to the broken-down state of its roads and my reasons are entirely practical. My family still lives in Suzhou and I often go there to visit. I would like Suzhou to become Shanghai or New York and not always be the 'Venice of the East' selling itself on broken-down buildings and a few muddy canals.

I really would rather tourists didn't go to Suzhou and I would like to raise the rallying cry for the city's municipal planning; demolish what needs to be demolished and discard what needs to be discarded. I particularly have in mind those rows of ancient bucket toilets on the old streets. Even though there are always people taking photographs of them as though they were made of gold and studded with jewels, actually they stink and are unhygienic. I am not going to agree with those people who themselves long ago started using flush toilets yet still advocate the pursuit of antique authenticity. They say we should preserve everything ancient but they are just armchair experts. If they really like those toilets so much, they can take one to use at home. And they can have it for free!

Maybe I'm being selfish but when I hear visitors to Suzhou putting the tourist's point of view, my uncivilised, unaesthetic self reveals itself. Perhaps it is because I lived in Suzhou for so long without ever finding any benefit from its antiquity (I have to buy a ticket just like the tourists to go up Tiger Hill or into the Humble Administrator's Garden); perhaps it is because I can still smell the stench of those old toilets; or perhaps it is just because a rather unkind friend once said of Suzhou, "What exactly are you Suzhou folk so proud of? The old women there chatting to each other sitting on toilet buckets with just a cloth screen between them?"

So I for one do not share the tourist's viewpoint and I reckon it has more than a little to do with envy of my native city. But what could I say in reply to something like that? I couldn't think of any great glory of Suzhou to thrust back in their face. It was at that point that I began to really hate those bucket toilets, as all they do is bring hurt to the innocent. No matter how ancient the houses with bucket toilets, or how plain and authentic the streets that have them, I don't like any of them.

But now, as even more time has passed, I find myself a staunch advocate of the preservation of man's ancient heritage, especially in connection with cities where other people live. In those cities, I advocate the preservation of anything that is more than one hundred years old, including bucket toilets.

A TIME TUNNEL

People are strange: they can calmly face life and death but are often unable to face the reality of their own age. You can be happily chatting away to someone and then happen to ask their age, and they fly off the handle at you, as though you have some unkind thoughts about them: if not that they are too young, too inexperienced and lacking in any credibility, then that they are too old, fit for nothing, insipid and lacking in dynamism and creativity. Or they suspect you of prying into whether they are a suitable match for their partner.

Lots of people seem shifty when asked about their age, actresses particularly so. They will happily tell you their bust measurement but not their age. If they have to fill their age in on a form, they do it in secret, or write unclearly or remain eternally eighteen. You can see at a glance they are being dishonest and it really riles you. Some women who aren't actresses adopt the same mysterious approach and roll their eyes at your gauche question, saying, "You shouldn't ask such a silly question. Have you no manners? Asking a woman her age!"

Men have a much healthier attitude to age but there is still no lack of rudeness. If you ask how old someone is, he will reply, "Of course, I'm older than you; I could be your father!"

When I was younger and was at a loss for something to say, I used to like to ask someone's age. But after a few knock-backs, I stopped doing that. Then gradually I found myself lying to other people about how old I was. When I was a youth of twenty, I would always say I was twenty-two and when I was twenty-three, I would make out I was twenty-five. It was a natural defence mechanism that stemmed from a fear of being considered a member of the younger generation, a young lad without facial hair who can't be trusted to do anything right. It puts you at a considerable disadvantage. In fact, just adding a couple of years like that didn't stop other people thinking of me as a youngster and I was often put on the wrong foot in conversations at work. Memories of those times meant that as I got older and had a little capital of my own in the age department, you should have seen how I treated the young people around me!

Time flies like an arrow and, before you know it, you are in your forties, where you find that age brings all sorts of problems. Of course, there remain some loud-mouths who ask you your age and I discovered that I was still not sufficiently comfortable with the question. If the other party was older than me, I answered evasively, keeping my expression polite, meaning, "I'm a lot younger than you and have a lot longer to live." But nowadays, I'm always bumping into people who are younger than me and they make me feel that my posture, movements, speech and even my facial expressions are somehow not right, and that I have no connection with young people. I don't know what makes me feel so gloomy, although I do know that if I do tell my real age, I am thinking to myself, "You nosey little bastard! What has my age got to do with you?"

I feel that I myself have finally become shifty about the question of age. Old age or youth, I don't want either of them. Youth is an old t-shirt that I have grown out of, that has been ruined by washing and that I can't wear any more. Old age is a pair of pyjamas: I put them on ready to go to bed and go to sleep but I'm not sleepy, not even drowsy, so what am I supposed to do? There's no point getting agitated about it. If there really were such a thing as a time tunnel, I would want one go in it, no matter what the ticket price was, just to solve the mysterious problem of age. Once I was inside it, I would grab hold of everyone there and shout at them, "Look me straight in the eye and tell me how old you are!"

LADIES AND GENTLEMEN, WHERE ARE YOU FROM?

Almost all city folk are the descendants of migrants. If you go back several generations, maybe a dozen or more, without exception they will have an ancestor from the countryside. So, in the box on their identity documentation for place of ancestral origin, the name is likely to be some place in which they have never set foot. This is of no real importance, as people are used to carrying their ID with them all over the world and a place of origin is just a place of origin. It may, in fact, be an area of considerable size but on your ID it is just a few characters and that's all. Very convenient and portable.

Previously when people were chatting on their travels, they might use this question as an opening gambit with someone sitting next to them, "Where are you from, Sir (or Madam)?" The person answering would invariably give their place of ancestral origin. In some cities that still cling to rather old-fashioned ways, like Hong Kong for example, as you walk along the street you can see the names of hometown associations and meeting houses written up on the old tenements in large characters. The sight of them gives you a cosy feeling. In the past, people seemed to take the idea of fellow countrymen and ancestral homes very seriously. The explanation for many such communal activities is very simple when you hear it, "We are fellow countrymen; we're from the same place."

Recently, travellers have changed their opening conversational gambit and now the frequently heard question is, "Where do you make your money, Sir?" This question isn't about your past history, it is about your present and your future. It is clear from this that people's outlook has changed and, to explain it using a literary analogy, the old-fashioned way was a classical historical novel while the new-fangled way is more like the new realist school of literary criticism.

Mankind today is in a confusing swirl of motion. Foreign devils are poking all round the land of we descendants of the Yan and Yellow Emperors while we ourselves are running around on the other side of the oceans, prodding this and looking at that. Of course, with even more finality, we have spread our bedrolls out in foreign countries and settled down there. So now, when we are strolling down the street in New York or Bangkok, we may bump into a whole host of our compatriots, to the extent that we could mistake a foreign country for our homeland.

There are some people who make the journey but are caught in two minds. They have made it to the ends of the earth but still want to turn back to look at their old home. I remember once a fellow countryman was visiting a compatriot in San Francisco and he discovered that the man's house was right next to the Pacific Ocean, with an incomparably beautiful sea view from its windows. The guests all said that the rent must be sky high. The host confirmed that it was but said that it was worth it, saying, "The other side of the ocean that way is China and I can look towards my old home every day."

As soon as he said it, everyone felt a rush of emotion but there was one straight-talking older woman who disagreed, "For a thousand dollars, I can buy a discount air ticket and fly back to Beijing. There's nothing to beat a trip home, is there!"

To use the literary analogy again, this older woman was a new realist contradicting a new romantic. The man who was renting the house, being of the new romantic faction, hummed and hawed for a bit, then sighed and said, "I've got a lot of work on over here; it's not easy to get back home."

FIXED PRICE

In the free market, you can haggle over the price and that's the advantage of the freedom. But haggling also brings a major headache, which is that it forces both sides of the transaction into a weird kind of warfare, using great amounts of force, tactics and pyrotechnics, sometimes just for the sake of a single copper coin.

Some people think time is money and don't waste time haggling over price; when they go shopping, whether it is for vegetables or a leather coat, they just take what they want and go. These people are the ones street hawkers give the warmest welcome. Honest pedlars appreciate their straightforward approach and they are their ideal customers. There are some pedlars, however, who have the bad habit of buying cheap and selling at sharp prices. As they watch the rapidly retreating figure of such a customer, they cover their mouths to hide their smiles and say to the pedlars next to them, "That idiot X still hasn't learned to haggle." I once heard exactly those words in the market one day applied to myself and from then on I developed a habit of my own whenever I went there: whatever I want to buy, I adopt a take-it-or-leave it tone and I make sure I haggle. My thinking is that I don't mind being scolded for being too sharp but I don't want the pedlars to call me "that idiot X".

Once I had developed this habit, it became ingrained: if someone says eight, I have to say five. As a person, I have many bad habits but this is one I am proud of. The advantage it gives of blunting the sharp tongues of the pedlars goes without saying but it has also helped my wallet avoid countless bad purchases. Although it is only a matter of a few *yuan* or a few tens of *yuan* here and there, small amounts become big ones, and over the years at least I have been able to snatch back enough money from the pedlars to buy an eighteen-inch colour TV.

Habits follow you around and this one has remained unchanged when I go abroad. I was in a market in Germany once and I saw a porcelain plate on a middle-aged woman's stall. When I went over to talk to her, I was amazed to find she knew a few words of Chinese. She had studied it a little at school and this was why she was smiling at my little group of Chinese, not just because she wanted to attract our attention. When I asked the price of the porcelain plate, she hesitated for a moment and then named a sum that I thought was quite reasonable. But, as I say, a habit is a habit. I looked at her with my best open and honest expression, and said, "That's a little expensive, can you make it a little cheaper for the sake of Chinese-German friendship?" She looked puzzled at first, but when she understood my meaning, she went bright red in the face. I realised that my automatic response had hurt her feelings and her self-respect. She rather huffily took back the plate and refused to do business with my sort any more.

I still remember that incident and sometimes it makes me angry. I get cross with that German woman for hurting my pride. If she didn't want to bargain, why didn't she put a sticker with the price on that plate? Moreover, she was in the wrong for not bargaining because these days you can bargain over the price of anything anywhere in the world, so why couldn't she do so too? I will let you, dear reader, judge who is right and who is wrong.

MORE THAN HIS FAIR SHARE

Airline passengers are very taciturn. It is not a great opportunity for conversation and even a wordsmith like me is disinclined to talk to the person sitting next to him, let alone anyone else. The only people passengers talk to are the stewardesses, and then only when they are wheeling their trolleys of food and drink down the aisle, and you have to tell them what you want. On one occasion, I was flying back from Shenyang to Nanjing when I came across a not-very-talkative but very memorable neighbour. He was sitting in the window seat and was not particularly fat but right from the start, he was clearly dissatisfied with the width of the seat. He kept discontentedly shifting his legs to the side, trying to occupy a larger area and encroaching on my space. I didn't think he was deliberately trying to inconvenience me, so I didn't argue with him. I suspected that he was a property developer by profession, so he was used to taking possession of space and it was something of an occupational disease with him.

The first time the stewardess went past with her trolley, my neighbour failed to reveal his true heroic colours and just asked for a can of beer, which he drained in two gulps, and emitted a grunt of appreciation. After that, I thought I felt him looking at me but it wasn't me his gaze was fixed on, it was the stewardess, who was busy about her work in the aisle. I didn't know what his cause for concern was this time, until the stewardess came back down the aisle and he said, "I'll have a glass of orange juice now!"

I looked at him a bit more carefully this time, thinking to myself that all I asked for was a cup of tea, so why is he only going for the expensive stuff? And two different sorts, at that! I hoped that the stewardess would refuse him but, keeping a faint smile on her face, she poured him a generous half glass of orange juice. My neighbour spoke up again, this time in a bantering tone, "Come on now, pour a little more!" I looked at the stewardess, who just smiled automatically, and filled his glass with orange juice.

My neighbour was making me feel as though I was at something of a disadvantage but I didn't want anything to drink myself at the time and I had no reason to get the stewardess to even things out. Not long after that, it was lunchtime and the stewardess asked, "Would Sir like the beef or the chicken?"

I didn't want either but the man sitting in the window seat piped up, "Could I have two portions, Miss? One chicken, one beef? I missed breakfast this morning."

This time, I looked almost hostilely at the stewardess, secretly willing her not to agree to this insatiable fellow's request. But she blindly maintained her scrupulous manners and said, "If you want more, I can give you two portions." And it wasn't long before the silly girl was back to give my neighbour his extra food! All I could do was watch my neighbour eating more than his fair share and silently demonstrate my disapproval. Of course, this disapproval was pointless, as my neighbour paid absolutely no attention to me, concentrating only on the stewardess and his food.

I did not enjoy that flight as sitting next to someone like that gives one an indefinable feeling of defeat. When we finally got to the end of the flight, because I was sitting in the aisle seat, I naturally stood up first and as we waited in the queue to disembark, I made sure to keep in front of my neighbour. Just as I was feeling pleased with myself, I heard an excited voice behind me shouting out, "Let me through! My luggage is stowed up front!" I automatically got out of the way and, in that instant, forfeited the only pleasure I had got from that flight. I would rather not talk about my sense of loss and defeat as I watched my neighbour making his way to the front. I was just too slow and dull-witted and the final victory was his, that man who always got more than his fair share.

NOT BOTHERED WITH TRIFLES

What kind of man is it who is not bothered with trifles? You are bound to have met him on your travels: he is the man with smelly feet who likes to take his shoes off. He is the kind of man who likes to share his bounty by way of taste and smell: he puts his feet up in front of you and reads a newspaper or goes to sleep, magnanimously sharing the secret of his feet with everyone, completely without embarrassment or shame. The man who is not bothered with trifles is the kind of man who blunders into your home, touching everything and picking it up; then he pulls a book out of your bookcase and announces he is taking it away to read. The man who is not bothered with trifles is the kind of man who enthusiastically invites you to join him for a meal, tells you to order the best food and drink and not to mess about, the meal is on him. But when it comes down to it, he reaches into his pocket and says, "I forgot to bring my wallet. Why don't you pay this time, and next time I'll take you to such and such a place (he names some really high-end expensive restaurant) and treat you properly to a slap-up meal."

The man who is not bothered with trifles makes the punctilious man feel very inadequate. The latter greatly envies the former's way of doing things, thinking to himself how much better it would be if he could imitate it. Not only would he be more heroic-seeming and expansive wherever he went, so many things would come easier too. Easier in material matters is not so important to him but praise in the moral and ethical sphere makes life much easier for a person. Don't you feel this too, deep down? Suppose you hear someone criticising you, saying you don't bother with trifles. Would you be angry? Of course not! Not only would you not be angry, you might even say modestly, "What can I do about it? That's how I've been since I was born and there's no changing me!"

And why would you want to change? Every time I hear someone who is not bothered with trifles talking like this, it gets me really agitated and I'm itching to tell them my story, "Don't even think of changing! If you change, you'll be just like me and turn into an old fusspot!"

Please don't misunderstand me when I talk like this, dear reader, and think that I'm being ironic. I really wish that right from my childhood I could have been someone who didn't bother with trifles, for no other reason than I think that living that way is much happier and more worthwhile. Nowadays, everyone says that the free-wheeling, insouciant type is the one who gets the most out of the world.

Of course, the man who doesn't bother with trifles often has some shortcomings, but most of these are the kind of shortcoming that other people find endearing. Take carelessness for example. When summarising his own shortcomings, the man who doesn't bother with trifles will say, "I'm really careless; not like you, you're always so careful and so prudent. I wish I was as good as you!"

This kind of self-criticism leaves the punctilious man confused and he says to himself, "What does it matter if you're a bit careless?" But then, if you think about it, a careless man doesn't make a good accountant. He might put a zero too many or too few on the books and mess everything up completely.

But a punctilious man naturally complicates things and might think, "What's so wrong with not making a good accountant? What you are good at is the kind of work that involves breaking the mould and creating a new one."

I have always been very sympathetic to the man who is not bothered with trifles but, not long ago, I went to the post office to send something to Hong Kong. A few days later, however, I actually received the item myself. At first glance I thought it had been returned but when I looked more closely, I saw that it was a stupid mistake by a careless postal worker. I couldn't stop myself exclaiming, "Did he have his head down the toilet or something?!"

When I look at how I am, I know I can never change the petty-mindedness of the punctilious.

A DISCUSSION OF THE PHRASE *CHUJIA*

There is something rather tragic about the sight and sound of the phrase 出嫁 (chū jià) meaning for a woman to get married. In fact it has very much the same sound as 'sell off' does in business. I don't know why our ancestors started saying '出嫁' for when a girl gets married. It brings parents the pain of parting from a loved one, on the happiest day of their daughter's life, and hot tears spring to their eyes. But no one takes any notice of their tears. Their daughters get married one after the other, and only when they reach their husbands' homes do those daughters understand the meaning of that phrase '出嫁': the character 出 means 'to go out of' or 'leave', and the character 嫁 is made up of a woman 女 and home 家, so it means 'a daughter leaving her mother's home'.

Chinese people have many sayings and proverbs that plainly illustrate the laws governing human life. There is one that says 'a girl should get married when she comes of age'. Its meaning is quite clear: when a girl grows up, she shouldn't hang around at home, but hurry up and find a man so she can move out. It is alright if you don't want to do so, but then you must accept that you become an old maid or an old spinster. At first sight, those epithets don't sound too bad, but after a few hearings they seem more problematic. The nuances of Chinese characters are very powerful: someone calling you 老人 (*lǎorén*) 'old person' is about the most polite usage of this character 老 (*lǎo* = old), but there are people who like to insult you as 老东西 (*lǎo dōngxī*) 'an old object', 老不死的 (*lǎo bù sǐ de*) 'old but never dies', 老流氓 (*lǎo liú méng*) 'old rogue', and 老不中用 (*lǎo bù zhōng yòng*) 'old useless'. In those phrases, the epithet is used to suggest that all manner of people are old and worthless. Moreover, when a woman reaches her thirties or forties, because she is still not married, she begins to be called '老', and how is she supposed to take that with equanimity? Of course, you may come across a linguistic obsessive who wants to dissect this, "Is it that these women are opposed to marriage? Or do they not believe in the truth of that saying 'a girl should get married when she comes of age'? Or do they think there is nothing good about men and have no desire to share a bed with one?" That question puts me in a position of some embarrassment because I don't know. I just know that there are all sorts of reasons that women don't get married and I know that women who do get married do so for a variety of reasons. They are like sheep being driven by a shepherd headlong into the pasture where they either start grazing or not, depending on whether they find the grass tasty or unpalatable. In the same way these women either enjoy the fruits of marriage or find them not to their taste, but either way, they've taken the plunge and are wet through.

Meanwhile, the women who haven't got married are still standing on the shore, fresh and dry, some of them maybe playing the innocent, and waving to their sisters as they call out, "What are you splashing around in there for?"

I can only guess at their thinking and, if there are such women as that, is it because they strongly object to that saying: 'a girl should get married when she comes of age'? Are there indeed the kind of women who think that way and say, "You want me to go and get married but I'm not going to!"? Of course, these are just the pointless musings of a boring scholar but I do think that if someone wanted to keep worrying away at the question of marriage and stir things up a bit, then maybe those armchair moralists wouldn't be quite so quick to keep saying things like 'a girl should get married when she comes of age'. If everyone stopped getting married, then all they could say would be, "Get married or don't get married, suit yourself!" Or, at the very least, they could stop using the old-fashioned 出嫁, and instead employ something more cosmopolitan like: "Miss, please consider whether you would like to bring a husband home."

DOGGY PADDLE

Swimming is my usual form of exercise. The pool isn't close to where I live but it's not too far either. When I get there on my bike, carrying my swimming things, I have a quick shower, as required by the pool regulations, then rush over to the pool, dive in and begin my 500-metre swim. It's an unvarying routine. I've been doing this for almost two years and, until recently, I have felt I'm really enjoying life. But now, I've begun to think that my swimming is boring and pointless.

This has been brought about by the appearance of a new family at the swimming pool: a young couple with their son. I am very focussed when I swim but the cries of pleasure that come from this family make it impossible for me to blot out their presence. The three of them are particularly eye-catching in the winter pool. Why is that? Because everyone in the winter pool swims in the same way but those three all use doggy paddle! Their idiosyncratic style looks rather comic in amongst the regulation breaststroke and occasional butterfly but, at the same time, it does distinguish them from the common crowd. Some people glare at them disapprovingly but they take absolutely no notice. You may care about the way they are swimming but they are blissfully unaware of you. They are just enjoying their version of domestic bliss in the swimming pool and, from time to time, mother and son burst out in unaccountable peals of laughter.

I don't know why but when I looked at it dispassionately, I thought they were the only three people in the pool who were truly enjoying themselves. I felt that my own regulation laps of the pool were dull and wearing, and a wild idea sprang into my head: I remembered that, when I was little, I used to swim doggy paddle in the moat of my old hometown. Why not give it a go now? Holding that thought, I tried a few strokes in imitation but almost immediately, I unexpectedly began to feel ashamed of myself, as though I had just urinated in front of everyone. I spontaneously stopped my doggy paddle and resumed my freestyle stroke. But I kept watching the family doggy-paddling away with huge enjoyment and immediately felt that not only was my own swimming pointless, it was also as irksome and tedious as if I was operating a machine.

So, from then on, I felt that my swimming was an irreconcilable problem: why couldn't I be happy doggy-paddling in the pool? Why did I have to adopt an orthodox stroke and why did that orthodox stroke make me feel that swimming was no longer fun? What had caused this? I felt that I, like many others, had been caught in the snare of public opinion. If we all follow the scientific and technological model, we lose originality and enjoyment, and everyone ends up the same.

As to whether this is an intractable problem, or something quite easily solved, some might say, "If you are not enjoying your swimming, why don't you just stop?" I had this thought too, but the trouble is, I still want to exercise. And again, the answer might come, "If it is exercise you want, stop looking for fun as well. Do you think you can have your cake and eat it too? Nothing is that easy!"

So here is the problem: even in the advanced state mankind has reached, can we still not have some cake and eat some too? Why are the two things mutually exclusive?

FACE TO FACE

Today, I want to discuss one of my bad habits and that is staring at people. Because I am short-sighted but don't wear glasses, I squint when I look at people, and the more I am focused on them, the ruder I seem.

I'm not going to prevaricate; I know there is a reason for everything and I am going to look at this bad habit of mine in two parts. One is my own lack of self-discipline but the other is not my fault; it is those self-inflicted casualties who walk around in front of me. It's not that I deliberately stare at them, it is they who are asking to be stared at. If I don't look at them, I would be being a bit aloof but they are completely unconcerned if I do look at them. So I feel that there is no connection between my looking or not looking and insulting or being insulted. Now, wherever I am I maintain the old straightforward working man's attitude: if you interest me, I'll stare at you: I'll stare at your eyes and at your nose, and what does it matter if there's a pimple on your nose?

I am very grateful to trains, buses, public restrooms and shopping malls, as these are the optimal places for indulging my bad habit to the full. Sometimes I take a stroll around a shopping mall and I always get annoyed about losing my way just as I am getting anxious about it being time to go home. It is only when I calm down a bit that I realise that I am not lost at all, it's just that the crowd is blocking my way. You're staring at him, he's staring at you, and you've both forgotten to keep walking. But that's nothing. The occasion that made the most profound impression on me was in Beijing back in the 80s, on a public bus, when I almost lost my precious spectacles in the crush. It was a rush-hour bus and it was so full it was about to explode. When I got on, my feet were hardly touching the ground and I felt almost as if I were floating, which was both stimulating and worrying at the same time. I remember a young black man, who looked like an overseas student, standing as tight to me as if we were glued together; if someone had been able suddenly to pop up and take a photograph, I'm sure there would have been an avid audience for it. I've already thought of its title: it would be called 'Long Live Sino-African Friendship'.

But at the time, the two of us young men, one yellow one black, were very embarrassed, and all I can do now, later on, is make the best of it: take the opportunity to consider this occurrence of my old bad habit, and study what it was about him that made me stare at the unusual sight of this young black man. I got a big kick out of it at the time, looking at his gleaming black skin, his impossibly tight curly hair and his unimprovably white teeth: such a comprehensive, close-range inspection made a very deep impression on me. I also very distinctly remember that there was a little face in the pupils of his eyes: it was the yellow-skinned face of a young man. In fact, it was my face. I also remember that the young black man could do nothing about being stared at by me, and just said in not very good Chinese, "Too minny peeple!"

The reason I call this habit of mine bad is to show that I am indeed a civilised and polite person but, even so, I have no intention of correcting the shortcoming, and I will continue to stare at people wherever I go. If I found myself in the desert, where there is no one to see, I wouldn't complain; but, as it is, I live in the city and even if it isn't some great international conurbation, it still has a population bigger than a country as rich in natural resources as Sweden at more than five million. Apart from when I'm asleep and have my eyes closed, everywhere I go I see people, so it is very difficult to rid myself of this bad habit. So, what I am asking of the people I stare at is that they don't curse and swear at me – of course, I'm not expecting them to thank me - but just let it pass.

GHOST STORIES

Ancient Chinese literati were very fond of writing and telling ghost stories, and the most famous of these are Pu Songling's *Strange Stories from a Chinese Studio*. Most of the ghosts in those stories are beautiful, red-lipped, sparkling-eyed female spirits such as Ying Ning and Nie Xiaoqian: not only are they generally very well known, they are also film stars, often gracing the silver screen. Because Old Pu Songling made them very beautiful when he wrote about them, the studio bosses always sought out the most beautiful actresses to play them.

But when ghosts appear on the movie screen, they leave the spirit world and, however you look at them, they are human. No matter how magical their appearance, no matter that they leave no shadow or footprints, you remain sure that they are only people dressed up as ghosts and spirits, and movie-goers don't get the full magical transformation that happens in the story. Some people like me go even further and say, "You're better off not watching these so-called ghost-story movies at all, because they take proper ghosts and turn them into something that is neither ghost nor human."

There is something disappointing about all this. Lots of people really want ghost stories: they both love and are afraid of ghosts though, of course, what I mean by 'ghosts' here are those beautiful, bewitching female ghosts. Most people reckon that stories involving visitations by female ghosts are romantic thrillers but male ghosts never bring any good and their stories are just straightforward murders, which really aren't very interesting at all.

The most exciting thing for those who read ghost stories is the way scholars or people born as peasants are seduced out of their minds by female ghosts, and the way scruffy smelly men are made to feel they are heart-throbs and god's gift to women. Although as readers, they are not actually participants in the action, their feelings are just as conflicted, complex, poignant and sentimental as men who actually get involved in affairs with women. The only difference there is that the men who get involved with women don't have ghosts but real women hoping to get intimate with them, whereas the male readers all harbour a kind of jealous wishful thinking towards the hero of the story and say, "Don't be too pleased with yourself, that's not a human, it's a ghost!"

But suppose there is a real woman involved, even if she is a devastating beauty, she will not bring that frisson of excitement that a female ghost can. The wonderful thing about ghost stories is that they never come true. Because female ghosts rise from the grave at the slightest pretext, reincarnate themselves for you at the drop of a hat, and confuse and enrapture men's hearts as they please, the danger lies in their glamorous fascination. Of course, there are also men who know there are ghosts in the mountains yet still go up into them because what they are looking for and longing for is a love affair with some vigorous rumpy pumpy between a human and a ghost. Not only did such men exist when Old Pu Songling was writing at the beginning of the Qing Dynasty, they are still with us now at the end of our 20th century.

The reason ghost stories are passed down from generation to generation is probably because people's idea of paradise has stayed pretty much the same. A human making love to a human is not so exciting but a human making love to a ghost, now that's exciting!

PEOPLE FRIGHTENING PEOPLE

Whilst we are on the subject of ghost stories:

It was the tail-end of the Cultural Revolution when I started at primary school. The slogans about 'sweeping away superstition' were deeply ingrained in us and, normally speaking, there should not have been any ghosts manifesting themselves in the schoolyard. But some naughty child or other, I don't know who, came up with a very scary ghost story: he said that a ghost called Queen Little Feet was haunting the lavatories and that anyone who went for a dump would see Queen Little Feet's little feet, wearing red embroidered shoes, under the stall partition.

Children love ghost stories and are scared by them at the same time, and I was no different. Once when I was sitting in class, I found myself thinking about that ghost in the lavatories and my heart started pounding and my head throbbing. I raised my hand and told the teacher that I had a stomach upset and needed to go to the lavatory. The teacher gave me permission, so I had the chance to go and investigate. I rushed over to the lavatory. Usually it was very busy and noisy but this time there was no one else there. I could barely contain my fear, but I really wanted to get some first-hand evidence of Queen Little Feet, so I knelt down and stared at the floor on the other side of the partition. I stayed there looking for at least five minutes but all I saw were some flies crawling around in the filthy muddy water. There was not a pair of embroidered red shoes or a ghost to be seen. I hurried back to the classroom, disappointed but exhilarated because I felt I had established my credentials as an authority on ghosts.

On that occasion my childish courage allowed me genuinely to 'sweep away superstition', not to be afraid of ghosts and never to be scared by ghost stories ever again. But there was one occasion when I was frightened by a real person. It happened when I was playing mahjong with some friends, and gambling for small change. Of course, even gambling for small amounts was illegal, and we all knew it, so we did it in secret behind closed doors. We played merrily on late into the night and everything was quiet. Then one of my friends went downstairs for a piss (the place I was living in at the time didn't have its own toilet); everything was normal when he came back and we went on playing. Then, suddenly, and to our surprise, we heard footsteps on the staircase which quickly became thunderous. My head went into a whirl and I thought my luck had run out. Dear readers, have you ever heard footsteps thundering up the stairs at the dead of night in a condemned building?

I really wanted to gather up the coins in front of me but my hands wouldn't move; my three friends were sat there like wooden dummies too. Then, just as we were all resigning ourselves to being led away in handcuffs, we saw one of our other friends rush in through the door, shouting, "Nobody move!" Even when we realised who it was, the four of us round the table still sat there, faces white as sheets, for a minute before suddenly coming to our senses. Then four mouths exploded into furious curses directed at our friend.

I asked the wretch how he had got in and he said, "I was just passing and I saw the door was open. Of course I wasn't going to miss the chance to give you all a good fright." It was all the fault of our friend who had gone downstairs for a piss, so we all turned on him, cursing him for his weak bladder.

I think the reason I seldom gamble anymore is connected with that night and from then on my belief has been confirmed in the saying, "When people frighten other people, they put the fear of death in them." I don't retell this story just to fill up space; there is a genuine purpose to it. I really hope that people who have a liking for scaring their friends will correct this failing. Ghosts only scare people to death in books and stories but people scaring other people to death really can happen. So whatever else you do, be careful with your footsteps at the dead of night!

THE SPENDTHRIFT

The edge of the desert is not really a good place for people to live but there are some who have lived for generations with sandstorms for neighbours and have absolutely no intention of moving away. They feel that if people are only willing to knuckle down to it, sandstorms are quite manageable. I once watched a TV programme about the true story of an old Mongolian man who spent his whole life planting trees to control the desert: I saw him standing on top of the sand dunes in the setting sun, planting row after row of trees; I saw his stooping silhouette, his back bent by years of hard toil; and I felt both moved and deeply saddened. I remember that special documentary particularly clearly and I recall the narrator saying in an approving tone of voice, "In the shade of its trees, X village (that is the old man's village) no longer fears the onslaught of the sandstorms".

A couple of years later, I happened to turn the TV on and chanced on a programme reporting on the destruction of trees, and the location and people involved reminded me of that old man. The reporter was interviewing the village headman of X village and asked him why they had felled the trees. The headman replied simply, "We are a poor village and we sold them for cash." At that point, the voice-over was reporting that the headman had used the biggest bits of timber to make furniture for his newly-married son's cave house.

I watched wide-eyed and dumbstruck, and thought to myself, "What about the old man? The one who planted the trees! Why aren't we seeing him? Let him have his say!" He did, in fact, appear later on, looking not to be in very good health. I saw him on the TV screen, hobbling along, touching the stumps of the trees that were left behind. He didn't speak but the experienced reporter had the camera focused on the tears running down his cheeks, which spoke more eloquently than words.

However, I wasn't really happy with this and thought to myself, "Why stop with just tears?" For my feelings as an outside observer to be properly satisfied, the old man should be allowed really to show his feelings to the headman. I almost found myself shouting at the television, "Box his ears! Box that spendthrift's ears!" But in the end, TV is TV: all it can do is make people stop and think, and tears are its preferred method for doing this.

I really don't want to keep going over and over such a black and white issue but the reason I am fixated with it is because I am still angry about it; I can't help being baffled that everybody let that village headman off so lightly. From ancient times, the number of profligates and spendthrifts has done nothing but increase and the most objectionable of all are those who make free with other people's households and with public property. Admittedly there are entrepreneurs as well as profligates; in the case of that old man, he planted a lifetime's worth of trees and it seems almost as if he was just waiting for the village headman's son to grow up and get married so that those trees could be used to make furniture: this is pretty much the definition of an entrepreneur. The reason I am dissatisfied with the old man may not be obvious to you but you have actually already seen it quite clearly for yourselves: he wept as he touched the stumps of the trees. I don't like it when someone uses tears to demonstrate their anger: it's pointless! If I were him, the first thing I would do would be to get hold of that village headman and box his ears nine times, then nine more sets of nine. If there really is anything about all this that merits consideration, it is that I would ask you to consider how richly deserved those eighty-one blows would be.

CHATTERBOX

Over the last few years, I have come to realise that I have turned into a chatterbox. My closest friends may well have noticed this and have found various different ways of letting me know how they feel about the change. Some of them say, "You used to be so quiet", by which they mean, "Where has all this vacuous chatter come from?" Others are even less direct, "I think your character has changed", but they don't specify whether the change is for the better or for the worse, and are clearly leaving it for me to work out.

I don't know how it has happened either but advancing age has brought with it a completely unexpected physiological change: I've become garrulous. I have had quite a few extraordinary experiences: in the course of heated debate with my friends, I have actually heard my own voice rising high and clear, and resounding confidently through the air. It is not without some regret that I now have to recognise that I, Su Tong, am no longer a taciturn man. It is a peculiar thing to be a man who doesn't know what silence is, nor to have any belief in its poetic qualities and inner strengths. Its virtue, that was so evident to me before, is immediately rendered tawdry and vulgar by my answer to the question: what is silence? It is when no voices are heard and no farts are dropped. You could say that, no matter what void it leaves inside me, no matter how wild and inevitably irrational my thinking, since I have now become a chatterbox, I want to find out what this garrulousness is founded on and, in particular, what its advantages are.

It isn't difficult to find a convincing foundation: I am not a youngster any more and I am taking advantage of a clearer voice and more agile mind to speak more and not to just stay silent for no good reason; now I'm older, I can cough and splutter through congested lungs and thick, old-man phlegm, and nag away at sons and grandsons, telling them they ignore their elders' advice at their peril, and other such pearls. For my own part, I never particularly appreciated the advice of older people, so now I make sure I get the first word in and I'm not afraid of being garrulous.

This thing called language is all very well as long as you are adaptable: if you don't speak it well, no one is going to issue a summons against you, but you do invite people's criticism. Besides, God gave you a mouth and it is not just for eating and drinking, it is for talking too. If you never speak, someone who likes talking may say to you, "You're a taciturn sort; one mouth isn't enough for me and you keep yours closed all the time, why don't you lend it to me?" If you are faced with such a request, what reasonable grounds do you have to refuse it?

So what are the advantages of garrulousness? Well, let me put a positive spin on the subject. The biggest advantage is that it keeps you mentally and physically healthy, and there is plenty of scientific material to illustrate this: depressed and cheerless people die early. There are also people who just listen but don't interact, and people who are prone to this kind of behaviour are even more at risk. They are like a permanently inflating balloon and there is no escaping the resulting explosion. Why should I want to be the balloon, when I can be the air pump? I think garrulousness is a kind of release, like the exhaust of a car. People following behind you may be uncomfortable but you are allowed to be a little selfish: ensure your own comfort first and then see about others.

It is only after I gradually made the transition into being a chatterbox, that I finally realised what a beautiful thing language is. Even when it comes to vulgarity or obscenity, all you have to do is get it out and not keep it bottled up inside and, one way or another, it is going to have an effect on people. Of course, this is all the self-perception of a chatterbox. Self-perception is a fine thing, as it makes you feel you are making a positive contribution to the world: it is the chatterbox's greatest merit and also their biggest failing.

IMITATING SO AND SO

'Celebrity' basically means somebody famous, and I guess 'famous' basically means that everybody knows your name and knows all about you. Celebrities inhabit the television and the newspapers, and they have no idea how many pairs of eyes belonging to ordinary people are staring at them with unabashed adoration or envy; but they are undoubtedly itching to comment on your appearance, or your voice, or even your backside, "You're on the way down and I'm on the way up."

It is said that the majority of Americans want to be a star at some point in their life even if only for an hour. I don't know whether it is Americans who say this, or it is something put about by other nationalities; so it is either a label they are proud to give themselves, or it is dirty water poured over them by others. The way I see the desire for fame, all roads lead to Rome and it's all much of a muchness.

Every country's press and media are expert at exploiting the mentality of their own population. I remember watching the international news quite some years ago and hearing that some organisation or other was holding a Marilyn Monroe look-a-like contest. In the face of hot competition, the winner whom all the judges decided most resembled that famous beauty turned out to be a man! I was speechless with surprise, thinking what an extraordinary man he must be, and wondering how on earth he had learned to imitate Marilyn's trademark pose with voluptuous hips and rear end.

This perhaps has something to do with the effect celebrities have on the lives of ordinary people. If you think about it, a celebrity's fame is based on this posture or that facial expression, on this song or that monologue: nothing very difficult, however you look at it, and how are you going to be able to stop other people mastering it? Moreover, if they can have a bit of fun and also make money at the same time, they really are killing two birds with one stone without having to expend much effort on it.

Anyone can be a celebrity. First let us consider the indirect way of becoming famous, by imitating a celebrity. This is a kind of shortcut to celebrity resulting from globalisation. Not long ago, I was lucky enough to attend a very lively evening show, the theme of which was something like "Guess who they are!" A number of brightly-clad guys and girls wearing masks mounted the stage one by one. At first, you had no idea who they were but once they started singing, their identities became obvious and they left the stage to tumultuous applause. But when the performers took their masks off, one look showed that they weren't actually who you thought they were; in fact, you didn't recognise them at all. At this point, the audience exploded with applause again. The compere then solemnly announced the names of the impersonators, and the strange thing was that the applause that greeted these was much less enthusiastic. I felt that there was something wrong with this and that it was unfair on those artists that they had been singing their hearts out just to enhance the reputations of already established stars. What about their own names? What happened to them? Once they left the stage, they were forgotten. It can't help but make you wonder about the thinking behind this way of becoming a celebrity.

Most unforgettable of all was the performer imitating some beautiful young starlet or other, who gave an almost perfect rendition of one of her songs then, to everyone's total amazement, when the mask came off, proved to be a young boy of no more than ten or so. Even as I was gasping at his abundance of talent, I couldn't help worrying about his parents' intentions. However I looked at it, I couldn't fathom it. Why did they let their son imitate that starlet? Were they really willing to go as far as to let their son turn himself into a glamorous woman just so he could become a celebrity?

PATERNAL LOVE

Everyone says of paternal love that it is moderate and controlled. The vastness of maternal love makes us overlook its existence and significance but, for many people, the distinctively calm and unruffled form paternal love takes, has a particular influence on them. The odd thing about it is that it is ashamed of expressing itself, shies away from ostentation yet remains towering and majestic – which is why a perceptive person once said, "Paternal love is like a mountain."

Not long ago, on a trip to Shanghai, I was idly flipping through a magazine I had brought along to while away the time, when I chanced on an article that certainly merited more serious attention. It was written by an American who was telling the story of paternal love as he experienced it. As I read the article, although it was an American writing about his father, the details of that American father, every day for so many years, squeezing orange juice for his son, immediately made me think of my own father. My father used to get up early every day to make congee for me and my sister, right up until each of us finally left home. I immediately started making comparisons as I read that article. The author said that every time he finished the orange juice his father had squeezed for him, he would hug his father and tell him he loved him, before leaving the room.

When he received that hug and that expression of love, the American father never said a word in reply. In America, hugging is an essential part of the relationship between a father and son but I never hugged my own father. However, when I was little, I routinely greeted him with a 'Daddy' the first time I saw him every day. When I was a little bigger, I felt that this greeting was becoming a bit of a chore, thinking to myself that he was still my daddy whether I called him that or not, so once I just skated over it. My father's way of dealing with this was to come and stand in front of me, wagging his finger under my nose, so I had no choice but to greet him just as before, "Daddy!" The weird thing was that that American boy was just like me: he said that one day he got fed up with that routine hug and tried just to slip out of the room after drinking his father's orange juice. His father stopped him at the door, saying, "Haven't you forgotten something today?"

Even now, I still make comparisons, and think that if I had been in his place, I would have said, "Thank you for reminding me", then hugged him and been done with it. But in the end American sons and Chinese sons are not the same, and that American lad overthought things and was too demanding. He rashly took a tougher line and asked, "Dad, why do you never say you love me?" And it was after this, when the American son forced his father to say "I love you", that the most moving part of the article presented itself. The father had great difficulty uttering this common sentiment, and when he finally did manage to say "I love you", he lost his self-control and burst out crying.

I almost burst into tears myself when I read that, and I still kept making comparisons with the paternal love that I experienced. I thought I could never force my father to say "I love you", and that was the one difference between me and that American son: I knew it, and that was enough. If a father's love remains unspoken, so be it, and let us forever immerse ourselves in that unspoken love.

CEMENT RELICS

I don't know when it started but all over China there is a new craze for developing tourism centred on the land's natural resources. Of course, it is great that we have such natural resources readily available, as it would be a terrible waste if beautiful mountains and lakes were hidden away where no one knew about them. So why should they not be loudly advertised for the benefit of the economy? But there are many places that do not have any such resources, so along comes a trend to create culture by remaking nature. They are making a whole host of concrete palaces, concrete caves, concrete halls and even concrete cities but, when you see them, you can't help being disappointed and feeling that you have been cheated.

Disdainful of their profession, tour guides are tramping all over sites where the concrete was only poured last year, enthusiastically claiming that this is an ancient relic from so many years ago in such and such a dynasty, and that that is where some famous scholar of several hundred years ago studied; that this is where he made his reputation and that is where he was banished to; or that this is the spot where he recited poetry dressed in his finery. Every time I hear some tour guide spouting off like this about some concrete relic or other, I can't stop myself saying to the girl, "What are you on about!? Can't you see the place!?"

I'm not being harsh, it's just that these concrete relics are poaching business from the Forbidden City in Beijing and the Terracotta Army in Xi'an, and it's not a fair competition. Sometimes when I see hordes of these mindless tourists being dragged by coach from this fake site to that, I think to myself,

"What idiots! Traipsing all over the place looking at the scenery or the ruins. Who told you that you were paying homage to history by visiting concrete halls and palaces or concrete ancient cities? But I know for sure there are people who believe the guidebooks on the question of these concrete relics, when they say that the historical records tell us that such and such happened here, or that this was where so and so was born, and that although the original has long since been destroyed by the vicissitudes of man and time, blown up in warfare or burned down, we have restored them to their original state, so you can snap away with your cameras and take home some precious memories! I think this is where the real misconception lies: if they have been destroyed, what are you doing rebuilding them? If something is gone, no matter how cleverly you rebuild it, it won't be the original, and if you have a group photo taken on some red-lacquered concrete verandah, you might just as well have your picture taken holding a sack of concrete."

Of course, I have considered the Old Summer Palace in Beijing; people who have been there all know that it is in ruins, but is still a genuine site. If something has been destroyed, it can be preserved as ruins, and this is the only other acceptable sort of ancient relic. If we truly want to pay homage to history, we really only have two choices: either sites that are preserved intact, or those that are in ruins. We absolutely mustn't visit those concrete relics: it goes without saying that they are not worth seeing, but how much worse is it to know that you have been swindled out of your ticket money and your ice-cream money!

VERBAL CORRUPTION

I don't know where the expression 'verbal corruption' comes from but I do remember that, when I was young, I heard my schoolmates talking about how A had corrupted B, and I knew it had something to do with extramarital sex. Although, of course, I had no personal experience, I knew what it was all about, and felt that it was a transgression confined to the world of grown-ups. Over the years, society has progressed and a whole new world of jargon has sprung up around sex, so this word 'corruption' has been able to return to its original meaning, which is principally to do with abuse of power, bribery, graft and other such contemptible conduct. Its sexual connotations have gradually faded away. But there are some folk who feel a certain nostalgia for such vulgar and indecent speech and have formed a kind of 'verbal corruption' faction.

On the whole, this faction is formed of men who outwardly show no sign of corruption and are neatly dressed and bespectacled. These people like to showcase their abilities in appropriate circumstances and wait for the right opening or someone else who appreciates vulgarity provides the opening and sets the ball rolling. The vulgarian then takes over and starts telling his locker-room stories, one after the other. These stories are all plausible but unsuitable for children, who wouldn't understand them in any case. But most adults do get them and most adults, including not a few unembarrassable women, enjoy them. These vulgarians are of varying levels of talent and ability. Some of them like the sound of their own voice particularly when being foul-mouthed: the kind to whom the expression 'what do you expect from a pig but a grunt' applies. But there are some brilliant and supremely eloquent people, of whom it is said that they can turn that grunt into an aria.

For many years now I have been a faithful audience for this verbal corruption faction, believing that, during a long and boring journey, or during a long and tedious meeting, it is always they who bring a little light relief. After all, if you are some pure-tongued individual who recites the bible from memory, you're not going to attract much of an audience. I sometimes get some enjoyment from pondering the imponderable and trying to work out exactly what special ability these folk have that allows them to put this corruption into operation; they don't actually do anything, the corruption is all verbal, but it has all sorts of little tricks, it brings out humour, it has a profound effect and it manages to be even more corrupt than real corruption. Not only does it satisfy the vulgarian's craving, it allows others to satisfy old cravings of their own. Everyone is happy and no one has done anything wrong.

People often reckon that the verbal corruption faction are very restrained in the way they live their lives, and their actions and speech are in complete contrast with each other. This appears to be a fact and it is also the thing that others most envy about them. If you think about it, man's own understanding of himself often surpasses anything science can tell him. Everyone knows the physiological functions of the mouth, so there's no need for me to go into them here, but who can say why the mouth also works as an overflow pipe. If I may be allowed to show off my layman's understanding here, I think that guilt about sex is the most forgivable of all the things you can feel guilty about, so it's no big deal if it spills out, it's just a safety valve.

The most worrying thing is that verbal corruption is now being threatened by the female sex; there are some women who are particular about the purity of what they hear. They say that verbal corruption is a form of sexual harassment and they want to take people to court over it. But the law is specifically concerned with fact, and I believe that when the verbal corruption faction stands in the dock, it has no reason to panic. One simple sentence will garner everybody's sympathy, particularly the men's: "I didn't actually do anything!"

SELF PRESERVATION

It is certainly true that children should never be underestimated and even at an early age they have the first buds of the instinct for self-preservation. When a child has done something naughty outdoors, if they can cover it up they will, but if someone tells on them, and one look at their parents' faces tells them they can't get away with it, then they say, disingenuously, "I'll tell you, but you mustn't hit me!" Then they admit their crime, doing their best to minimise it, all the time watching for their mother's or father's slightest movement. If there is any sign of danger, the child holds their hands out in front of them, like a boxer defending himself, and says, "You mustn't hit me!" But grown-ups are grown-ups and break their promises when they are angry, so the blow lands. At which point the child begins to wail and yell, "You promised you wouldn't hit me! You don't keep your word!"

Any trouble can be mitigated by self-preservation so the consequences are lessened, and even children can master the secrets of the art, "I've owned up, so you mustn't hit me!" This kind of plea may not be completely effective but it is always better said than not said; it may lighten the blow a little and save a few bruises.

Of course, the situation is a little more complicated and multi-layered in the adult world as, if grown-ups do something wrong, they don't end up facing their parents but if it's not their partner, it's the police. In private life, if it is the man who has done something wrong, he will say to his wife or girlfriend, "I had a sudden rush of blood to the head and crossed the line. From now on I won't have anything more to do with that temptress, so let's make a fresh start together."

If the woman is having an affair, then she will say, weeping and wailing, "I am so sorry, and I'm so ashamed; just let me go away and die!" This is what is called "getting it all out in the open from the start".

Even a murderer shouldn't show weakness but should say that there is too much violence in the movies and on TV, and suggest that he has been influenced by that, with the result that he killed someone without really thinking about it. There are perfectly intelligent people who, on the one hand, spare no effort to exonerate themselves whilst, at the same time, being happy to see confessions squeezed out of offenders like toothpaste from a tube because they firmly believe in the probity of officers of the law. In the olden days there was a standard policy that the judge would give you a stern talking to, you would confess all and the judge would spare you. Nowadays, the sentence is ordained by the law but as soon as the defendant looks up, he sees the sign that reads "Leniency for those who confess, severity for those who refuse to". He ponders this and feels he ought to confess. After all, confessing is easy, and if you do it properly, you'll probably just get a slap on the wrist and be sent home. When it comes down to it, man is a higher order of creature, not some bird circling in the sky, at first sight so free and easy, but which can be brought down with a single shot. Man is expert at self-preservation, so he doesn't fly around in the sky but keeps his feet firmly on the ground, especially if he is doing something wrong. If you go to arrest him, all he does is put his hands in the air and say "I surrender". With those simple words he saves his life. And if there is a next time, he can do the same again.

HIV POSITIVE

Once, in an idle moment, I picked up a photography magazine and suddenly came across a group of photos entitled *Face to face with AIDS victims*. I remembered that I had looked at the same magazine before and seen the same pictures but not paid them any attention. It simply hadn't occurred to me that every one of the people in them was an AIDS sufferer. It wasn't at all that I am unobservant, but rather that those unfortunate people all looked too open and relaxed, just like ordinary photographic models.

Most opinions expressed by non-experts on specialist subjects are trite and banal, tending just to follow the herd, so a hobbyist photographer only takes pictures of lotus blossoms, kingfishers, mothers and babies, and so on. An expert photographer, however, always shows imagination and creativity, and at the same time as they give expression to an idea, they also give expression to the thinking behind the photograph. A careful inspection of this particular set of photos reveals that what the master photographer wanted to capture was the calm, relaxed, unafraid smiles of the AIDS sufferers, and not the grief-stricken, fearful, death-haunted tears that we naturally expect to see.

The most unforgettable shot is one of a little girl, maybe seven or eight years old, guileless innocence writ large on her unblemished forehead. Her two little hands are up to her mouth, and she is smiling into the camera lens: I am sure you can imagine, dear readers, her coy but scintillating expression. Purely because of that expression, I experienced a sudden, irrepressible pang of heartache.

There was a simple caption underneath the picture, 'Veronica: Veronica and her mother are both HIV positive but she doesn't yet know she is different from other children'. That is what made the photograph so heart-rending. So much so that I couldn't bring myself to look at it again.

I would rather look at the other fourteen photographs of adults. I am sure they all knew why the photographer wanted to take their pictures and also endorsed his creative concept. They had given him the utmost degree of cooperation and, because of this, when we look at this group of people facing death with smiles on their faces, we see one of them sitting happily on a big wooden barrel, one of them wearing ice skates and one, a grandfather, hugging his granddaughter in a picture of domestic bliss. I particularly noticed that in those fourteen smiling faces, there was not a single trace of those smiles being forced and they were all completely natural.

I was astonished at this and I don't know whether it was because my understanding of reality had been turned on its head or because I realised I had absolutely no understanding of photography and had to admit that I had not fully understood this group of photographs. I thought I understood the basic rules of human emotion that if it is appropriate to smile, you should smile, and if it is appropriate to weep, you should weep, but now people are rewriting those rules and replacing tears with smiles. I don't know if this augurs the imminent arrival of an age of optimism but I do believe that optimism and freedom from fear are the children of the sun, and fear and sorrow are the children of the night. They are interdependent but they are not interchangeable, nor should they ever be.

GROUPIES

So what are groupies like? Previously I knew very little about them because there was no one in particular following me and I wasn't following anyone else. I only knew what I had read, and that made me imagine some star or other running helter-skelter down the road as if their lives depended on it, pursued by a crowd of these 'groupies' yelling and whooping. But imaginings are just that, imaginings, and they do not represent reality. Once, I was watching a concert that was being broadcast on the television, and the moment a male popstar who was all the rage at the time mounted the stage, a young girl came flying in from the side, seized him in her embrace and kissed him. Then, no doubt stunned by her incredible good luck and not knowing what to do next, she just stood on the stage, tears of excitement spilling from her eyes at the idea of performing on the same stage as her hero. At which point, she was hustled away by nearby stewards and it was then that I observed that she wasn't really some crazy weirdo, and the further away she was dragged from her idol, the more she turned back into a simple, shy young girl. I don't know whether it sprang from natural male envy or from a feeling of protectiveness towards the young girl, but I found myself saying to the television set, "What's so attractive about a wrinkled old face like his?"

I know that my rather sour question would mean nothing to a real groupie and stemmed only from my own hypocrisy. If, by some good fortune, I were to become a popstar, and if some young girl threw herself at me and planted a kiss on my wrinkled old face, I would certainly not be asking the same question then. So, as you can see, I have a conflicted attitude to groupies. What's sauce for the goose is sauce for the gander and if, by some chance, one day I am poking fun at groupies, and then by some other chance, find myself repackaged as a popstar and those groupies bear grudges and not a single one follows me, I really would have no complaints. In the end, all fame is empty fame and all you can do is keep up your self-deception with assertions that you are happy to be a loner and a maverick.

Of course all this hypothesising does is expose my own self-regard. How is anything like that ever going to happen to a middle-aged man like me? When it comes to groupies though, they still make me feel frustrated and uneasy, but also pressurised by a pressure that is entirely self-generated. I have a daughter of my own, just beginning to grow up and at present she is infatuated with Miss Zhao Wei and Mr Su Youpeng in the TV drama *My Fair Princess*. So, although I am nervous about the future, I have no concerns about the present as I am pretty sure she isn't able to hurl herself at her two idols. She has, however, recently become rather envious of one of her classmates, and says, "So-and-so is really popular in class right now." When I ask her why, it turns out the reason is that so-and-so has the same birthday as Su Youpeng, right down to the hour and all the other astrological details, so obviously she is going to grow up to be just as famous!

I thought this clearly demonstrated my daughter's future groupie potential and, in my agitation, couldn't help exclaiming, "You're not allowed to be a groupie!"

She looked at me in surprise and said, "Who's being a groupie?" I could tell from her expression that she wanted me to explain what was wrong with being a groupie, and I found myself temporarily unable to justify myself. As I floundered for an explanation, belittling TV stars and movie stars alike, I couldn't help making it personal. In doing so, I cut off my own retreat. A father has to live up to his children's expectations, so I have no choice but to abandon my own dreams of stardom.

LOVE IN OLD AGE

I believe in love. I have read many profound and splendid essays on love handed down through history and the majority of them are about the touching emotions of love, its craziness, its conception and its destruction. My subject today has nothing to do with any of those but is concerned with love's ordinariness and its old age; you might say it is about a kind of grey-haired love which has no aesthetic beauty, no element of suspense or conflict and which, either deliberately or otherwise, has been overlooked by those scholars and literary types who revel in chaos and disruption. Nevertheless, I assert that it is to be found wherever you look and it touches on what people call eternity. I suggest you look around you amongst your neighbours and work colleagues, and I further suggest that you exclude all those young lovers joined at the hip, and ask you to look instead amongst the withered old couples. Maybe you will find the couple I am talking about there.

Dear readers, you will have worked out that I have a particular example in mind, and indeed I do. They were my neighbours and have now been dead for many years.

They were no longer young when I first remember them. Their two daughters had already left home to get married. I recall that the wife was a tall lady and you could see that she had been beautiful when she was young. The husband was rather shorter but his features were also very regular and handsome. On many a fine day, they would appear on the street, the wife carrying a basket of clothes to wash at the well, and the husband following behind with a bucket; or the wife beating their quilt with her hands in the sunshine, with the husband then coming out of the house to give her a rattan beater. Once I saw one of their daughters arrive with her husband and son for a visit, and the little boy knocked on the door, shouting, "Grandpa! Grandma! Hurry up and open the door!" Then, from inside came the clatter of footsteps, the door opened, and I saw the faces of the old couple, wreathed in smiles, one to the left of the door and one to the right. I was surprised to discover that, when they smiled, both of their mouths slanted to the right. But identical smiles are not enough to illustrate love in old age. The whole truth of it was revealed on the day the old woman died.

A person can never escape the ultimate calamity of death but, even so, the old woman's death was very sudden. It was a heart attack. When the neighbours were mourning the death of the old woman, they also expressed their concern for her husband, saying, "What is the old man going to do now she is gone? Will he be able manage by himself?" He just sat by his wife's body and everyone who came to offer their condolences noticed his expression: there were none of the expected signs of grief and he just sat there, calmly watching over his wife, the last wife he would ever have. In the early hours of the next day, when the last of the mourners had finally left, the neighbours heard the sound of the two daughters begin to wail again. Everyone thought the girls had been overcome by grief again at the death of their mother but, come morning, they saw the old couple's daughters setting up another bier for their father, who had also passed away!

This is not some story I have made up, it is true and I really did know an old man who followed his wife up to heaven, hot on her heels. The daughters said that when their father died, he was sitting there, watching their mother, then he just quietly closed his eyes. They thought he had fallen asleep. Who could have expected that the old man's death could have come so gently and so voluntarily?

Everyone was astonished at how devoted a husband he was. But did he die with no obvious cause? No, the way I see it, it was love that took away what remained of his life, because sometimes love itself is a terminal illness. From that time on, I have had a superstitious belief in what I call the tree rings of love, and if there is such a thing as eternal love, it is the love found in extreme old age.

THE FATE OF THE BOULEVARD

If some outsider were to be planning a trip to Nanjing, and I was the tour guide, I would arrange the following itinerary for them: we would enter the city from the Shanghai-Nanjing Expressway, so we would pass through the eastern suburbs and the Zhongshan Gate, then on by the Historical Archives, the Wuchao Gate, the Yixian Bridge and the Daxing Palace until we reached the Jinling Hotel (taking a room on the lower floors as it wouldn't be wise to let them view the city of Nanjing from too great a height: in the city centre there are still too many roadside food stalls and flat-bed trikes selling cantaloupe melons, and it's not a very pretty sight). After a short rest, I would take them to the two mausoleums of Sun Yat-sen and Zhu Yuanzhang, the first Ming emperor, and then, tired with sightseeing, we would go and eat: salted duck, wormwood celery with dried stinky beancurd, chrysanthemum and egg soup, and so on. As the night drew in, I would take them in the fading light to the bus station at the Zhongyang Gate to wait for their bus home. Any tourist lucky enough to follow this itinerary will go away with an unforgettably good impression of Nanjing.

This same tourist will have had the good fortune to pass along the two finest remaining boulevards of Nanjing, Zhongshan East Road and Zhongshan North Road. These two boulevards were originally tree-lined on all four sides, and although they have each sacrificed one row of trees, like a human body losing one of its arms, their foundations are firm and the remaining plane trees are strong and resolute, so they still provide Nanjing with two large stretches of shade.

So, these are the two boulevards we are most proud of. I have been a resident of Nanjing for sixteen years now, and every time I am out of town I always meet people who tell me their impressions of Nanjing, "The most beautiful thing about your Nanjing...." At this point, I can never resist finishing the sentence for them: "….are those plane trees!" When you talk about Nanjing there is no limit to what you can say about the gaiety and splendour of Qinhuai, the ancient capital of the Six Dynasties period, as a literary and cultural model, but there is a simplicity and directness about the boulevards of Nanjing.

Outsiders say, "Those trees of yours on Nanjing's boulevards…" and I interrupt: "Hah! So many of them are gone now…." and just those words cut straight to the heart of the matter. They are all men of the world and there is no need to say any more; everyone knows that those plane trees sacrificed their lives for the sake of the city's traffic, and so died in a worthy cause.

People aren't stupid and no one expects that all the ins and outs of the relative merits of ideal traffic and ideal shade can be fully covered in one lightweight article but I do want to be open about my love of Nanjing's famous boulevards. It is winter now, and those plane trees in the cold wind only serve to enhance the oil painting effect of the views of the city but in the height of summer, the beauty of the boulevards is much more practical. I remember the boulevards of a dozen or so years ago; I was making my way from the Nanjing University of the Arts on the main road in the west of the city to a friend's place near Yudao Street. I had ridden all the way to Beijing West Road inside the Caochang Gate with my head completely shaded from the sun. Just think about it: I had ridden for half an hour in the shade. What kind of high-status treatment is that? I think that of all the tens of millions of cyclists in China, the cyclists of Nanjing receive pretty much the level of privileged treatment accorded to a head of department. I thought of those classmates of mine who had stayed in Beijing and wondered what they might be doing. If they were also cycling, good for them. But what about staying in Beijing and what about Chang'an Avenue? They are all right, I suppose, if you like baking in the sun!

But perhaps I've let myself get a little carried away, so let's get back to the question of the boulevards and the benefits they bestow on us. It is the year 2000 now; things in Nanjing have changed and the city has become more rational without so many surprises and irregularities. But I still have some regrets and I find myself with ambivalent, not to say, contradictory attitudes to the city's development and its boulevards. I still remember one summer day some years ago when I was cycling through the Drum Tower district and I suddenly hit some fierce sunshine. I was temporarily lost for what to do. I got off my bicycle and looked all around me. It was only then that I remembered that in the spring, a whole load of plane trees in the Drum Tower district had sacrificed their lives for the sake of an underpass. I have been prejudiced against that underpass ever since.

Prejudice is prejudice however you look at it. I have no intention of being so unreasonable as to say I want the plane trees not the underpass. In the end, I can only return to the customary view of the residents of Nanjing: what does it really matter if there are a few less plane trees? In any case, Nanjing still has a lot more trees than other cities and although the status of Nanjing's cyclists may have been reduced a little, they are still at least at section-chief level, so my previous certainty also now sounds a little alarmist. Can I really say that the fate of the trees is the fate of civilisation itself?

So who do the trees share their fate with? I am undecided. But what I can say is that the fate of the trees is most certainly their own.

INDEPENDENT TRAVEL

Baiyangdian was my first ever travel destination, and in those days the expression 'independent travel' hadn't even been invented; there were no travel agencies to help you arrange your itinerary – I wouldn't, in any case, have gone looking for them as, at that time, I was a poor university student financially reliant on my parents and I was as likely to go to the moon as I was to go anywhere expensive.

I had a classmate who had a knack for taking one unawares in putting words into action. He came running up to me one day and said, "Baiyangdian is drying up and it's going to disappear. Shall we go and see what it's like?"

Luckily, I was just as impulsive and straightforward as him, and I replied, "Let's go!"

So this first trip was arranged impulsively and in a rush. We needed two bicycles for transport but back then, at the beginning of the 1980s, bicycles were prized possessions and who was going to lend us theirs to go off on some far-flung expedition? Luckily, we found a generous and optimistic classmate who, first of all, lent us his own bicycle and then took us to a relative's house to get another, an even more beaten-up one – but that didn't matter, we had our two bicycles and we set off.

I remember it was a beautiful, bright, windy day when we rode out of Beijing heading for the interior of Hebei Province. We had been riding for a long time but we were still in the urban county of Beijing. Frustrated, we stopped for a rest. As we were sitting at the side of the road drinking some water, I finally had a revelation and understood why people went wherever they were going by train or car. But there was no magic medicine for such regrets, so we girded our loins and got back on the road. As my legs turned to jelly and the shining ribbon of the road seemed to have no end, I turned to look at my classmate and said to myself, "Why did I listen to you, you bastard! What does it matter to me whether there's any water left in Baiyangdian? I've only got myself to blame!" Of course, I couldn't actually voice these thoughts, and all I said was, "I can see you're out of breath. Shall we stop and have another rest?"

Hurrying along the highway in this manner, it was already night by the time we made it to Ba County in Hebei. Our original plan to save money by not paying for overnight accommodation became entirely theoretical and when we saw a small hotel, we looked at each other and made a beeline for it. It wasn't long before we were sprawled across a large, filthy communal bed. The only impression it left us with was the stench of smelly feet that filled our nostrils.

The next morning, our physical and mental strength restored by a night's sleep, although our backs hurt and our legs ached, the two of us were determined to see the thing through and headed for our destination like two racing cyclists. Hardly aware of how we did it, we reached Anxin and, barely aware of what we were looking at, we saw an expanse of water. My classmate gave a great shout of joy and I merrily followed him and his bicycle to the water's edge. It was then that I saw there was a problem: Baiyangdian calls itself a *dian* (an expanse of shallow water), but in fact it is really a lake. The words are different but they are both large areas covered by water and, as I come from Jiangsu, I'd seen lots of this kind of lake already. Had it really been worth it, cycling for two days just to see this stretch of water?

Thus, my first experience of independent travel ended in a sense of disappointment at our destination, and that disappointment was really for my classmate: he was from the northwest; he had never seen a *dian* and, of course, he still hadn't.

A DAY IN THE DESERT

A visit to the most beautiful part of Xinjiang starts in what is least interesting. We must leave the newly flourishing oil town of Korla City and cross the famous Taklamakan Desert into southern Xinjiang.

There is a road through the desert. It is not a camel caravan track but a top-quality modern desert highway. I feel that cars penetrating into the heart of the desert are just like ships on the boundless ocean, except for the red tamarisks and black saxaul trees that remind us there is life everywhere on this earth. Where fish represent the oceans, red tamarisk and black saxaul represent the desert.

Of course, the most beautiful thing about the desert is the sand. The sand dunes, shimmering in waves under the sun, take on a golden sheen that makes me think of the desolate but gilded lens that Bertolucci's film *The Sheltering Sky* turns on the desert. But, of course, the camera lens can never be as meticulous in relaying reality as the human eye. I was delighted that we ended up choosing such a taxing but rewarding route. We were able to feel the edges and textures of the desert.

Someone in the tour van got out a map, but none of us, not even the driver, knew exactly where we were in the desert. It was just too big. Then someone in the front row suddenly called out, "Look at that sand!" We all bent forward to look, and up ahead we saw drifts of sand blowing across the road like little streams, spreading across from one side of the road to the other. The grains of sand were like tiny living things, holding hands and ever so carefully crossing the road.

"Sleep inside the car, piss outside it" is what the locals say about the tour vehicles in Xinjiang. At one point we stopped in front of a stand of desert poplars and there was a touch of rarely seen rain in the desert air. We all ran up to the top of a sand dune where one of our number spotted seven rocks. They were formed of beautifully veined and multi-coloured stone, and my fellow travellers eagerly suggested that we collect them up. As we unthinkingly went to pick them up, once we had them in our hands, a problem suddenly occurred to us: the appearance of these rocks in the middle of the desert was something quite out of the ordinary – we all reckoned that they must be some kind of symbol or marker, so perhaps there was something exceptional about the dune too. Who had put those rocks there? There were all sorts of wild guesses, but in the end it was decided that, however you looked at it, the safest course of action was to leave those mysterious stones where they were in the middle of the desert.

You can't cross the Taklamakan in a single day and, as evening drew in, deep in the desert we saw one of the control posts of the Central Taklamakan Desert Oil Field, shimmering away like a mirage. We spent the night there and in the early hours I dimly heard a vague and mysterious sound. I got out of bed and went over to the window. When I looked out, I saw the moon high in the desert sky and the sand dunes laid out in the night, looking just like the most vivid and precise of papercuts.

"Did you actually hear something?" you ask.

Yes, I did. I heard the wind blowing across the shifting sands.

HOW TO WELCOME THE NEW CENTURY

Time always slips by quicker than people expect. A few years ago, I encountered the phrase 'trans-centennial' in the media and in my children's essays, and thought to myself that this was referring to something in the distant future. So it is greatly to my surprise that this idea of crossing the century has become a reality. The millennium! Those fortunate people who are alive at the time have a shared celebration in which they can cross the century, just like that. It sounds like a really difficult thing to do but in reality it is as easy as anything.

Half of my life has been lived in the twentieth century and it has been a period in which I have made many mistakes which I have no chance to rectify. I am sure there have been many things which have caused people pain but I cannot recall them and all I can do is say to myself, "We'll cross those bridges when we come to them". What am I relying on to say that? I am relying on time, that most amiable, cunning and intelligent of playthings. You think you are the one toying with it but in the dead of night, when all is quiet, you hear the sound of the wind outside your window and you see the moonlight beside your bed, and you suddenly realise that you are beset and surrounded by time, and that it is time that has been toying with you all along.

So here I am in the twenty-first century and the future I imagined as a child has become reality; it is a future that has unaccountably lost its poetry but is there anything to grumble about there? No, there is not. In the end, as we live our lives, year in year out, what we should really be welcoming is each day the sun rises and the moon sets. That is the eternal arrangement Mother Nature has made for her sons and daughters and it is indeed the only constant.

There is a novel by the Italian author Italo Calvino called *The Baron in the Trees*. The hero is discontented with the reality of his life and escapes from it by climbing up into the trees to live. Over the last few days, as I read about people in the newspapers and see them on the television, looking forward to the millennium, I somehow always find my thoughts turning to that man in Calvino's novel, and I want to be like him, surveying the scene from up in the treetops. As he lives up there, can he discern every detail of time as it slips past? Perhaps he is aided by the wind and the rain, the thunder and the lightning, and even by the coming and going of the green leaves on the trees, but can he really discern the deep-seated enmity and inexhaustible menace that time holds over us? Time says, "Because of my existence, you are pre-ordained to be just another kind of plant and, in the end, your destiny is also just to wither or decay."

It would seem that I can't ascend to the treetops. Many brave and intelligent men have taken solemn vows that they will create boundless glory in their limited lifetimes, so that their names will live on in the pages of history. But this great achievement really exists only on paper (or perhaps on a multimedia CD ROM), and when it comes down to it, I have not yet anywhere found a comprehensive plan for how to defeat the march of time.

WHY ARE YOU DISAPPOINTED IN ME?

At a book fair once, I met a most extraordinary reader. He was standing, empty-handed, in the queue of people waiting for my autograph. When he got to the front, he fixed me with a piercing look, of a kind which made me feel strangely uncomfortable, and I heard him say, "You shouldn't come out signing things willy-nilly. I am one of your readers but now I've seen you, I am very disappointed."

I have always remembered that scarily forthright middle-aged man. He shocked me and stopped me from being able to look at myself in the mirror. What exactly was the nature of his 'disappointment'? That is something I have given a great deal of thought to.

I can't confront my reader's disappointment. I love my readers and it was because of that, that at the book fair that day, I became even more of a disappointment; I even felt disappointed in myself. In fact, I didn't know if that reader's disappointment in me stemmed from my tired expression or from my fixed smile. Or was it that he felt deceived because my looks and manner didn't live up to the expectations he had formed from my work? He didn't say! I felt as though I had been guilty of some kind of negligence, and the experience made me steer clear of book signings and sales promotions for fear of falling short of expectations.

When you lock the stable door after the horse has bolted it is hard not to overlook something important. The kind of people who dislike me are not easy to avoid completely. Not long ago, some other authors and I went to Taiwan and on the first day we were there, we went with some other friends who knew the area to have a nice quiet time in a teahouse. Before we had exchanged even a few words of conversation, one of the local girls told me openly that she was disappointed in such-and-such an author. She said she hadn't expected him to be so taciturn, just like an old man. I don't know why but I had that same feeling of negligence and I was sure that her disappointment extended to me. I wondered what exactly was going on and why it was that it was so easy for an author to appear disappointing in other people's eyes. Events proved that I was not being over-sensitive in making these connections that day as, when we were about to leave Taiwan, a reporter friend who I had been getting along with very well over the last few days said to me, in the same direct way, "I should tell you that we are very disappointed in you."

This time I suddenly lost my temper. I didn't have that wimpish feeling of having to apologise to everyone and I realised I had nothing to feel guilty about in front of these disappointed people; nor did I have to accept responsibility for their disappointment. I saw that their disappointment stemmed from their expectations but why should they have these expectations of some stranger they have never even met? Suppose I was a pear tree but other people took me for a peach tree? Was that my responsibility? If those other people liked peach trees, all I could do, as a pear tree, was say diplomatically to them in their disappointment, "I'm very sorry but you've got it wrong. I'm not a peach tree, I'm a pear tree."

I don't know if this experience is in any way connected to interpersonal relationships but I do believe that there is nothing dangerous or scary about close personal relations. Nobody should feel responsible for somebody else's expectations; if you can please everybody then you are a lucky man, and if everyone dislikes you, then you are very unlucky, but there is absolutely no need for you to breathe, eat, speak or joke around according to the expectations of others. A person can only live in their own words and expressions, even if they are full of faults and defects. My natural disposition will always make me grin awkwardly under the gaze of those who are disappointed in me but I would urge my younger, braver friends, "If anyone tells you they are disappointed in you, then you can simply reply like this: I am very disappointed in your disappointment."

PART 4

Reading and Writing

translated by Haiwang Yuan

阅读写作

- Reading
- Reading Vladimir Nabokov
- John Denver
- Bel Canto, *Xintianyou*, and Shackles
- Whither the Night of Horror?
- Let the Woodcutter Awaken
- A Little Anger; a Little Fear
- Stream of Consciousness
- Mirrors and Biographies
- Groping for a Lamp's Pull Chain
- Why Can't I Write Essays?
- Passion for Fiction
- The Path of Essays
- Some Elements of Short Stories
- A Few Words about Short Stories
- Answers to My Questions
- Seven Prefaces
- Why Did I Write *Wives and Concubines*?
- Why Did I Write *Pusaman*?
- Send Him to the Trees
- A Peak in the Day-to-Day Account
- How to Play a Joke on the World?

Because people's minds in this era are generally in a state of drifting, prose as a record of genuine feelings and thoughts is also lithe, piecemeal and messy. And because this era emphasises individuality, writers are scrambling to pick their costumes, props and dubbing equipment in the creation of their prose. Looking around, those who choose to banish themselves can no longer find the pasture where Su Wu, an unyielding Han-dynasty diplomat kept in captivity in the enemy's territory, could herd his sheep or the isle where Robinson Crusoe could live all by himself.

READING

A long time ago, I read almost indiscriminately. I would pick either a masterpiece or a book that fascinated me with its beautiful and vivid title, and put it by my bedside for night reading. In this way, I have read a lot of fine works and works of third or fourth class, or even poor quality. There were also special circumstances where I found it hard to concentrate on reading some classics. Take Melville's *Moby Dick*, for example. It is highly praised by almost all European and American writers who consider it to be a must-read by practitioner writers. However, I tried reading it for two months before I gave up halfway because I felt it too boring. I returned it to the library with frustration. That was years ago. I have never read *Moby Dick* again since. If I start re-reading it now, I wonder if I will still like it. But anyway, I dare not deny the great value of *Moby Dick* and Melville.

Reading for pleasure occurs several times a year.

The one incident of reading for pleasure that impressed me the most was when I read J. D. Salinger's *The Catcher in the Rye*. At that time, I was studying at Beijing Normal University, and a friend of mine recommended and lent the book to me. It only took me a day to finish it. I remember that by the time I finished reading the last page, the classroom was empty. The janitor turned off the lights one by one in the corridor as he walked by. When I stepped out of the classroom, my heart was also filled with sad darkness. I envisioned the American boy's travelling experience in the city. I imagined that I also had a little sister like 'Old Phoebe' so that I could either make jokes with her or confide my vexations to her.

During that time, Salinger was the writer that most fascinated me. I read all his works that I could find. I cannot explain my adoration for him. Perhaps it was the youth-enlightening nature of his works and the author's free and happy intuition for the language that had a powerful appeal to me. Therefore, I regarded *The Catcher in the Rye* as a literary masterpiece model contrary to the academic model. Its impact on me was different from that of *Quietly Flows the Don* that I read at the same time. The former directly penetrated my heart and soul, whereas the latter edified my mind as a classic.

Until now, I haven't been able to shake off Salinger's shadow completely. You can see traces of his style and language as gentle as water in some of my short stories. Today's literary world has entered an era when people are scrambling to destroy idols. People think that Salinger is a superficial, second-class writer who misleads others. This makes me sad. I hope that people won't slight him in my presence. I cherish the first gleam that Salinger gave me. This is human nature. No one should tear up a worn-out banknote. At least I won't.

Now let's talk about Jorge Luis Borges. About 1984, I found Borges' *Short Story Collection* in a box of new book catalogue cards in the Beijing Normal University Library. I borrowed the book and fell deeply into Borges' maze or trap—the thinking of a special three-dimensional geometric novel, simple and elegant narrative language and a black hole-like profound artistic charm. Frankly, I couldn't understand Borges but I could feel him, which puzzled me. I cannot forget how much of an impact Borges had on me. A few years later, I received a piece of prose in my editorial office. Entitled *The Light of Borges*, it was from a Sichuan poet named Kaiyu who I didn't know. In the prose, he told a story about a Borges fan who purchased books by Borges and mailed them to his friends. It also described the sadness into which Borges' death plunged them. I liked the prose very much, perhaps because it gave expression to my deep feeling for Borges. Although I couldn't publish the piece, I believed as Kaiyu did that Borges had brought us light. He illuminated a dark and unexplored literary space and inspired a group of young writers with a kindred spirit to display their skills.

Reading is beautiful. Reading often kindles your excitement and pleases you. The feeling of immersion in a work is refreshing. It often happens like this: you can remember some extremely trivial details of a book you like, such as tongue-twisting names of people and places, an insignificant scene, a few dialogues between the characters, even the names of the flowers and plants described in the book, the colour of a girl's skirt, and the furnishings and the odour in a room.

I read Truman Capote's *Breakfast at Tiffany's* two years ago. I still remember Miss Holly Golightly ringing her neighbour's doorbells randomly when she lost the key to her flat and recall her country accent and a square rattan basket.

One hot summer, I was reading *Herzog* in a mosquito net. I still remember Herzog peeping out through the window at his wife's lover, a lame man, bathing Herzog's little daughter in the bathroom. His gentle movements and loving eyes made Herzog heartbroken. From *Humboldt's Gift*, another book by Saul Bellow, I learned about rectangular mattresses and a lot of American vulgarisms.

I have read Carson McCullers' *Ballad of the Sad Café* twice. I first read it when I was in high school. I bought the first valuable literary book in my life with my pocket money, the *Collection of Contemporary American Short Stories* published by Shanghai Translation Publishing House. It introduced me to American literature and enabled me to read *Ballad of the Sad Café*. At that time, I thought that the characters in the short story were so strange that I could not understand their significance. When I re-read it later, I could not but say that one only needs to read *Ballad of the Sad Café* to understand the meaning of characters and atmosphere, the ins and outs of a story, and the intention of an author.

Reading is beautiful.

READING VLADIMIR NABOKOV

There is a long list of American writers I love and admire. Needless to say, Ernest Hemingway and William Faulkner are on top of the list. I have read a few translations of the others like John Barth, Philip Roth, Robert Coover, Norman Mailer, Truman Capote and John Updike, and they have still left me indelible memories. Now, I have also included Vladimir Nabokov in the list.

Laughter in the Dark was the first of Nabokov's novellas that I read. It seems that he wrote it while he was still in the Soviet Union and that it did not leave an overwhelming impression. There is not much difference between it and other ordinary Russian works. He probably also inherited the tradition of Anton Chekhov and Ivan Bunin. Other than a love story of a girl who works as an usher in a cinema, I cannot think of any more details. It's probably because I don't much like it. I have never liked novels of the Old-Russian style.

Later, I read selected translations of Nabokov's *Pale Fire*. I find Nabokov's obscurity and depth to surpass those of postmodern writers such as John Barth and Donald Barthelme. The only impression of the novel I have is that there is a professor named Kinbote who behaves strangely, speaks inexplicably and thinks in a banal and boorish manner. It seems that this is the only image of the character I can capture, as I can't see the complete picture from selected translations. Nevertheless, *Pale Fire* shows to me the significance of Nabokov as a brilliant writer. Awe-inspiring is not only the bizarre structure and narrative style but also the keen intellect and unrestrained abilities he exhibits in his work.

I read *Lolita* this year. I don't know how the quality of this translation compares with others. Anyway, I finished reading the book in one breath because I was already fascinated by the first few sentences. I like this beautiful and concise language: "Lolita, life of my life, fire of my loins. My sin, my soul. Lo-lee-ta: the tip of the tongue taking a trip of three steps down the palate to tap, at three, on the teeth, Lo. Lee. Ta." The image of Lolita is no stranger to me and somehow I would associate her with the cute little prostitute in Capote's *Breakfast at Tiffany's*. They are both lively and lovely girls, full of youthful vigour. Such girls often live in a sinful atmosphere in writers' works. The more lovely and seductive she is, the more tragic her fate becomes. It's true with both Capote's little prostitute and Lolita, except that the latter is younger, only twelve years old. She is under the sway of her stepfather Humbert's desire, so her fate is more sorrowful and moving, and her literary flavour is more intense.

What's important is Humbert, Lolita's stepfather and her lover. It's the image of this character that has made *Lolita* world-famous.

I think Nabokov wrote the book because he became interested in Humbert. The basis for writing *Lolita* is the intrapsychic basis of Humbert's life. Then what is Humbert? Is he a young middle-class gentleman? An incestuous father who dominates a young girl? Or a jealous murderer who kills for romance? I see him as none of those. Humbert is a desire, a dream, a life, an experience of suffering and an embodiment of happiness. A symbol of concepts and rules is the only thing he is not.

It is meaningless to analyse the romantic 'father-daughter' relationship between Humbert and Lolita from the perspective of psychology. Besides, this is a novel, not a medical case. In my opinion, Nabokov's novella is a pathetic and touching life of hardships rather than a typical story of incest, which is but a framework to tempt readers. No other sin is more passionate and moving than Humbert's; no other soul is more desperate and pessimistic than Humbert's, and no other life is more stressful and crazier than Humbert's. Humbert escapes with Lolita from reality, morality and everything else. He lives the life of a vagabond concerning the only thing he needs, namely, the twelve-year-old illicit lover Lolita. With her, he wanders in the realm of the spirit, which is the gist and the most charming quality of the novel.

Humbert says, "I am not, and never was, and never could have been, a brutal scoundrel. The gentle and dreamy regions through which I crept were the patrimonies of poets—not crime's prowling ground". Humbert is not the social rebel portrayed in many novels, nor the rebellious image of a powerful man. This has to do with the tint of privacy and sinfulness in his behaviour. Therefore, I would say that Humbert is just an image of an individualist who advocates the spirit for spirit's sake. This image is independent and personalised. If it is well written, it will never be repeated in other works. Therefore, Humbert is the unique character of the many contemporary American writers I have read. When he pops his head out of the motel window, we should wave to him and say: Hello Humbert!

As a literary disciple learning how to write, I'm in awe of Nabokov's superb language ability. With his accurate and minute descriptions of the details, and his complex and passionate flow of emotions, his entire work, imbued with broiling fascination, never gives the impression of interruption and dissociation. I assume that a book so packed and coherent throughout reveals its author's literary attainment. I always exclaim with admiration when I read a detailed description like this:

> And less than six inches from me and my burning life was nebulous Lolita...! And then she sat up, gasped, muttered with insane rapidity something about boats, tugged at the sheets and lapsed back into her rich, dark, young unconsciousness.... She freed herself from the shadow of my embrace—doing this not consciously, not violently, not with any personal distaste, but with the neutral plaintive murmur of a child demanding its

natural rest. And again the situation remained the same: Lolita with her curved spine to Humbert, Humbert resting his head on his hand and burning with desire and dyspepsia.

In actuality, it is with this detailed description that Lolita attracts me. While incest and seduction are obscene and filthy, an excellent novel about incest and seduction can be so noble and fascinating. This is exactly where Nabokov's glory lies as an excellent writer. When he rebuilds the world and it melts into his fantasy. How beautiful it is!

Nabokov says, "My characters are boat-rowing slaves". The twelve-year-old girl Lolita gives rise to Humbert. And Lolita and Humbert give rise to the masterpiece *Lolita*.

If we have Nabokov without his Lolita and Humbert, what can we get from him then?

JOHN DENVER

There was a country music singer named John Denver who had a song called *Country Roads, Take Me Home*. Few master country musicians hold this person and this song in high esteem. But for a long time, when it comes to country music, what I have in mind has been this person and this song.

My obsession has to do with my puberty or memory only. During my college years, John Denver was quite a hit on college campuses. Young people who could speak a little English and loved to sing happened to learn to sing this song at the same time. At almost all the evening parties, there would be a young man singing it on a podium to the accompaniment of a guitar that he was playing with a sure or nervous hand. And as an extremely loyal listener, I stood in the crowd listening with my mouth open, my ears pricked up and my body trembling. In the song, I envisioned a mountain and a river in the United States and then a horseback wanderer chanting in high spirits in that country. When the line "country roads, take me home" suddenly arose in its high pitch, my youthful body shivered as if malaria had hit me. The notes of the song tugged my every heartstring.

When you are twenty, a non-existent country road can take you not only home but also to heaven.

I don't know whether what I felt then was rational. Neither do I know why a song having nothing to do with me could make me tremble all over. Maybe it was all because I was young. Maybe adolescence is an age apt to tremble, anyway. Of course, the time machine is constantly obliterating the traces of our youth. The song you liked when you were young became a swan song unknowingly in your toiling, weight-gaining life in middle age, and you think little of it any more. Once, I happened to lay my hand on a cassette tape of John Denver's song. The so-called nostalgic urge forced me to load it into a cassette player. However, all I heard was but a harsh and distorted vocal voice. Revisiting an old dream by listening to a falsetto likened to a dubbed voice of a cartoon character plunged me into a sense of loss. It tears at my heartstrings to realise suddenly that many things have expired: music, memory and even proof of my adolescence. Not only have they expired but they have also fallen apart.

Of course, people entering their middle-age have waved goodbye to their adolescence. They'll never say that a certain song or a certain singer deceived them, though on their faces is written a mature expression of watchfulness for deceit. They still listen with tolerance, however. If John Denver could still sing "country roads, take me home", they may hum along but they already know that it's not the country roads that can take them home now. It's a train, a car or a plane.

I'm not prone to sentimentality. But I'm timid. Sometimes, I flounder in an indescribable fear, just as I felt this time. For example, when facing the tape recording ruined by the passing of time, I was afraid that I didn't know whose singing would make me tremble again in the future. What shall I do if I lose the ability to tremble? Allow me to make a tasteless joke: it's not enough for a human to tremble in bed only!

BEL CANTO, *XINTIANYOU* AND SHACKLES

To have someone sing bel canto with an indefinitely high, brisk and beautiful voice requires that the voice be pristine and untrained or the voice of an eight-year-old boy castrated to perpetuate his puberty. That was exactly what the Italians did centuries ago. They had a fervent urge to pursue the true beauty of art. Therefore, choir boys could sing opposite singers like Farinelli in halls of human music, thus creating the miracle of continuing the so-called 'sounds of nature' in adult singers.

I once watched a film about Farinelli. The most unforgettable part of the film was that Farinelli's elder brother castrated him with his own hands and lived on his money to rise high in the world. Despite that, Farinelli loved his elder brother as always. Apart from the plot, what perplexed me was also Farinelli's singing throughout the film. It seems impossible that this was his original voice. Whose voice was lent to him? The real singer must have as good a voice as Farinelli's. But I'm certain that the voice was feminine and from a contemporary world-famous female singer.

Thinking about it, I find it confusing. Since the female voice can cater to the need for 'natural sound', why did the Italians bother to castrate their boys then?

Human art has become what it is today because it has gone through misunderstandings, and twists and turns, through which humans have created such brilliant art as represented by Farinelli and the architectural structures of the Baroque, Rococo and Gothic styles. Nowadays, people celebrate natural things and oppose polished ones. But they still feel awed by Farinelli and the Cologne Cathedral. They must admit that while running counter to nature, some works of art are still great. The universally applicable artistic concept of celebrating nature has turned out to be a specious slogan. Those who are keen on summarising the laws of art are now faced with a dilemma.

People who have been nurtured by modern civilization are committed to the development of human artistic heritage, but at the same time, they are tirelessly correcting and removing parts of the art that violate human nature, including singing by castrated singers. Take bel canto, for example. The representative figures of this century are Stefano Langone, Luciano Pavarotti, Elisabeth Schwarzkopf and Maria Callas. They are normal men and women with good looks. We are in a time when there's no need to gain a particular singing voice by creating a new generation of singers like

Farinelli. That's because we are confident that the tenor of Pavarotti is the highest of human voices. People aren't fervently and excessively demanding for singing voices any more.

But we admit that we have confined some artworks to the grave forever, just as the Italians can no longer hear Farinelli sing at county fairs or the prudent and hardworking Germans can no longer duplicate the Cologne Cathedral no matter how hard they try. This is a choice made voluntarily by nature-celebrating people of modern times. Perhaps no one has ever thought that seeking the true meaning of art sometimes may destroy it and we're unaware of the consequences. But only when we look back occasionally will we see tomb after tomb of artworks popping up behind us.

Recently, I read in a magazine about a writer dwelling on literature and dance, to the effect that he opposed dancing with shackles in literary or artistic creation. He argues that modern dance is healthy and graceful while ballet is morbid. This is not a fallacy because it is completely correct in the elaboration of a certain realm of artistic creation. But I realise that the assumption points to a dubious direction when it comes to the essence of literature and art. It somehow reminds me of *Xintianyou*, a folk music style from Shaanxi, and a folksong singer from the province. When the singer sang a *Xintianyou* song at a contest, the judges proclaimed that his treble was higher than Pavarotti's. We don't have to differentiate bel canto from *Xintianyou* as if they are oranges and apples. *Xintianyou* singing is usually regarded as a form of folk art that is unadulterated and therefore natural. However, when we listen carefully to the treble of *Xintianyou* and that of bel canto simultaneously or separately, we may be surprised to find the two to be both technical and unnatural. To decide that the former is natural and the latter unaffected is equally hypocritical. What is even more surprising is that, where this troubling treble is concerned, this *Xintianyou* singer's spurt for success heightens the melancholy nature inherent in *Xintianyou*, whereas Pavarotti's obvious bel canto skills bring the gorgeous atmosphere of operas to a climax.

People tend to ignore that art is not born in pursuit of nature. Therefore, the shackles in the art are part and parcel of art. Take the vocal method of bel canto as an example. Its control and application of the chest, throat and nasal cavity is close to science rather than the so-called natural state where people sing as they like. And all the famous tenors and sopranos often sweat profusely at concerts. The attentive audience can find their larynx as busy as an exhausted rabbit being chased by a beast of prey and their chest as tense as if buried with a bomb to be ignited by a burning fuse. The amazing thing is that the unpleasant vision disappears when you close your eyes. And you hear wonderful, high-pitched and incredible singing. You even hear the shackles in the music sounding melodious. At that moment, we may wonder what bel canto is. It is nothing but decorating every note, making them more resonant and beautiful than the natural sound of humans.

This is not the case with *Xintianyou*, which is known to be the product of shepherds in northern Shaanxi wooing girls while leading their flocks of sheep or goats on arid highland. *Xintianyou* doesn't seek to enter music halls. Unlike Western operas, it's a folk art that expresses feelings candidly. It's considered simple, free and unrestrained. People think that original *Xintianyou* songs should be hoarse, melancholy and passionate. They should be tainted with the smell of the soil from the Loess Plateau. But people are unaware that generation after generation of shepherds has been repeating the tunes handed down from their ancestors. Shepherd singers of *Xintianyou* have no idea who will carry on their songs to eternity. Therefore, they try their best to sing it in alternating pitches regardless of whether they're touching or not. Eventually, when people like us from outside the Loess Plateau get to know *Xintianyou* songs and know how to hum them ourselves, *Xintianyou* then has become an art, thereby losing its freedom. On what basis do we distinguish Qinghai *Hua'er* from *Xintianyou*? It's our understanding of what 'authenticity' really means.

It's difficult for people to accept the idea that authenticity constitutes the shackles of art, but it's precisely these shackles that are the prerequisites for art to become art. We allow human thoughts to fly high but we cannot take it for granted to free art from these shackles, which are tempered with the essence of art itself. Therefore, the shackles aren't instruments of torture. We should see that freedom can coexist with shackles. The magic of art is that it can fly freely with them.

WHITHER THE NIGHT OF HORROR?

It happened on a hot summer night about twenty years ago. A boy was sitting under a street lamp outside the gate of a factory. He was reading a novel with its cover already brown and brittle. After a while, he suddenly looked antsy, struggling to remove his eyes from the pages. He looked about and moved his stool to a group of people playing Chinese chess. He sat there and resumed reading. But the chess-playing people were boisterous and the boy yelled angrily, "Don't make so much noise! When you're doing so, how can I concentrate on my reading?"

That boy was me. What helped me remember that night was the book I was reading. It was an unknown detective novel, giving me a kind of unprecedented fear and excitement. That night, I suddenly felt the air was permeated with crime or the smell of blood. I suspected that the shadow under the wire pole in the distance was a vicious perpetrator wearing his gloves. A book threw me into a world of boundless imagination. I didn't dare to go back home because there was no one at home and because ghosts lurked in the otherwise peaceful house that night. Holding the book, I lingered under the street lamp and did not dare to enter the dark doorway until my parents returned. Only after a long time did I realise that the book was *Sherlock in Shanghai*, written by Cheng Xiaoqing.

Now it seems that the people who are frightened by Cheng Xiaoqing's text are probably the timidest readers. What needs to be explained is that it was the first time I had read so-called popular novels. Like many first times in my life, it also had an unexpected effect on my subsequent reading. I enjoy it if a novel can scare me without reason. I have a strange yardstick in my mind by which to measure a readable novel, that is whether it can scare me.

I seldom read romantic fiction. Neither do I read martial arts novels. I have barely laid my hands on the books by Jin Yong and Gu Long—books uniformly praised. But I've had a singular love for horror stories. I've become immune to horror, partly because of my profession of writing and partly because I am old and knowledgeable enough. Some told me how horrifying Steven King's stories were. But I found them hard to read and myself unfazed. I'm uncertain if that was his or my problem. Sometimes, when I recall the stories told by adults when I was a kid, such as *The Plum Gang, A Case of a Bronze Ruler*, and *A Green Corpse*, I have no idea where my fear came from. Everything seems to be related to age and experience. Why does an adult forget the taste of horror? That is something very disappointing.

Like me, many of my friends have also lost the facility to be scared by horrifying text. When we got together, as usual, we tried all we could to have some fun. Eventually, the only fun we could enjoy was fear. Each of us would share the most horrifying story they knew. Under such circumstances, I came to hear a few genuinely scary stories. One of them was set in the era of the 'Cultural Revolution'. Initially sounding true, it was about a man who blocked the way of another man on a secluded path and insisted that the latter give him something. The only thing the other man had had to give him was his blue checked handkerchief. The two thus became friends. What happened next was uncanny: the man who had gifted the handkerchief was said to rendezvous with the man who had received it. The address that the handkerchief-receiving friend had given him led him to a hospital morgue. There, he found the friend lying on a slab, holding the blue checked handkerchief.

It truly scared me this time. I had been trying to write a horror story. Later, after repeated editing and patching up, I came up with one, a short story entitled *Cherry*. I shared it with quite a few of my friends, only to be frustrated: I ended up scaring none of them. One of my friends told me that horror stories had to be told orally. Once written, they have a different flavour.

I had to agree with that friend of mine. It's hard to scare cool-headed and worldly-wise adults with texts or stories now. Feelings of horror can only be experienced in person. Even they don't know where those scary nights have gone.

LET THE WOODCUTTER AWAKEN

This poem by Pablo Neruda is an ode to labourers, almost a must-read for lovers of poetry throughout the world. Passionate poems such as this always appeal to young, romantic hearts and upright, unsophisticated souls, thereby leaving an indelible and deep impression on their minds.

The only forests I've seen were in Xishuangbanna, Yunnan Province, China. Travelling by car from Jinghong to the China-Myanmar border, we passed through endless tropical forest on our way. I remember the lush foliage of the forest appearing nearly dark, probably because those century-old trees completely blotted out the sun. Sunshine worked to no avail in the forest and lost its beautiful effect and shades of light. That is why tropical forests impress me as black and humid.

I have never been to the Greater Khingan Range in northern China. I have only seen images of those frigid-zone forests featured in films or illustrated magazines. The photographed images must have been retouched and re-laid out by photographers. However, I have no idea why I stubbornly believe that the forests in the Greater Khingan Range that I have never seen are supposed to be forests extolled in poetry and eulogised by Pablo Neruda.

The forests of the frigid zone are aesthetically unique in that both the mountain ranges and the forests are undulating and that the colours of the forests change ostentatiously with the four distinct seasons. They are also unique in that the forests appear uprightly unyielding and awe-inspiring because of the innate masculinity of the pines and firs, and that silvery winter turns the snow-covered forests into a beautiful and spotless wonderland. When lumberjacks trudge up to the mountains in the snow, when they start their chainsaws and let them roar, we hear the sound of labour and the rhythm of resonant poetry.

Am I expounding on the relationship between forestry and poetry? The answer seems to be yes or no. I live in an eastern city half a thousand kilometres away from any forest. I can only sniff at the Manchurian ash furniture at home and get a vague odour of the forest. But I still adamantly assert that I love forests and those lumberjacks who are extolled in poetry. If this sounds a bit sentimental, I am not to blame. It's the fault of Pablo Neruda or poetry.

Now I have to say something about ecological balance and forest conservation, buzzwords I borrow from many others. People who have some conscience don't have the slightest doubt about their validity. The floods taking place in the drainage areas of the Yangtze and Nenjiang rivers in recent years are related to the deforestation in the surrounding areas. This is a fact known to all. The latest news about forest conservation is that logging has been stopped in the Greater Khingan Range. What I want to mention is a TV interview between a microphone-wielding news reporter and a lumberjack who had just given up his chainsaw. I noticed the absent expression on the lumberjack's face when he was asked about his plans. He paused a little and responded that he wouldn't fell trees. He said he was going to plant them from this point forward.

At that very moment, I felt that a type of labour sound in my imagination came to a sudden halt and the poetic sound was also hushed. In the real world, Pablo Neruda passed away in remote Chile. I find the world realistic, where everything must be reasonable and scientific. Those who eulogise manual labour are just deluding themselves. I suddenly realise that some kinds of labour in the world are intrinsically erroneous. Take poetry, for example. It isn't the truth, no matter how beautiful it may sound. I must understand clearly that each era has its sound of the forest. The imagination of forests in the future may not be filled with the sound of sawing or cries of 'Timber!' In an era when trees are planted everywhere in the world, Neruda must pass away. If we want to sing of the forests, we must call for poets who extol afforestation.

This is the new poetry of forests. Woodcutters, wake up! Woodcutters have awakened! Then, they go down the mountains with their chainsaws. This is the poetry of forests already turned from unrestrained enthusiasm to reasonable sobriety. Woodcutters, wake up! Let's all cast aside our axes and chainsaws and go home. As for those of us who have fallen in love with forests through Neruda, it's up to us to make it a priority to read these new poems.

A LITTLE ANGER; A LITTLE FEAR

The Yilin Press published two new translations last year, namely *The Public Burning* and *Libra*. The authors are the backbone of postmodernist American writers Robert Coover and Don DeLillo, respectively. None of the two novels are their recent works, the former published in 1977 and the latter in 1988. But I believe that these are the first translations presented to Chinese readers. What's interesting is that both novels belong to the genre of 'political novels', relatively unfamiliar to us. Therefore, they have aroused high reading expectations among us, prompting us to find out what trick these political novels are playing.

The trick is, of course, politics, or rather, discussing issues and writing about them in terms of political events. Let's discuss *The Public Burning* first. The political event chosen is the well-known Julius and Ethel Rosenberg case of the 1950s. Coover first familiarises us with his work through his novellas and short stories such as *The Gingerbread House, A Pedestrian Accident* and *Spanking the Maid*. These works may be clever, secretive and neurotic, but they seem to be lacking a dose of stimulant compared with John Bath, another famous master of postmodernist literature. But *The Public Burning* is exciting. Throughout the story, one can see its spurning of reality, the state apparatus and the political order. An intellectual accustomed to resorting to cynicism and sarcasm, Coover displays his great courage by pulling everyone's pants off in his story (There is a classic description of a spectacular scene of all the people taking off their pants in public). This courage derives from the writer's self-confidence that makes him think that everyone is in a slumber except him. This lovely self-confidence arouses such anger in the writer he sneers at everything. The writer even devalues the dignity of the history of which he is making use through the mouth of 'Uncle Sam', who says, 'My child, history is a pile of cold ashes. If you fumble in it, all you can get is dirt'.

The novel is about the 'New American Dream' with the Rosenberg incident at its core. The writer doesn't care about whether the couple leaked the atomic bomb secrets to the Soviet Union and whether the couple was guilty. What he wants to play up is the befuddling and chaotic atmosphere of the 'New American Dream' era on the execution ground, Times Square (where historical facts are concerned, the author's relocation of the execution ground was reasonable). What he wants to convey is that people go crazy when the state machine runs amuck and that the 'dream' era can go both crazy and astray. Another shocking aspect of the novel is that it uses the then Vice President Nixon as the key narrator and portrays him as a 'clown', who is not only sympathetic and conscientious but also able to think straight. This Vice President 'clown' should have the guts to enter Ethel Rosenberg's cell and have sex with her (I doubt if Nixon ever sued Coover for defamation at that time). In the end, she was willing to endure Uncle Sam's sexual assault, which was the last climax and the most absurd and yet resplendent ending of the 'New American Dream'. Meanwhile, it's also the most heart-throbbing politics!

It seems that *Libra* does not have such an impact on its readers. Although classified as a novel of the political genre and set in the 1960s when Lee Harvey Oswald assassinated John F. Kennedy, the exact details of the novella seem to follow the writing rules to a T. As for the element of politics, it's already assimilated in the nuances of the characters as a literary element. Don DeLillo is known for his realistic literary style. By copying buzzwords of the time, this novella depicts the 'inner journey' of a rebel growing up in the slums of New York City, and the 'inner journey' has to do with life's experiences and vicissitudes. Therefore, readers can see in the book a delicate literary description of Oswald's military service in Japan and his quest for ideals in the Red Soviet Union. The brief life of Oswald looks like that of a dissident but, in essence, his is the life of a person who doesn't fit in with society. Such a person walks to where people are sparse after his birth, away from the crowd until he finds a new life through some type of self-destruction and, in the end, achieves a balance through a certain leaning. This isn't a tragedy related to political beliefs but one of a person's fate. I'm convinced that this isn't only my thoughts after reading but also an idea that DeLillo wants to express.

Coincidentally, I just read in a newspaper that the mistress of Lyndon Johnson, Kennedy's successor, recently broke the news that Johnson was the manipulator behind the assassination of JFK and claimed that the news was conclusive. This coincides with Don DeLillo's 'inference' in his novella. Certainly, the writer has no blood relationship with any of the parties involved in the case. He has no conclusive evidence. He only uses his intuition to fictionalise the real culprits behind Oswald, that is, two grumbling CIA agents. A writer's intuition isn't credible. He's accustomed to complicating and intensifying things, and prone to exaggerate the pros and cons. Though never authoritative, his conclusions depend on his understanding of politics, which is very compartmentalised. You know that there are stains and bullet holes in them but you don't know where the stains came from and where the bullets were shot from until you open all the compartments.

The biggest difference between *Libra* and *The Public Burning* lies in the writers' political stance. Don DeLillo's attitude towards politics differs from that of Robert Coover in that he is more respectful and composed, and there is a modicum of fear in his respect and composure.

STREAM OF CONSCIOUSNESS

ONE

Various signs show that our literature has gradually entered the realm of art. Today we see a lot of writers and works with real artistic spirit emerging. This is a little capital, with which we may as well discuss some internal and external issues of literature. I'm striving for neither pompousness nor excess. As we'll discuss all the prospects and difficulties that literature may face as art-related issues, we can do it in an even-tempered and good-humoured manner. Each speech is a performance, just like the music performed by street musicians: their performances are as mutually connected as they are mutually independent. But their attitudes are all composed and sincere.

TWO

The paleness of the sense of form once caused Chinese literature to appear cloddish and rigid, which is almost a tragedy of ignorance. The emergence of an excellent writer or a good literary work largely depends on the establishment of a sense of form. Now the sense of form has been awakened in the minds of a generation of writers. Ma Yuan and Mo Yan are two prominent examples.

When conceiving and writing a novel, a good writer must have a strong sense of autonomy. They expect to put their unique brand on every part of the novel and organise every detail or dialogue in their tentative way and form. Then, they'll erect the structure of their novel according to their aesthetic attitude, which takes the courage and wisdom of a loner. A writer sits lonely and aloof in the house he has built, whereas readers look at it from outside with curiosity. To my mind, this is an artistic effect, which achieves the aim of entry (appeal) through alienation.

The sense of form has a life just like a plant, which has a meaningful life cycle of growing, blossoming and wilting. Once established by writers, the sense of form becomes a contradictory entity. As an individual entity, it not only has irreplaceable advantages but also presents a potential crisis. And this crisis comes from the reader's rebellious mentality and instinct to reject the old and crave the new. Therefore, it seems difficult for writers to maintain their charm forever. Is there a need for a writer to transcend and sublimate their ego constantly? Do they need to provide some convincing spiritual entity before they become the embodiment of a sense of form? There are many examples in the world.

Jorge Luis Borges—maze-like style—his philosophy of wisdom and virtual reality; Ernest Hemingway—succinct and sprightly—bewilderment at survival, death, human nature and war; André Gide—sensitive and delicate—suppressed dejection and a wandering spiritual orphan; and Milan Kundera—rebellious theme—the embodiment of resistance and evasion in Eastern Europe.

A critic comments that the merit of a good writer lies in their contribution of a certain language to literature. In other words, the merit of a good writer is to provide a sense of form with eternal meaning. It's imperative that you integrate yourself with the sense of form, just like two hydrogen atoms merged with one oxygen atom to become the water used by all of us. This is an arduous task and yet a sacred purpose of art.

Three

A novel must reach a certain pinnacle of perfection which can be simplicity and unconventional grace or oddity and profoundness in the sense of either humanity or philosophy. Such a peak of attainment doesn't have to be superior or inferior but it must support the soul of the novel.

In actual reality, we have read many novels that can't reach a certain pinnacle of perfection. In other words, they have only a false, pragmatic shell. This is because their authors did not engage their souls during their creative process. Their works have nothing to do with their souls. This is another tragedy of creative writing.

A person with special life experience and the gift of being enriching and sensitive can often become a talented writer and reach their exquisite and substantial peak of perfection.

Whenever I read Shi Tiesheng, I always sense the light of his soul, which may be luckily attributed to his conversion to the beliefs of fate and religion. Serene, moderate and relaxed, his works amass artistic strength through his casual narration. I consider him to be simple and honest. When I read Yu Hua's novels, I can also feel his sensitivity and his indulgence in fantasy. He complements tenderness with cruelty and rationality with irrationality. And he does it in a clever and sharp-witted manner. I maintain that he has reached a bizarre and changeful peak of perfection.

A novel is the backlight of a soul. You inject part of your soul into the work so that it has your flesh and blood, and attains the peak of art. This involves two issues: first, a writer must examine the true state of their soul and shape themselves accordingly; second, the strength of sincerity is immense and its significance lies in not only overcorrection but also the abandonment of the malpractice in writing manifested as affected, fawning obsequiously, cajoling the public with claptrap, and acting as the occasion dictates. They are not supposed to scratch at an itch from outside the boot, that is, fail to strike things home, or to take off their pants to fart, namely to be redundant. Neither are they supposed to sell quack remedies as sincerity. I believe that sincerity is the attitude towards survival. This is especially true with writers.

Four

There is a saying in the circle of poetry known as 'Let Bei Dao pass'. It comes from the voice of a new generation of poets who have risen. Such a slogan hasn't been heard of to this day in the world of novelists, probably because a spiritual leader with a far-reaching influence like Bei Dao hasn't emerged among them. I have no idea if this slogan is good but the term 'pass' means 'let him go through' rather than 'overthrowing' him. To my mind, it has a positive and progressive connotation.

Who are we going to 'pass' in the world of novelists? It's a different world, where no one has ever put forward such an ambitious slogan. This is because an artistic norm and order have never been established in our novel writing. (It needs to be explained that there is no corresponding relationship between artistic norms and order, and the contention of a hundred schools of thought). The contingent of novelists has always been in disarray with different schools among them. These differences are reflected in the various aspects of the writers' cultural literacy and artistic attainment, as well as their creative attitude. But the fact is that each claims a sphere of activity. For that matter, I have no idea if such a situation is good, either.

We rarely feel the pressure from our compatriot writers. Who sets up the barriers to block our way? Who casts a shadow over us? The barriers and shadow are attributed to the lack of classical styles or spiritual seekers in this era. They're also the result of being bogged down with a lot of wrong experience. Under the pressure of the shock waves of American contemporary literature, European literature and Latin American literature, this generation of Chinese writers is shrouded in confusion and a mood of implicit obedience. You must rebel, but to do so, what weapons do you need? Neither the quintessence of Chinese culture nor the advocation of foreign cultures at the expense of our own. As for the doctrines of Laozi and Zhuangzi, Zen Buddhism, the 'Cultural Revolution', or 'economic reform', you can write about them and achieve spectacular effects but none of them can be your weapon. Some ask how our fiction can go out to the world. Since no one can show us how to, we'd better quit thinking too much about the question. The responsibility of a writer is to shape themselves first. It's of perpetual significance for them to file a golden key and show it to the world before they can become a true model.

FIVE

Some think that a writer must start writing their fiction from the outside to the inside, drawing parallels from inference, before getting to the innermost literature. Those who embrace this thinking are mostly scholastic writers.

We seem to be accustomed to unitary artistic thinking. That is, we are afraid of being cast out of literature. This subjects a writer's experience to various kinds of limitations and causes the writer's image to appear relatively self-enclosed in society. There are many brave iconic rebels overseas. One example is Irwin Allen Ginsberg's tour lectures and poetry-recital events, which were all the rage in the United States in the 1960s. Another is the non-fictional texts in the excellent works by Truman Capote and Norman Mailer, such as *In Cold Blood*, *The Executioner's Song*, and *Some Children of the Goddess*. They even launched long-term columns on TV to discuss literary and non-literary issues with the audience. We can describe this line of thinking as effective offside. In it, there lurks the desire to dominate, or at least influence, ideology. It empowers and completes the image of a writer and increases the self-confidence of literature to some extent.

I think the lifeless literary world results first and foremost from lethargic writers. Authors who have no rights because they fail to fight for them. There are certainly other causes, but none of them are catastrophic. Catastrophe is caused by our withered mental attitude.

MIRRORS AND BIOGRAPHIES

Writing an autobiography is akin to setting up a mirror on one's desk. But how to portray the person in the mirror requires particular methods and conventions. Therefore, while reading autobiographies, we will see various real or vague images of the biographers.

We are always convinced by a person's account and description of themselves. We always think that an autobiography needs to be as accountable as testimony. We always believe that the mirror of an autobiography will accurately reflect the image and the expression in the eyes of the biographer in front of the mirror. However, such reading expectations may be naïve and detrimental. This feeling deepened after I recently read the autobiography *Le Miroir Qui Revient*, (translated into English as *Ghosts in the Mirror*) by Alain Robbe-Grillet, a leading French novelist of the *Nouveau Roman* (new novel) trend. After closing the pages, what I saw in my mind's eye was, instead, the images of the biographer's mother and some unrelated people. I also saw the expression in the eyes of Alain Robbe-Grillet, but that look was directed at another famed French literary figure Roland Gérard Barthes with contempt and sarcasm.

A wife who is always accusing her husband of neurological problems, a mother who is always telling her son not to have babies, and a middle-class woman who almost kills her husband with a knife simply because he can't light a candle in time—this lively character has subverted my old impression of this author's ignorance of characterisation. The image of this mother in his novel is unreservedly true to life. Let's look at Roland Barthes then. 'In the last days of his life, Roland Barthes felt the least worried about his consciousness of himself being a swindler'. As if that is not enough, Alain Robbe-Grillet also describes him as a 'hypocrite' and a fake 'thinker'. I am truly stunned by such a relentless and incisive attack by this author against Roland Barthes, another literary master (he had just been killed in a car accident at the time).

I trust that the author was sincere when he wrote the book. But after reading it, I feel a sense of loss. I have the feeling not because I doubt the author's virtue, which is meaningless, but because I see Alain Robbe-Grillet in the mirror looking sideways. I don't mind looking at his sideways-looking eyes but I do want to see his eyes directed at the world and the people at large, and I also want to see the expression in his eyes as he examines his inner self. But that kind of look is just evasive and fleeting. Only his description of his life as a worker in post-war Germany is detailed and peaceful.

Somehow, I think of another great Frenchman, Jean-Jacques Rousseau, and his famous *Confessions*. Back then, I was deeply moved by this self-exposing and self-flagging soul. One day, I read a book and found some text in it saying that the Rousseau described in his autobiography was not the real Rousseau. I have become more cautious since then. A mirror of autobiography must mostly be a bronze mirror covered with a green patina. We must learn to feel the image of a person in a bronze mirror. Just as Alain Robbe-Grillet puts it, 'I am not an actual person but I am not a fictitious person, either'. This may just divulge the very secret of autobiographies.

GROPING FOR A LAMP'S PULL CHAIN

Writing has become the most important part of my life for years. It results from being active on my part and having no choice. I have tasted the sweet bitterness of writing. But I hate to describe it in detail, let alone in a dramatic, autobiographic language. I just want to say that I'm trying to get close to my dream. I want to write more fictional works while I am still young and, as a disciple of literature, to leave a few more novels and fictional collections behind as the best memorial of literary masters.

Because of my occasional fascination with the American writer Jerome Salinger, I wrote ten short stories, including *Going Away on a Kick Scooter*, *A Sad Dance*, and *An Afternoon Story*. I set the background in a street in the north of Suzhou City where I grew up. In this short story series, I depict an adolescent looking at and living his life from a juvenile's perspective. The mood of the stories is casual and childishly simple. Few critics pay attention to this series but it's extremely important to me. On an autumn afternoon in 1984, I wrote my 4,000-character *Marking the Occasion of the Mulberry Garden* in a single dormitory. It was an afternoon worth remembering because it witnessed me taking my first step. And I cherish these immature and yet genuine works of literary exercise.

Friends generally think that my three novellas *The Escape in 1934*, *An Opium Family*, and *Wives and Concubines* are the most important of my literary works. I agree with their assessment. In retrospect, these three novellas bear the obvious trace of my plodding forward in the mire of fiction. I'm therefore very grateful to *Harvest* magazine for accommodating me to help build my self-confidence.

The good luck that *Wives and Concubines* brought me was both fortuitous and coincidental. In my experience of literary creation, it was but an artistic attempt. Through this novella, I tried to get out of the trap of the form that I previously employed so often and filled the space of the work with a classical spirit and original life. I tried writing characters, character relationships and their related stories with a technique of exquisite, realistic depiction. It turns out that this is also a pleasant writing process. I have therefore really discovered another possibility of fictionalisation.

Song Lian, the female protagonist of *Wives and Concubines*, became a 'complex' in my later literary creation. In the few following novellas, I spontaneously created female characters of the 'Song Lian' style, such as Xiao E in *Petulia's Rouge Tin*, and Xian and Xiao in *Women's Life*. I have finished writing the so-called 'female series' as of now. I will continue to 'move about' in a quest for alternative possibilities in literary creation.

Fiction is a gargantuan maze in which all the contemporary writers and I are groping cautiously. All our efforts seem to be fumbling for a lamp's pull chain, hoping to shine a brilliant light on our fiction and on our entire lives.

In a brief article that I wrote last year, I discussed the style of fiction. I always maintain that as soon as a writer has established their writing style, they face an imminent crisis: tackling the most urgent task of figuring out how to get out of the 'trap' of form and how to develop and enrich the connotation of literary creation. The writer must constantly say goodbye to the works of yesterday, dare to smash everything in existence, and shape a brand-new look and style of created works. I think this is the most meaningful stage in the life of writing and the most challenging process of creation. To carry on my extended metaphor, we must have the courage to walk into each of the doors and dark spaces in the maze of fiction.

Go around yourself and find your way out of the maze!

Try it and see if you can find the hidden pull chain.

WHY CAN'T I WRITE ESSAYS?

Regarding non-fiction, I like to read great essays by prominent writers the most. I remember reading Lu Xun, particularly his famous caricature of the follow-the-crowd mentality: someone gazing at his spittle on the ground would attract a curious throng of spectators around him. Reading the passage gave me such a shocking pleasure that I had a hearty laugh. Since then, I have had a model and criteria for such a style of writing in my mind.

In the eyes of writers, the world is a heavyweight giant. Novelists run around his body to glimpse the expression in his eyes, describe every detail of his life, and even assiduously tell their own stories about him or make their assumptions about the giant's dream. Novelists have deified the world. Nevertheless, the emergence of some great essayists has disrupted the relationship between the world and literature. These people who have broken away from superstitious beliefs treat the world as a patient. They are truly brave and daring. Knitting their brows, they auscultate (examine) the giant here and there with their home-made stethoscopes and have identified that the patient's focus of disease is festering and bacteria are multiplying. Then, they accurately mark the infested locations on the patient's body with flags. Since then, we have been able to read a kind of text that deviates from traditional literary concepts. It opposes the practices of beautifying things, being sentimental, sighing all the time, making a mountain out of a molehill, skimming the surface without going deeper, and failing to get to the root of a matter. Here, we have learned about the combative quality of the text, the spirit of which is as sharp as a scalpel ready for an operation on the world.

A writer like me has been watching this giant of the world wide-eyed for many years, trying to observe the expression in his eyes. But sometimes, he's asleep and I cannot see it. I then sit near his mouth, where I hear the breath exhaled from his nostrils mixed with a faint touch of halitosis. A writer like me sometimes tries to treat the world with a scalpel and some flags to mark the focuses of diseases. Busying myself around the giant, I find that I can't turn its massive body over. I don't know where to start. When my hand reaches under the giant's armpit to locate the point of balance, I feel his actual power and weight. I feel that his body temperature is as high as the melting bath in a furnace that gives me a burning sensation. Scared, I let out a scream of alarm like someone timid and hurt. A writer like me wrings my hands in frustration, at a loss what to do. Unable to stand their master's hesitation and incompetence, the carefully prepared colourful flags held in my hand have decided to betray me. Going against their original intention, they turn themselves into festive flags and make clamorous utterances to the effect of 'Welcome! Welcome!' Their betrayal puts me in a more absurd situation and causes me to be more scared. A writer like me makes a last-ditch effort to point out in an uncertain voice that the world is suffering from periodontitis. After hearing it, the world says, "I have known it for a long time. Almost everyone suffers from periodontitis, anyway". I feel extremely embarrassed. I lean over to auscultate the world and hear some rales or irregular breathing. I know that the lungs of the world may be infected. I want to tell others about this discovery. But the listeners also betray me. They leave me without saying goodbye. I find the effort of my labour is ultimately lost. What's more important is that I don't think it a problem for anyone to have some rales. Medical common sense doesn't see it as a big deal. I'm thinking, "What have I kept myself so darn busy for and why don't I go to sleep while the world is in a slumber"? Therefore, with an illusory passion, I fall asleep by the head of the giant.

A person can do nothing but dream in their sleep. Therefore, the yield of my dreams is very high. That's why I've never been able to come up with essays like Lu Xun's.

PASSION FOR FICTION

I have met many of my readers frequently and they have put a lot of interesting questions to me, mostly related to a specific plot or character in one of my novels or stories. On those occasions, I often sigh with wonder at the magic functions of words and language, which have penetrated the lives of many strangers under circumstances that I can't foresee and enabled their imaginations and memories to be in direct contact with me. That makes me pleased.

On several occasions, I have felt embarrassed by a common question from a reader. The question is usually to this effect: how did you write a certain aspect of the life described in a certain novel without experiencing it? Each time I can't respond succinctly and to the point. To my close acquaintances, I just tell them I made it up. To strangers, though, I choose a more elegant term, namely, 'fiction'.

We can't equivocate with my readers by using the term fiction. Undoubtedly, they are unsatisfied with such a simple and sloppy answer. The problem lies in that I don't think that I'm making irresponsible remarks, that I think that I'm telling the truth and that our understanding of fiction is far from enough to explain its true meaning.

All fiction is based on the subjective world and rooted in real life but its branches and leaves should extend beyond the subjective world of a writer and above the real life that the writer can hear and see. It should be richer and more colourful than the subjective and objective worlds combined. What ability can a writer possess to generate such energy? We place our hopes on their great soul and their profound thinking. But, rational and vague, such hopes also apply to a politician, a musician, a painter and even a star performer. To a writer, however, fiction is essential to their life's work; for it must become an important means of their cognizance.

Fiction is not only fantasy but it is also an assurance, one that transcends the limitation of concepts. Fiction can be so powerful that it can settle the impurities in real life to turn it into a cup of pure water held in the hands of a writer. In this sense, this cup of water becomes a secret recipe for an elixir with which the writer can eternalise their life of literary creation. Fiction is not just a kind of writing technique; it is more of a passion arousing in you an insatiable desire for the world and the multitude of people that inhabit it. It enables you to record the world or its inhabitants in your own way so that what you put down will differ from historians' historical records, from newspapers' news features, from street gossip, and from the writers and works of your time.

Fiction has become a writing technique and blood at the same time. It provides a new point of growth for an individual's limited thoughts and a broader space for the limited vision of the individual. It turns textual history into the history of their mind.

Nowadays, when we talk about Jorge Luis Borges, Gabriel García Márquez and Italo Calvino, we see the light of fiction which we often ignore. We are amazed at Franz Kafka's accurate summarisation of the human predicament and alienation. And we are shocked by William Faulkner's depiction of human life in a place as tiny as a postage stamp. We extol the virtues of these great writers and yield to their leadership while we often forget that the power of leadership is but personal creativity, and what we are led into is a world of fiction—a world in the process of creation and simulation, both real and imaginary. Mankind's homeland and the home to return to are between the light of early dawn and the afterglow, also both real and imaginary. We are led like this so that an individual's momentary monologue suddenly becomes a classic in others' lives. An otherwise isolated and helpless mental world can now shroud tens of thousands of souls through its text. This is the charm of fiction. In the final analysis, this is also the charm of novels.

To my mind, many contemporary writers encounter similar thorny questions: what kind of world should we describe for readers? How should we attach equal importance to the philosophy and logic of this world, to repentance and forewarning, to conscience and innocence, and to ideals and morality? How should we merge sunshine with moonlight in this world every day? Though difficult to do, this task can only be our choice.

THE PATH OF ESSAYS

From the eight great prose masters of the Tang and Song dynasties to Lu Xun, the tradition of our essays has been imbued with the ardour of being concerned about our country and people. Lu Xun's extraordinary poignancy and acumen made his prose roar and thunder for a time. Through Lu Xun, people have fully realised that words are also herculean. It was a power of the first half of the twentieth century. Today, the herculean Lu Xun is being piously worshipped in the temple of literature. A role model's power is infinite but the high standard of the role model is too difficult to emulate. Therefore, we see a very strange phenomenon: people have faith in and worship Lu Xun but shun him silently in their writing. The spotlight of Lu Xun has lit up the path of prose but there is no traveller on it.

Then we should talk about Shen Congwen, another great writer of the first half of the twentieth century. He wrote his *Xiangxing Ji* (*Random Sketches on a Trip to Hunan*) in 1934, two years before Lu Xun died of illness in Shanghai. Aside from their personal relationship, they grandly shook hands with their writing but people tend to overlook this hidden symbol and its meaning. Since then, Lu Xun has been great and Shen Congwen has been excellent but Shen Congwen's graceful and feminine writing style has overshadowed Lu Xun's influence. This is not the result of the comparison of the two camps but the facts are amazing. Later, in the long voyage of prose, Lu Xun was the captain but the helmsman was Shen Congwen. On this beautiful and gentle course, this big ship sailed to the 'Island of Extremely Good Disposition'. However, we know that the destination that Captain Lu Xun had designated might be a volcano, hell or heaven. What led them to this 'island'? It's hard to say. Perhaps it's the balance of the power of text that resulted in the course's alteration, or perhaps it's the alteration of the course that led to the balance of power.

Who can make it clear whether the prose has been loyal to the captain or the helmsman during its voyage in the past years, or whether it has been loyal to the ship itself?

We are all confined to a whispering pattern of prose. No matter how you look at the prose tradition, it must be a double-edged sword. Sometimes it gives you strength and sometimes encumbrance. Because people's minds in this era are generally in a state of drifting, prose as a record of true feelings and thoughts is also lithe, piecemeal and messy. And because this era emphasises individuality, writers are scrambling to pick their costumes, props and dubbing equipment in creating their prose. Looking around, those who choose to banish themselves can no longer find the pasture where Su Wu, an unyielding Han-dynasty diplomat held captive in the enemy's territory, could herd his sheep or the isle where Robinson Crusoe could live all by himself.

SOME ELEMENTS OF SHORT STORIES

In reality, I don't know how to select some classic short stories for a collection, let alone how to make it authoritative. The only thing that I can do is to select my favourite ones so I can share the joy of reading with my readers.

Where short stories are concerned, masters both at home and abroad have left their immortal voices. Sometimes, I think what originally motivated writers to write fairy tales was to lull children to sleep. For that matter, short stories are bedtime stories for adults, who'd better read them under their bedside lamps and read one story a night before going to sleep. Then, they can relish it for three or five minutes, either to be moved, to smile understandingly or to feel that they have something to say but find it hard to. If reading can achieve such a result, it means that this brief time spent reading is not a waste of time. How wonderful it would be to cultivate such a habit to make a dreary day glorious!

Of course, to do this, there must be a prerequisite, that is, a collection of many good short stories by the pillow.

What I have selected here include the works favoured by seasoned selectors, such as *Vanka* by Anton Chekhov and *Boule de Suif* (*Ball of Fat*) by Guy de Maupassant. I meant to exclude those that have become 'classics' to give people a brand-new collection to read. But I can't bear giving up these two stories. Therefore, I've included them in the belief that every reader has already realised the classic significance of each. Forgive me for my refusal to pick up the comments made by others.

First, let me share my impression of Nathaniel Hawthorn's *Wakefield* after reading it. I don't think that its impact on me is less than his *Scarlet Letter*. A man who has strayed to another subdivision is still observing his wife's daily life. The creation of such a character itself is already of extraordinary significance. What is the man afraid of? What is he avoiding? The straight-line distance of this man away from home may not exceed a kilometre but we, as readers, can't help measuring his distance from society, ethics and morality. This is the uncanny workmanship that the author displays in his *Wakefield*. A man who runs a few hundred metres away from home therefore attracts more attention from the reader than a man who runs across an ocean as described in many other novels. The old, crafty Hawthorn doesn't want to destroy social norms because he lets Wakefield finally return home: 'One evening, in the twentieth year since he vanished, Wakefield is taking his customary walk towards the dwelling which he still calls his own'. Hawthorn makes the man enter "the door one evening, quietly, as from a day's absence". In this way, after causing us to give out a panic-stricken scream, Hawthorne then soothes our uneasy senses empathetically. Meanwhile, he also calms down many a nervous conscience and, so to speak, stops many a moral tree from shaking.

What earns Isaac Singer respect is his simple and sincere concept of novel writing. He always spares no effort in 'characterisation', persistently planting an old-fashioned Jewish forest of characters. He works untiringly on characterisation like a farmer who won't quit until he dies of exhaustion. That's why Singer's characters are usually so colourful and lifelike that you can even smell their body odours. *Gimpel the Fool* is his most iconic textual description of a character. Compared with Isaac Singer, William Faulkner, the literary master we are more familiar with, has always used the most extreme wisdom and means in the history of human writing to establish a monument for humanity itself. Reviewers think that Gothic fiction has influenced *A Rose for Emily*, but how can Gothic fiction compare with the great Faulkner? This is the subconscious reaction of many readers who love Mr Faulkner but this is not the reaction of Faulkner himself. He is not ashamed to ask questions. A holy hand has consecrated the 'rose' we know through reading Faulkner, so it's gloomy, weird and full of the atmosphere of death, but every part of it transcends the so-called 'artistic atmosphere', making people eager to explore the inner world of Miss Emily, which likened to the dilapidated house where she resides, has a door covered in dust. Faulkner wants to open two doors for us but he's more interested in opening the door to her inner world. Therefore, he pushes it open before our eyes, revealing what's in the house where Ms Emily has lived in seclusion for forty years. We see the body of her lover who died years ago lying on the bed, and "a long strand of iron-gray hair" on the pillow. We also see Ms Emily lying there along with her inner world. It has been lying there all the time because, as Mr Faulkner tells us, she's the loneliest woman in the world. We feel scared when reading this part, not by something frightening, but by loneliness.

The inescapable loneliness and self-salvation of the soul are the stark realities that people must face and we, along with literary masters, pay attention to these realities. Jorge Luis Borges's *La Instrusa* (*The Intruder*) is not as rigged with traps as his other works. The story is simple and striking. That's why I've chosen it only after looking carefully and hesitantly through his countless exquisite works. *La Instrusa* tells of two poor brothers depending on each other for survival. They fall in love with a prostitute at the same time. That's why I refer to the story as simple. But we can feel the impact of the story at its ending. To prevent an unstable romance from destroying fraternal solidarity, the older brother chooses to break away from the love affair and kills the woman with his own hands for the sake of brotherhood. It's the madness and rationality that shock us. They sometimes integrate into magma and erupt. How can you not be shocked? The heinous atrocities turned out to be the best way out for the brothers! I think the reason Borges turns violence into an element of his exquisite works is that the best writers don't have to avoid anything, because he preaches nothing, and because what he cares about is still human plight: all kinds of loneliness and all kinds of difficult but ineffective methods of self-salvation also constitute the most important details of human life.

Serious topics are always the spiritual coffee that we need. But I also love some literary works that don't say much but are still moving and unforgettable. This is true with James Joyce's *Araby* from one of the short stories collected in his *Dubliners*. It describes the love life of a boy in puberty. It involves the boy's first romantic encounter or nothing at all. With a silver coin in his hand, the boy is taking a train alone at night to a distant Arabian-style bazaar. He planned to buy a souvenir for 'Mangan's sister'. However, after all the effort spent on travelling to the bazaar, he ends up buying nothing and the bazaar has also closed. This is the major part of the story. You can speculate as you wish to have a deep understanding of the writer's intent. What adds to our imagination is more interesting to me. Imagine an early teen sitting unaccompanied on a train at night, imagine him standing alone in an already closed market, and recall if you had a similar night tour at his age, and you'll come closer to the author's original intention. This is also a way of reading short stories. The same method should also apply to reading Capote's *A Christmas Memory*. Strictly, instead of a fictional work, it's more like a casual memory, a reminiscence of the trivialities coming to pass when the author and a childish old woman enjoy the fun of Christmas despite the hardships in their lives. The narrative is toned-up and simple because of its casualness. All the sorrows are condensed into gems shining brilliantly before us. Especially for the death of the old woman, the writer writes: another 'morning arrives in November, a leafless, birdless coming of a winter morning, when she cannot rouse herself to exclaim: "Oh my, it's fruitcake weather!"' Arguably, *A Christmas Memory* is not a very famous short story but I am sure that readers will be moved by such a spontaneous and yet sincere work and will never forget it.

I love Raymond Carver entirely because I admire him for his extraordinary insight into the lives of ordinary people and his fair and exquisite attitude to observation, and because his sympathy is as unpretentious as his writing style. The farmer named Holits in his *The Bridle* is a character living at the bottom of society that Carver is best at describing. After bankruptcy, he and his family move to a new place to start a new life but fail. Eventually, they relocate to a place even stranger to them. All the members of this frustrated and unlucky family have left, leaving behind a bridle that makes it hard for their neighbours to forget them. It also makes us feel a hint of melancholy. Carver is not an ordinary advocate of 'minimalism'. That's because his economy gets him many results with the least effort possible. We can always feel that he points gently with a thick finger at our souls, our wrinkles, our bruises and our ambiguous places. His calmness and serenity thus become powerful.

Zhang Ailing is the only writer in this anthology writing in Chinese. I must clarify that I don't think she's the only one who has made a name for herself creating short stories in China. My selection of *Hongluanxi* (*Great Felicity*) is for its tone of Chinese literature, which is a model for the traditional literature familiar to Chinese readers at large. She chooses every word in concise Chinese vernacular ingeniously and crafts each figure of speech with as much effort as the famous Tang-dynasty poet Li Bai exerted to compose his poems. Therefore, traditional Chinese fiction is famous for its tremendous accomplishment through the accumulation of small ones. A masterpiece must be penned with tremendous endeavour. Take Erqiao and Simei, the two unmarried young women characters in her short story, for example. They painstakingly try to find the best wedding costumes and accessories for their brother and sister-in-law. But according to Zhang Ailing, while each of her characters thinks of themselves as having the most important role in the wedding, "Erqiao and Simei see Yuqing (the bride) as nothing but the snow-white text 'The End' that concludes a motion picture whereas they are the advertised film to come out the next season—a film more fabulous". What makes Zhang Ailing's writing powerful is the clever metaphors used here and there. I've been maintaining that works like this are authentically made in China. Her writing is more casual than poetry but more rigorous than vernacular prose. It becomes fiction in approaching it, thus making itself subtle and marvellous. This short story of hers gives its readers a reading experience that differs from the above-mentioned works by foreign writers. This is also the amplest reason for my inclusion of *Great Felicity* in the anthology.

A FEW WORDS ABOUT SHORT STORIES

Whether it is a novel, a novella or a short story that I'm going to dwell upon here, the texture must be beautiful, and the structure of the flesh and blood is especially important. The most important thing in the structure of a short story is control. For a writer to control a narration with imagination within the limit of a few thousand characters is like dancing on a round table. Any movement, however beautiful it may be, mustn't be overdone. Any elaborate account, however accurate, must take thrift into account. To an overzealous writer, a short story cannot satisfy his or her zeal because zeal will eventually transform into the power of keeping a balance.

A short story can tell a story but we can no longer design a dramatic conflict. A short story also calls for characterisation but we can't detail their personalities with too many words. The only issue we need to address is still the exercise of control.

The control of words is, to a large extent, the control of the rhythm. As Italo Calvino puts it, a short story is like a horse-drawn carriage. How it runs and how fast it runs depends entirely on the traffic conditions on the road. So, when writing a short story, we must keep our eyes wide open so that we can see the traffic ahead clearly.

ANSWERS TO MY QUESTIONS

1. TELL US SOMETHING ABOUT YOUR CREATIVE EXPERIENCE AND YOUR PAST LIFE.

To put it in a naughty way, my earliest creativity was doodling on a cement floor in my childhood. I once traced and copied a slogan on the wall of a chemical plant: 'Revolutionary committees are good!' I was praised by spectators in unison. I was then a pre-schooler.

I fell seriously ill when I was nine and stayed at home with my schooling suspended. Confined to bed, my daily companion was the novel *Yanyangtian* (*Sunny Days*), the first novel I ever read. Then, I had a strange hobby: jotting down a list of fabricated names and marking each with their title, such as Party Branch Secretary and Militia Battalion Leader. I had created a list of characters. I chanced upon such a list while rummaging in my chest of drawers a few years ago. Perhaps the practice was the earliest daydreaming of my literary career.

I wrote poems for a time in college. Nine out of ten of the college students at that time were poets. The creation of poetry played a vital role in honing the language skill. It's true with me, at least. Later, I learned to write fiction and published my maiden work *The Eighth One Is a Bronze Bust* in the July edition of the periodical *Youth* in 1983. I was bold enough to write about a veteran educated youth who had embarked on the path of economic reform. And I was lucky enough to receive the Youth Literature Award for it the next year. After I got the prize money, I called a few of my friends together and celebrated it at the classy Hongbinlou Restaurant in Beijing.

2. TELL US SOMETHING ABOUT THE INFLUENCE OF FOREIGN WRITERS ON YOU.

This involves a long list of names including the eminent writers known to all, such as Ernest Hemingway, William Faulkner, J. D. Salinger, Jorge Luis Borges and Gabriel García Márquez.

When I was a teenager, I was obsessed with picaresque novels like Maxim Gorky's *Unrequited Love*. The *Contemporary American Short Stories* published by the Shanghai Translation Publishing House exposed me to the actual scene of world literature for the first time. I found the image of the pedantic old bachelor in Isaac Bashevis Singer's *The Spinoza of Market Street* unforgettable. I was a high school student in Suzhou, Jiangsu Province, China. My interest tells me that the best contemporary literature of the world is in the USA. I cannot shake off the shadow that batch after batch of

American writers cast over me and the stimulation and shock that they gave me. Neither can I shake off the invisible shackles they have on me.

3. TELL US SOMETHING ABOUT YOUR WORKS.

We'd better not talk about them. I'm fully aware of the defects of my works, which others may not have discovered yet. If I talk about them, I'd be seen as showing the skeletons in my cupboard.

Sometimes, I study my works like studying others and often end up thumping my chest and stamping my feet in anxiety and sorrow. Defects in content and art are common in the works of popular contemporary writers. If one critiques them, everyone else follows; if no one says anything, no others will utter a sound.

4. TELL US SOMETHING ABOUT THE PROS AND CONS OF POPULAR AND UNPOPULAR WORKS.

This involves an understanding of the word 'popular'. It means something recognised and welcomed by people at a given point in time. In other words, if we don't count other literature genres, popular fiction is fiction that's generally accepted while exerting influence on the time of its popularity. Take 'Scar Literature', 'Reform Literature', and 'Root-seeking Literature' for instance. They made up the pre-1985 model of popularity. Chinese literature after 1986 underwent a qualitative change. A batch of works characterised by the unique personalities of their writers reached the pinnacle of literature. They also became a hit in a short time, like winning a horse racing bet, where both the horse and the rider have the significance of popularity. In the circle of literature, works like such horses include *Qiwang* (*The Chess Master*), *Biandi Fengliu* (*A Land for Life, A Land for Love*), *Ni Bie-wu-xuan-ze* (*You Have No Choice*), and *Touming de Hongluobo* (*Radish*). Writers like such riders comprise Ah Cheng, Liu Sola and Mo Yan. Undoubtedly, they are excellent in the first place before they suddenly burst onto the scene. Their works have established their popularity and influenced the style of many literary works.

There are, of course, two meanings of the so-called 'unpopular'.

One is that literary works are unpopular because of their poor quality, which makes it difficult for them to circulate. The other is, to my mind, that works by outstanding writers don't circulate well. These unpopular good writers usually do not catch people's attention. But even if they do, they can still be unpopular. The reasons are complex. They don't seem to write for the general public and cannot be emulated universally. They hide their individuality deep in their works and make it hard for readers to assimilate, thus producing an unexpected effect that alienates their works from the readers instead of promoting circulation. They want to attract readers through alienation. Examples of these types of writers include Can Xue from Hunan and Ye Zhaoyan from Jiangsu.

There are no pros and cons in 'popularity' and 'unpopularity'. They are both soils from which good literary works can grow.

5. TELL US SOMETHING ABOUT OBSTACLES TO LITERARY CREATION AND HOW YOU TACKLE THEM.

Every writer encounters obstacles in creating their novels. Obstacles come from all aspects, either political or personal. By personal I mean other people and the writers themselves which, I'm afraid, present the most significant obstacles.

Writers face lurking dangers with their success, which comes usually from the writers' artistic individuality and style. But the so-called individuality and style can easily become a beautiful bog, from which writers find it hard to free themselves. A successful writer often has a certain new-fangled mark. As time goes by, the mark will fade and pass its prime. Readers tend to prefer the new to the old and will become tired of them. But writers are reluctant to shake off their style and model, which are indeed hard to drop or even break down. Therefore, a lot of writers build their nests where they are like birds begrudging leaving their old ones. They're drifting with the tide of literature while entrenched in their positions. This state of self-deadlocking and self-stranding often results in an obstacle to writing. To avoid or overcome obstacles, writers must be determined to break with the past and dissect themselves to reshape themselves from scratch. This is no easy job and requires tremendous courage.

Obstacles stem from a wilted habit of mind. If I want to create a story different from the previous ones, I must write sentences without cliches and break forms apart as soon as I establish them. Then my literary creation will be full of vitality. Unfortunately, that is exceedingly hard to do.

What is an obstacle? It's a pair of small-sized shoes a writer puts on themselves. Writers feel their toes squeezed wearing them but begrudge throwing them away, which they deem to be wasteful. Besides, what if they can't find new shoes after dumping the old? This anxiety is universal.

6. How do you think personality is formed?

Successful works always have a strong personal style, through which we can detect the entire consciousness of the writer. When a writer brands a special mark of personality everywhere on their work, their personality is then highlighted in their works, and their style will thereby be elegant and pleasant. Good writers often have a rebellious mentality against tradition and norms, which they destroy forcefully in their works, robbing their own value through the violence of words. Deliberate innovation is always an effective weapon of offense and self-defense.

The essence of the personality style possessed by many writers is the artistic promotion of their complexes, which are usually abnormal and unethical. Personal complexes sometimes become potential opportunities for creation and have a strong explosive power. This is reflected in many famous writers at home and abroad. It's inconvenient to elaborate, but you can experience it for yourself. In other words, you can peep at it at your discretion.

7. What do you think is the supreme artistic realm? Do you think your fiction is charming?

I have a bad habit of living in the details of the past and having no plans. The artistic realm can be referred to as a kind of light, half hidden and half illuminating. The artistic realm I wish to enter is multi-layered. I hope it will be natural, tranquil and quietly remote. I also hope that it will be rich, complex and changeful. But they'll share the same common ground, that is, they must be pure and artistic.

The excellent works I have read do enjoy the 'light' which I look forward to. Examples include Raymond Carver's short stories *The Bridle* and *A Small, Good Thing*; J. D. Salinger's *For Esmé—with Love and Squalor*; and John Barth's *Lost in the Funhouse*. I genuinely love outstanding short stories like them. They always fascinate me and drive me forward.

Speaking of charm, it's an issue that puts us to shame. Charm, to some extent, has evolved from politics. I never play politics, though. I'm convinced that my works are not that charming but I don't deny that I do play some tricks in my literary creation. Therefore, I can't deny that they do have some charm. I must strike a balance here or I'll be seen as pretentious and affected to the extent of being coquettish. Charm is an illusion in others' eyes while fiction is tangible, so much so that you must create it word by word with neither affectation nor rashness.

8. WHAT'S YOUR OPINION OF AVANT-GARDE FICTION AND WRITERS?

Wu Liang has given a close-knit and honest analysis and explanation of the topic. I like one of his subheadings: 'True Avant-garde Is As Always'.

The so-called *avant-garde* literature is relative. In all the realms of culture, there have always been some cultural elements of a relatively extremist and rebellious nature. Either on the rise or ephemeral, they're certainly positively significant. Avant-garde artists and writers are adventurists. Tapping and striking broken bricks from the wall remains on the square of literature, they engage themselves in either destructive or creative activities, by which they push literature forward.

Chinese contemporary *avant-garde* is only relative to Chinese literature. Their literary works look like foreign ones in form but amble along different rails. Probably, they're doomed to be unable to surpass the world. Therefore, I feel they are tragically heroic with a tinge of holy martyrs. For them, ridicule is a sign of ignorance while indifference is a sign of cruelty. I hope that people are kind and at least should have a normal baby-protecting mentality.

True *avant-garde* must have a sober-minded understanding of their position and value. They're supposed to have the character and spirit of a saint. Therefore, true *avant-garde* is as always forever.

SEVEN PREFACES

1. PREFACE TO 'THE BLOOD OF YOUTH'

This collection, including three newly released short stories such as *Swimming Pool*, has taken me eight years to create. It's the brainchild of my years of hard work and fascination with short stories. I will cherish this collection very much.

The editing sequence is exactly the opposite of the chronological order of the stories' creation. The first short novella and eight short stories in the first series of the collection are the works I wrote last year. The works collected in the second series were all written between 1988 and 1990, and the third collection was all selected from works buried in the years dating back before 1988.

Cherished Memory of the Mulberry Garden was written in October 1984 when I had just graduated from college and came to Nanjing to work. I met a few like-minded literary friends. It seemed that I wrote this short story to change their negative impression of my previous works. I stuffed the manuscript of *Cherished Memory of the Mulberry Garden* through the crack in the door of a friend's house. I achieved my purpose: my friends who read it all expressed their love for it. Since then, my confidence in fiction creation has ballooned. But this short story wasn't officially published in *Beijing Literature* until after I had submitted it to other periodicals across the country in the previous three years.

I often mention *Cherished Memory of the Mulberry Garden* not because it is satisfactory but because it's of great significance in my life of literary creation. Reading this old work again seems to give me a beautiful nostalgic feeling. It reminds me of burning the midnight oil in my single dormitory with passion, despite mosquito bites and stomach-growling hunger. More importantly, the thread of my later short stories emerged in this story: a group of adolescents in puberty on a narrow old street in southern China, which I later named Toon Tree Street; unstable emotional factors; the smell of blood suddenly infiltrating a dark street; a few sprouting young lives festering in humid air; and some twisted souls hovering on a bluestone-slab street. Beginning with *Cherished Memory of the Mulberry Garden*, I recorded their stories and the vacillating conditions of their lives. Creating this story gave me keen pleasure and satisfaction.

I used to live in a street like Toon Tree Street. I know that the blood of youth is thick and rich in literary significance. I know how the blood of youth flew in the years of chaos. Anything that flows follows a certain course. I try to record this course in this collection.

The collection *Blood of Youth* also includes a different type of stories that also happen on Toon Tree Street, such as *A Radio with a Wooden Frame* and *On a Sunday Morning*, in addition to a few short stories featuring adolescent characters from the country, such as *Running like Mad* and *A Straw Scarecrow*. Can we, perhaps, treat them as a few branches of the same tree, or branches more touching than the tree itself, or branches that point to the future of my creation of short stories?

I'm uncertain that I'll still be indulging myself in the stories collected in *Blood of Youth*. Neither can I judge the true value of *Blood of Youth*. But it will undoubtedly be a work I'll cherish myself. Self-cherishing is especially important to a literary creator.

2. Preface to 'Both Sides of the World'

The title I give to the book is a bit abstract but, as implied by the title, it involves the two sides of the world.

One side is urban and the other rural. This is a unilateral, simple arrangement of the world.

Let me talk about the rural part first. Attentive readers can detect that in most of the stories, I use Fengyangshu (Chinese Wingnut Tree) as the name of the place in which my stories are set. It seems to be a deliberate and yet awkward imitation of William Cuthbert Faulkner's Yoknapatawpha County. In these works, I made up this Fengyangshu Village. Many of my friends regard it as a show of my 'nostalgic' and 'homecoming' mood. Fengyangshu Village may have a trace of residence by my ancestors but it's a drifting and unreproducible trace. With my method, I've picked up a broken history and stitched the pieces together. That's a wonderful process of fiction. In the process, I've felt the pulse of my ancestors and native land, I've seen where I came from and I'll see where I'm going as well. As some commentators say, creating these fictional works is my spiritual 'homecoming'.

The Escape of 1934, written between the autumn and winter of 1986, was the first novella in my life. Reading it now, I still find something in it I'm not quite satisfied with, but it's of special significance to me.

Now, I'll talk about the other side, that is, my fiction about urban life. *Burn* and two other short stories debuted in 1992. Four novellas, including *Calm as Water*, were written in 1987 or 1988. They were semi-popular fiction dealing with puberty, loneliness, confusion, love, loss and quest. I give these works of mine the proud name 'semi-popular' because they all share the clues and essence of the aforementioned fiction popular because of its wide circulation. It's these 'semi-popular' works of mine that have won me the first and widespread readership.

The shadow of my actual life can be seen drifting among these urban adolescents. Through the partly true accounts, I've recorded my personal life, something about my youth and dreams, my confusion and quest, my very self and my friends, and the transient youths on the urban streets. I include the two kinds of works in *Both Sides of the World* like a gardener planting two kinds of plants in the same flower bed, hoping that they will look harmonious and mutually enriching.

People live on both sides of the world, namely the city and the country. While my blood is on the rural side, my body is on the urban side.

3. Preface to 'Snapshots of Marriage'

This book contains my 'representative' novellas. Of course, 'representative works' refer to works that have attracted the attention of public opinion and a wide range of readers. In other words, they are the batch of my fiction that is not left in the cold.

Let me talk about *Wives and Concubines* first. It's widely known for its adaptation into the movie *Raise the Red Lantern*, a result that I never expected. The original motivation for writing *Wives and*

Concubines was to look for a change or rather, to write a classical and pure Chinese novel and to test my creative energy and skill. I've chosen a theme that's common in the history of Chinese literature, namely a tragic story of the concubines in a feudal family. The success of this story may be attributed to the literary nutrition I've got from the Chinese classics ranging from *Dream of Red Mansions* and *The Golden Lotus* to the trilogy of *The Family*, *The Spring* and *The Autumn*. I base my work on downright fiction because I've never seen a feudal family with wives and concubines. I don't know the concubines named Songlian and Meishan. Nor do I know Chen Zuoqian. At the time of writing, what I had was the confidence to write what I wanted on plain paper and a weird impulse to depict old times.

After *Wives and Concubines*, I also wrote *Petulia's Rouge Tin*, *Women's Life* and *Another Kind of Woman's Life*. This series of four novellas about a woman's life was published as a collection by the Zhejiang Literature and Art Publishing House. I thought I couldn't write fiction of this genre but I unexpectedly came up with *Gardening* this year. Though connotatively different from the abovementioned works, it seems to be also feminine. I can't help feeling sorry for what I published before on 'literary creation' that stressed the necessity of jumping out of the box of style. From the momentum of my writing habit, it follows that jumping out of the 'box' is no easy job. I'll never speak of 'jumping' or 'changing' any longer without carefully thinking.

A Married Man and *Divorce Guides* are written about men, or specifically about a man named Yang Bo in real life. The two works are a reaction to my literary creation. I try to pay attention to reality and to the description of a man's situation in marriage, in which idealism gradually fades and gives way to gloomy and banal practical life. The aspect of men marked by embarrassment and loneliness is thought-provoking. I try to present how the worldly bog traps the feet, the body and even the mind of men like Yang Bo. The fear and struggle of men or women constitute most of the marriage landscape. I assume that when they crawl out of the bog covered in mud, their fatigued souls are already ensnared by frightening nothingness. These are perhaps frightening novellas or, rather, frightening reality.

Over the years, I've taken great pains to realise and perfect my literary dream. It has been the happiest thing in recent years to publish most of my novellas together. For this, I'd like to thank Jiangsu Literature and Art Publishing House and related friends.

4. Preface to 'Love in the Last Generation'

The year 1993 witnessed people plunged into the abyss of misery in the distant, war-ridden Bosnia and Herzegovina. I often noticed young and handsome Slav soldiers coming and going through the gunpowder smoke (or lying on a stretcher with a broken leg) on TV. It was also on TV that I saw countless couples embroiled with each other in endless dramas broadcast on the dot every evening, each featuring an ear-jarring theme song.

That was precisely the two aspects of the world, one real and serenely bloody whereas the other was illusory and sentimental. We can only live in such a world as we savour others or are savoured by others; go to war or make weapons for war; or act or watch others act with appreciation. This was what we could do only, whether it was in 1993, 1992 or 1994.

To me, the year 1993, like all years, was also filled with joy and sorrow. It wasn't torrid in the summer of 1993 in Nanjing, and I don't think it was freezing in winter. Likewise, what I wrote in the attic alone was neither exciting nor disappointing to me.

For a writer to be apprehensive about the quality of what he writes is worrisome itself. But I don't want to evade this feeling of anxiety. Fortunately, with the completion of that novella, I could expect to write the next.

Ye Zhaoyan, a writer who lives in Nanjing with me, says, 'A writer must damn well write'.

For writers to feel comfortable or happy wherever they are, it's vital for them to maintain a good creative mood—isn't it? I think so. On a winter night in 1993, the icy wind was whistling outside the window and I heard a voice saying in the unseen world: *When are you going to finish it writing word by word?* Another voice said encouragingly, *Go on writing and don't look here and there! What do you think you are? What else can you do except write?*

That's true. What else can I do, eh?

. . .

5. PREFACE TO 'IMPERIAL HAREMS'
   There are two imperial palaces and two kinds of history here.
   My Life as an Emperor is a palace I casually built. It's a historical story I've concocted with my favourite formula. The time of the reign I set is always rife with mishaps. The characters are half-real. For example, an emperor that shouldn't sit on the throne becomes an emperor. But once sitting there, he becomes a juggler in the end. I'm obsessed with characters who live lives of vicissitudes. That is because I've always been frightened by the capriciousness of life and the relentlessness of history.
   I think of *Wu Zetian* as a historical novel that goes by the rules of fiction to the letter. I racked my brains to impregnate it with the functions required of modern fiction but it turns out to be a story of the only female monarch known to all, going beyond neither the readers' expectations nor historical records. Since I didn't have the desire to create fiction about a female monarch with the title 'Zetian Dasheng Huangdi (Zetian Great Sage Empress Regnant)', this novel and this famous woman have inevitably fallen into the set pattern of fiction.
   Is one fake and the other real?
   That's not necessarily so. Let's put fiction aside momentarily and look at history. The distance between man and history is neither close nor remote. When I look back at history, I only hear the music and song drifting out of the palace walls and horrifying anecdotes that startle me from my dreams. I assume that when history looks back at me, I'm but a frog in the well—a person with a very limited view. So, what's real and what's fake?

6. PREFACE TO 'RICE'
   Rice, written between the winter of 1990 and the spring of 1991, was my first effort to practice writing a novel. I was still young and aspiring when I began the first chapter. I became haggard when I finished half of the book. I was almost senile when I completed the manuscript in spring. To recall how I wrote *Rice* is not to make it

sound frivolous. I just want to say that it was the first time I felt how hard and tormenting it was to write a novel.

After *Rice*'s publication, I heard two completely different reviews. I'm still grateful to the friends who have lavished their praise upon it. And the sharp criticisms that have scrutinised it from the inside out aren't malicious at all in my memory. They're helpful for me to reflect on the quintessence of my work and even on my inner world. The novel makes me feel sorry for the conclusion I've drawn after self-examination: I feel that some detailed passages in the novel, especially the sexual descriptions, are kind of playing to the gallery.

No matter how it weighs on the scale, your soul must be pure. Of course, this is a precept given to me not just by *Rice*.

In the North of the City is a recent novel of mine. It's special among the small number of my novels because the characters are the group of adolescents in my real life, shimmering in the memories of my childhood. The Toon Tree Street in this novel is the longest and the most boisterous. And to review my childhood life through the language of novels has always been a wonderful experience for me. The reason why I'm obsessed with keeping these street stories alive is simple: there are always humans under cooking smoke and human breath always pervades Toon Tree Street.

As the sixth series of my fiction collection, this book happens to include my maiden novel and works that have just debuted. It happens to enable me and my readers to recollect what this writer is babbling about from that place to this one.

7. Preface to 'Butterfly and Go'

I've spent most of my time and energy creating short stories in recent years. I'm both joyful and fearful now that these short stories are being introduced to readers at such a fast speed.

I don't know whether readers will understand and appreciate these works with changing styles. In fact, I can't determine the value of this change myself. Many writers' views on art are wishful thinking, and literary creation based on dreams usually leads to two results: either gaining a truly unique artistic life in a difficult situation or watching the darkness gradually engulfing the last candlelight in your hand.

A writer spends their entire life trying to build the literary edifice in their imagination. At least there must be a few walls to enclose its space and the construction of these walls requires painstaking efforts. In J. D. Salinger's best story *For Esmé—with Love and Squalor*, a boy asks a soldier to guess a riddle: "What does one wall say to another?" The answer is *"See you at the corner"*. I often remember the riddle and its answer, thinking that a wall must meet another eventually. Many creative writers are therefore deliberately planning for the corners, hoping to make two walls meet perfectly.

But everything is still up in the air, and this makes me or all of us panicky.

WHY DID I WRITE *WIVES AND CONCUBINES*?

One night in the spring of 1989, I started writing *Wives and Concubines* in the attic where I lived alone. This story had been lingering in my mind for a long time.

'The fourth concubine, Songlian, was carried into the Chen family's garden when she was nineteen years old...' When I opened the novel with such a long sentence, I had almost defined the narrative style and type of story for this novel. However, such a plain description unexpectedly presented a challenge to me. It was a real challenge because I had never thought of beginning a novel with such old, banal language.

What aroused my desire for its creation is an ancient story known to all Chinese. I got the Chinese title *Qi* (wives) *Qie* (concubines) *Chengqun* (in a group) from a line in a friend's poem. It appropriately summarised the fuzzy story shimmering in my mind. So, I changed my habit of spending a lot of time deliberating on a fiction title and committed it to the first page of the manuscript right away.

Perhaps this was an auspicious sign. Just as I wished, the progress of the novel proved exceptionally smooth.

What would happen to Songlian, a helpless woman, after being taken as a concubine into the Chen family? If a novelist can raise such questions, it means that he has found a tunnel of popular novels through which he can travel freely. I travelled freely, and for the first time in my life, I discovered all the quirks of writing a classical novel in the style of plain description, a style too wonderful for words.

When I felt natural and relaxed, I was able to find a way to create female characters that was casual, coquettish, sentimental and hesitant. A story like *Wives and Concubines* had to be written in such a manner.

The world outside the window in spring became tumultuous. I locked the manuscript of a book, of which I had finished more than half, in my desk drawer. Then summer went by before autumn arrived and I found the trees outside the window shedding their leaves. That reminded me of a novel I needed to finish.

So, Songlian reappeared again in the autumn garden.

What I was going to write also became clearer. I wouldn't tell a story of polygamy. I found the structure of a typical feudal family with four female spouses a perfect fit for transplantation into the structure of a novel. Songlian was a newly placed beam that still exuded the fresh odour of wood, but was also the easiest to break.

I didn't want to reproduce the life of the Chen family garden in the novel. I was just moved by a certain sound in my imagination: the concubines like Songlian shuffling in the snow and sobbing in a dark room with their hands over their faces. It was painful not to be able to walk in strides but it was more painful not to be able to cry out loud. The concubines like Songlian dreaded wellheads as well as death but this is precisely where our widely diffusing and penetrating pain lies.

The four miserable women were all tied to a man in misery like four withered wisteria plants strangling each other in thin air to compete for soil to grow and space to breathe.

Misery often leads to tragedy, as with Songlian.

The truth is that a novel can't tell two stories well but people often interpret a novel into several stories.

Take *Wives and Concubines*, for example. Readers may read it as a 'story of women in the old days' or a 'story of polygamy'. If that were the case, I wouldn't be satisfied with the novel.

Can we interpret it as a story of 'misery and fear'?

If so, I'd be more satisfied.

WHY DID I WRITE *PUSAMAN*?

I've been trying my best to describe common people's existence as I see it. I've been sniffling and sighing over the quality displayed by that kind of existence. I've been feeling that some people treat misery and misfortune as their fate. It's these people that are living in this rambunctious world with both love and hatred. They cast others aside and are cast aside by others. I've been trying to represent this forlornness, which is the forlornness of the common people rather than that of philosophers or others.

That was how I started writing *Pusaman*.

This is a story that took place in the home of a commoner in South China. It's a story of a traditional family but narrated by the ghost of the deceased father, Hua Jindou.

The story took place in the 1960s to the 1980s.

The narrator Hua Jindou is a ghost full of grievances. He has already died and, as a wandering ghost, he doesn't have to eat or be clothed thereby saving the family food and clothing which makes him pleased. However, since death prevents him from meddling with the family's affairs, he's seized with anger in heaven. Unwilling to rest in peace, he's destined to be a painful and lonely ghost.

The aunt, the oldest of the father's sisters, is alive, so she must take care of the five children left by her brother and sister-in-law. Her love for the children is as messy as a pot of porridge. But it's this porridge that feeds the children and nurtures them into adulthood. During the long years, the aunt is adamantly reproaching the entire world while taking care of the children of the Hua family. Too busy and fatigued to think, she doesn't feel lonely. To me, however, not knowing loneliness is her loneliness.

Of the Hua family's children, none except the second daughter Xinmei makes Hua Jindou happy. He hates that they can't live up to his expectations apart from Xinmei, who has conceived a child with a deceitful young hooligan, and died young and pretty. Since childhood, the remaining three daughters and one son have been at loggerheads with their father's ghost. Though growing up with a lot of trials and tribulations, none is promising, especially the only son of the Hua family. He's incapable of carrying on the family line because he hangs out with men all day long. To use a term popular in Hong Kong and Taiwan, he's a *jilao* (*geilou* in Cantonese), a transliteration of the term 'gay'.

I've created a ghost who cries bitterly in my writing. He doesn't know why he must suffer like this. Later, he gives up meddling with his family affairs and worms his way into hell, leaving loneliness to everyone else, which includes me and all of us.

SEND HIM TO THE TREES

COMMENTS ON READING ITALO CALVINO'S *IL BARONE RAMPANTE* (*THE BARON IN THE TREES*)

When he looks up at the thick foliage of a forest, Italo Calvino finds that the crisscrossing boughs resemble dimly lit paths. As they zigzag in all directions, a kind of mysterious journey that is hard to outline begins to unfold in mid-air. Is it a journey of light? Or a journey of insects, moss or fallen leaves? Those may be the associations that come to the minds of those engaged in writing and painting. But Italo Calvino has exceptional insights: he sees something else. He sees a person and his home in the trees. This light of inspiration most probably strikes Calvino in the blink of an eye, when he sees the 'baron in the trees', jumping from one tree to another. That jumping figure is precisely the 'character' the writer is watching. This is a testimony to the saying: the emergence of 'an inspiration' is the emergence of characters in most times.

Someone climbs trees not to hunt or collect fruit. Neither is he as naughty as a child. He does so to start his life there! Readers find it hard to forget *The Baron in the Trees* because they can't forget the person who climbs trees to live there. Novelists are always crafty and create all sorts of strange characters. To borrow the vocabulary of today's business advertising strategy, 'the more bizarre, the more beautiful'. Expressly, a pervert is inherently eye-catching and inevitably impressive. But Cosimo, by climbing up trees, transcends our general reading experience. The creation of the character still seems shocking to this day and shines like a gem in the history of literature.

The Baron in the Trees was published in 1957, which was exactly a decade after the debut of his *Il Sentiero dei Nidi di Ragno* (*The Path to the Spiders' Nests*) that made his name and five years before the publication of his exceptional work *Il Visconte Dimezzato* (*The Cloven Viscount*). For an outstanding writer, a decade of his prime years should be an untrammelled history of literary creation, like a rushing river that could overflow its banks to cause grave flooding but may not flow backwards. But Calvino seems to dash out sideways and scampering like mad, not only betraying himself but also breaking away from the conservative Italian literary cohort. Calvino came to the fore when the wounds of the Second World War in Italy gradually formed scabs (and he had already touched upon the scars of the ulcerative period in *The Path to the Spiders' Nests*). During the war, he experienced the sorrows of Italy in the dilapidated streets and taverns. In peacetime, he had the leisure to look at his motherland Italy carefully, only to find his ancestor in the trees. Calvino was good at making people remember his novels with such beginnings. Even in *The Path to the Spiders' Nests*, the characters are hard to forget. A lonely boy who, cast aside by the children of his age, is accepted and used by adults. No one forgets that the boy's sister is a prostitute who sleeps with a German officer. I've tried to disassemble the chain of characters in the novel: Pin—sister—a German officer—partisans. I find them akin to recycled composite materials that can link up countless good or mediocre plots and character relationships (then there are the stories of Pin stealing a gun and Pin interacting with the partisan camp). While propagating more, faster, better and cheaper novel materials, this character chain is also risky, as are all super-efficient professional methods. It's true with *The Path to the Spiders' Nests*. The seemingly robust character chain is somehow uncoupled as the story of the novel unfurls, gradually giving off a mechanical, loose and feeble noise. The uncoupling might begin with Pin's encounter with a gigantic man named Cousin. From there, all the details seem to develop inexplicably in a direction that prevents the novel from being brilliant. We have a story of a young partisan plus a gun, eventually. It's more like a second-class film about a territory falling into the hands of invaders.

An overly deft and scientific chain of characters might not be suitable for an ambitious novel. A writer doesn't have to take serious themes such as 'World War Two' to heart. Calvino must have examined himself more thoroughly than I do. Five years later, Italy was poor and yet peaceful, and Calvino wrote *The Cloven Viscount*. Where the creation of characters alone is concerned, it has abandoned the familiar model. A decade later, *The Baron in the Trees* came into existence as the times demanded and with it emerged the shocking Calvino.

Calvino has come and nearly the entire traditional world of fiction must step aside. So must his relatives, his manor and even mother earth. He has turned a tree into a man's world and he has made the world forsake lonely people and made lonely people abandon other people's world. This was Calvino's vision of novel characters in the 1950s, and it was also the most decisive and brave practice of novel creation in his literary career.

The young Baron Cosimo can find any excuse for climbing a tree, not necessarily the refusal to eat snails. There are as many examples of rebellion and rejection in literature as in actual life. Calvino, however, deliberately climbs the tree. 'Climb the tree! Climb the tree'—the voice is as holy as evil, and it's the call that people can hear, be it the most light-hearted or the most heavy-hearted. For neither resistance nor rebellion, the story becomes strange and shocking when a boy's wilful and childish behaviour evolves into a choice of survival. Readers probably all understand that there's a huge philosophical significance hidden behind an adolescent's refusal to leave the tree, but everyone is also feeling jittery for Calvino's amazing talent. How will he end the drama? What will Cosimo do in the trees? Will he come down and when? (But everyone knows that the descent of Cosimo from the tree would mean the end of the novel.)

Without Calvino's permission, Cosimo can't come down. Cosimo's life in the trees relies on the writer's indomitable imagination and a sense of humour bordering on cruelty. Cosimo's careless love with the girl Viola, his neighbour in the trees, may be expected but his association and friendship with the arch robber Gian dei Brughi in the trees in the novel is grotesque and abrupt. The establishment of the character Gian dei Brughi also catches people off guard. He's romantic and fond of reading, so much so that he forces Cosimo to find him books that mustn't be tedious. It's also an unfinished book that leads to the eventual arrest of the robber who kills people like flies. What's more amazing is that Gian dei Brughi is still concerned about the fate of the protagonist in the novel he hasn't finished reading even before his execution. When Cosimo tells him that the protagonist in the novel has died by the noose, the robber, obsessed with mincing his words, kicks away the ladder beneath the gallows before saying to Cosimo, "Thank you, I'm going to get myself hanged, too. Farewell."

Calvino magnifies Cosimo's world in the trees. This character grows like the expanding boughs and branches, thus providing the writer with inexhaustible novel materials. Cosimo walks back and forth in the trees from twelve years of age until he is an old man. 'Youth hurriedly passed by on earth. You can imagine the situation on the tree. Everything there will inevitably fall: leaves and berries. Cosimo became an old man'. Still led by the writer's ambition to create myths, the old baron walks along in the world of trees to the distant forest, thereby keeping the legend alive: the baron in the trees experiencing wars first hand and eventually meeting Napoleon. The ending of the novel ruthlessly dampens the reader's yearning and kindness as a true legend. Cosimo never returns to the ground. The dying Cosimo encounters a hot-air balloon in the end. A story that begins with wonder and ends with it. The novel concludes before readers see him return.

Please pay attention to the inscription on the tombstone written by the writer for his character Cosimo. It helps us not only understand the character but also outlines Calvino's train of thought on the characterisation of Cosimo: living in trees—always loving mother earth—ascending into the sky. This inscription somehow reminds me of my interpretation of Franz Kafka's *The Metamorphosis*: becoming an insect—experiencing human suffering —nowhere to live.

We can trace the strongest artistic appeal back to its origin, which sometimes is so distinct: there is a person in the trees. I assume that *The Baron in the Trees* has become a classic fable about life. Like Kafka's castle, Calvino's trees also become the end of the world. But we must ask a classroom-style question: what move do you think has made this great artwork a winning chess game? If someone asks me the same question, my answer will be: it's a risky move, and the risk lies in the protagonist's residence in the trees instead of on the ground.

I always feel that beneath Calvino's elegant writing is concealed a heart of stone, and when I think about it carefully, it dawns upon me that sometimes a writer is a tyrannical ruler of characters: since no place is suitable for people like Cosimo, they'd better be resettled in the trees!

A PEAK IN THE DAY TO DAY ACCOUNT

Readers of Raymond Carver may find him strange. Those who don't like him consider him to be a writer only good at keeping a routine day-to-day journal like following a calmly flowing creek. In their eyes, he's an obstinate and meticulous journal keeper. Different opinions like this are normal. If readers who don't like him run into those who favour him and question him about the practice of day-to-day journal keeping, the latter would scratch their heads. That's because their devoted affection for a certain day-to-day journal is akin to dubious psychological abnormality, a condition where they have a lot to say but don't know where to start. This is where the strangeness lies. It's difficult to extol Carver's merits with rigorous and appropriate literary language. I find it futile to persuade an optimist to appreciate Carver and equally futile to talk a connoisseur of the classic literary value system into loving him. Carver is indeed a keeper of a routine day-to-day journal. It's a journal of men and the flowing-water-like journal can flow upwards. Carver's rebellion against literary models is also bizarre. Others try to rebel from above but he starts from below. He writes almost only in a language of middle-school level. He's obsessed with writing about real life. By doing so, he almost gives up all the convenience afforded by fiction writing. Is this explanation good enough? It's still unconvincing. The only explanation that matches the subject of my preface is that Carver can make people confuse fiction with real life and this sense of confusion is magical. Perhaps because most of Carver's stories are but an organic series of life scenes instead of stories, the moods of his characters are like peaks standing out of the dark clouds shrouding them in this series.

Therefore, reading Carver, the reader sees no cloud but the immobile mountains behind the clouds.

While reading the mood of a generation of Americans, we're probably reading the mood of our generation of us Chinese.

We have no alternative but to apply metaphors to Carver who hates metaphors. Talking about this so-called minimalist writer is not simple at all. We usually think that Carver's labels of literary creation are eye-catching, such as attention to daily life, concise and simple text, and near repellence of any figure of speech. But we'll eventually find that after exhausting all the labels prepared for Carver, we still find it hard to see him distinctly.

Carver has a compulsive habit of cleanliness in his writing, which is evident in his rejection of many of the normal elements of novel writing. Besides his taboo against rhetoric, he probably hates meticulous descriptions of scenery and psychology. Let's make a flippant guess. Carver might have said that he would rather kill himself by bashing his head into something if we had asked him to describe the 'bloodless sun' on the Don River as Mikhail Sholokhov does or to write about the dork Quentin's stream of consciousness amid the suffocating smell of honeysuckle by following the example of his compatriot William Faulkner. Carver has been challenging people's reading taste. He writes nothing that should or shouldn't be written except for characters. So, if we're going to talk about Carver, we can only start with his characters. The source of Carver's literary creation testifies to the theory of epigenesis in traditional realistic creation. Everything relates to personal experience. With this in mind, we must talk briefly about Carver's short and unsatisfactory life. According to his researchers, Carver used to work as a sawmill worker, a deliveryman, a gas station clerk and a porter. He married his pregnant fiancé at nineteen. Whether he took the initiative or had to be a breadwinner, Carver later complained that he had never enjoyed his youth. Carver might not have realised how he unintentionally became propaganda material for realist creation theory and how he naturally used the resources from his own experience to grow into an observer and articulator of the 'Hard Times' rare in American literary circles. The occurrence of literary creation is one thing but the created work is another. What we shouldn't overlook is the Americans in Carver's description. They exude the anxious alcohol breath that Carver himself breathes. It neither represents degradation and tragedy nor, of course, alludes to the vigorously pioneering American spirit in the popular impression. That bitter scent of alcohol at best symbolises a mood of depression. Yes, most of the men in Carver's novels are dejected, reminiscent of the author himself: his worker-like appearance and his sensitive inner world. His enthusiasm for the images of failed men almost makes us suspicious of his narcissism in disguise and of him presenting to us a written report of the analysis of his personality and destiny.

Everywhere are men who have failed or are in trouble and men who want to lick their wounds but can't find their tongues. In Carver's *Will You Please Be Quiet, Please?* that has made his name. Signs of the tension between the protagonist and his wife might not be obvious at the beginning but there are subtle hints. The sight of his wife dressed in white and a red scarf on the balcony reminds Ralph of an episode in a film. "Marian is in a drama where he has no role". While cajoling and coercing his wife to recall her adultery, Ralph feels that his wife is in the film again, only that humiliation causes him to lose his mind. The cuckolded husband now has a part and storms into the cast of the drama. Ralph's behaviour after he runs away from home is intriguing. He gambles and loses all his money. He's also beaten without rhyme or reason. He returns home totally hurt. And his conduct after returning is of great significance. In anger and dejection, he hushes his conscience-stricken wife repeatedly, "Will you please be quiet! Please!" His wife falls silent and eventually reaches one of her hands out to her husband's private parts quietly. What happens next is logical and thought-provoking: the husband quiets down as well! The couple are reconciled temporarily. Somehow, readers, particularly male ones, feel something is wrong. They seem to feel what I mentioned earlier. Readers, especially the male readers, receive a staggering punch in the face from Carver at the end of the story.

Everywhere are people who have become sensitive after being hurt, people who become more unfortunate because they are sensitive, people who have lost hope in life, and people who can't live up to others' expectations. Everywhere there is fragile harmony and deep estrangement. The narrator 'I' in *Feathers* somehow can't remember Olla, the name of his friend and colleague Bud's wife, even though he and his girlfriend have visited their house as guests. Scenes of two or more couples getting together are not uncommon in Carver's short stories, such as *What We Talk About When We Talk About Love*. But the beginning of the two couples' gathering in *Feathers* also means the end of their friendship. What in the world has happened at an evening party? We can say that nothing or everything has happened. Bud and his wife keep a beautiful peacock at home and they also have an eight-month-old baby who has been fussing behind the scenes at first. Then Olla brings him out without thinking but Fran, the girlfriend of the narrator 'I', insists on seeing the cute baby out of her female communicative instinct. As a result, something happens. This baby who finally appears forebodes danger. He's shockingly ugly! The appearance of this queer baby exposed Bud and his wife's wounds thoroughly to 'I' and Fran. But remember that there is a price to pay for seeing others' wounds. This rare family gathering becomes the only and the last one. No couple can see each other's baby any more. From that time on, there are only a few peacock feathers left to serve as a testimony of the friendship between 'I' and Bud. In another short story *The Compartment*, Myers, another man who can't withstand injuries, takes a train across France to see his son whom he hasn't seen for eight years. But an accident causes Myers to deviate completely from the destination of this trip. Myers' loss of his suitcase to a thief is like a flashing dark cloud. Then what we see is a man that only Mr Carver can accurately portray. This kind of man, in the face of misfortune, chooses to drift with the current of the unfolding event to continue his misfortune. Myers is an example. He saw his son (already a young man) waiting for him at the station in Strasbourg but he did not get off! He has rejected the station with indescribable sadness, fear, unknown anger and vengeance. He stays on the train and even feels impressed by the French countryside soon afterwards.

American film director Robert Bernard Altman has adapted nine of Carver's short stories and one of his poems for the film *Short Cuts*. He says, "I treat all Carver's stories as one". This is, of course, a film director's 'short cut' to using fiction. This statement, however, prompts me to assume that if I treat all the characters in Carver's writing as one person, then who would he be? No doubt he'd be Carver himself. It's not because I'm old-fashioned but because all perfect fiction evokes suspicion that the writer always exchanges his soul with some god or devil.

Everything in Carver's fiction is formidably sharp. As far as his mental pressure on his readers is concerned, if it's exaggerating a bit to accuse him of 'killing without spilling blood', more would agree that he hurts people in their tender points with a razor blade. Some critics speak of Carver's worldview as black. How can it be? That statement oversimplifies Carver's pursuit of minimalistic narratives. On the contrary, I think of Carver as a very complicated writer. Only complicated writers write with extraordinary cruelty, often using the words 'kill' or 'cut into pieces'. They leave the reader with a dagger forged with words. I have been trying to sum up my impressions of Carver's works in a standard commentary tone but I find it embarrassing to write them down. As a result, I've come up with some incoherent internet slang that I consider smart myself.

For instance, my comments like 'desperate hope, downhearted strength, moderate throe, emotionless affection, cleansed evil, simple complexity', and so on and so forth... would bewilder Carver's soul in heaven.

HOW TO PLAY A JOKE ON THE WORLD? THOUGHTS ON READING ISAAC BASHEVIS SINGER'S *THE MAGICIAN OF LUBLIN*

LET'S TALK ABOUT ISAAC SINGER'S 'THE MAGICIAN OF LUBLIN'.

Isaac Singer differs from other American Jewish writers. He's different not only because he's the sole American Jewish writer who writes in Yiddish but also because of his strange, closed subject resources. Compared with Saul Bellow's panoramic writing from the broad perspective of intellectuals, he appears narrow-minded and obstinate. Compared with Philip Roth's impulsive and rebellious writing, he seems pedantic and honest. But the result of his writing is an accident. Readers cannot but comment that Singer's works are the most old-fashioned and yet the most touching of the works by Jewish writers.

Singer immigrated to the United States from Poland at thirty-one. He was still young but seemed to have shut many of his windows to the New World, leaving only one to his gloomy hometown in Poland. From behind the window, he watches the world, which is then presented as lying on the *Old Testament* with a miserable expression. In Singer's inner world, there is sometimes a snowy winter and sometimes a thunderous summer, and the Jews coming from every part of Europe are like birds that, hovering in the air, find it hard to alight to the ground. Singer sets himself the task of helping them land with his writing. Of course, in textbook terms, the core of Singer's writing is the Jewish national spirit and character. Reading Singer's novels would be a shortcut to understanding the Jews if you want to do so without knowing how.

LET'S TALK ABOUT THE CHARACTERS; THE MAGICIAN YASHA MAZUR IN 'THE MAGICIAN OF LUBLIN'.

Yasha Mazur is a skinny magician who is very famous in Poland. According to his agent's vision, he'll most likely cause a sensation throughout Europe in the future. In the imagination of men of letters, the profession of a magician is like that of a wizard. It's related to the oppression of animals, the art of trickery, deceptive tricks and the life of a wanderer. The profession of the magician has an inherent advantage in characterisation. Somehow, instead of taking this advantage, Singer avoids the ordinary idea of creating a captivating beginning in his novels by making use of a magic show filled with the fanfare of fireworks. The author still concentrates on his writing with extreme honesty. Yasha is a man surrounded by four women. According to the narrative sequence of the novel, the first woman is his wife Esther, a virtuous and kind seamstress. Yasha comes back home to reunite with her every few months and treats her well. But he has a non-Jewish assistant named Magda. She loves Yasha deeply and takes better care of Yasha than his wife. Yasha reciprocates her kindness with kindness and provides financial support to her mother and even her brother. The third woman, Zeftel, comes from a village, a hotbed of thieves. She's not only coquettish but also knows how to use men like Yasha. The fourth woman is Emilia, the widow of a university professor in Warsaw, a woman who lives in poverty but in style. She's where Yasha's heart belongs and therefore his favourite woman. At this point, the relationships among the characters in the novel are bewildering, but they don't come as a total surprise. Singer, however, portrays the character Yasha with a narrative philosophy of practical jokes: Yasha even has a crush on Emilia's fourteen-year-old daughter Halina and already 'set a trap' for her.

It's clear that Singer first labels the character Yasha as a shameful licentious sinner and then cleanses him of the label to restore his religious Jewish identity to him. This is the great value of the character Yasha's existence, and the driving force and procedures of the novel's plot development. The story of Yasha with the four women has everything that can cause indescribable excitement among readers. But we gradually discover that the author doesn't treat lust and sexual relationships between men and women as the goal of his narration. This is a story about sin and self-salvation. The characteristics of the character Yasha, namely cleverness, craftiness, deception, greed and possessiveness, progressively sing a painful harmony with his conscience, kindness and religious education. The writer may have attempted to allude to his ethnic people with metaphors but, no matter how sober we are, we can't bear to refer to the destruction of Yasha as a Jewish writer's castigation of his own national characteristics. The most distressing thing is the path a man takes to destruction, and even Yasha himself feels that his life is suffocating. 'He feels that his life is like a novel whose plot is getting increasingly tense, even making the reader impatient to turn the pages'. What makes people tenser is the meticulous description of Yasha sneaking into a secluded senior citizen's house in the middle of the night, attempting to pry open his safe with his magician's skill. It's apt to remind readers of the plot in Fyodor Dostoevsky's *Crime and Punishment*, where the protagonist kills the old landlady. But we can heave a sigh of relief in the end. Different is the way a great Jewish writer deals with the tragic fate of his character from that of a great Russian writer. Also different is the tone of the violence caused by pleasure-seeking from that caused by a dejected loser. Yasha eventually gives up his idea of stealing and killing, and he even sprains his ankle. Then the reader may cheer heartlessly that a magician of Lublin should have stopped committing a crime halfway and sprained his ankle!

Yasha's awakening is food for thought. Is that the result of the change brought by his Jewish brethren's example of piety in the synagogue? 'The long-forgotten childhood devotion has now returned, a faith that demands no proof, an awe of God, a sense of remorse over one's transgressions.' 'I must be a Jew... A Jew like all the others!' This may be an explanation, but it's by no means persuasive. I see Yasha's as a passive and inescapable awakening which has come to him as he faces grim reality. Therefore, it seems thoroughgoing and makes the reader as sad as happy. We must go to the women for our conclusion. Seeing no hope in the love affair with Yasha, the loyal Magda has hanged herself. Emilia, coming from a decent family, has severed the otherwise close relationship with Yasha after discovering that her plan to improve her life with his help has fallen through. And the flirty Zeftel certainly hasn't become Yasha's life-saving slingshot. She throws herself into the arms of a human trafficker when she finds Yasha completely isolated and on the brink of a mental collapse. So, Yasha has finally come back to his wife in Lublin Village and completed his bodily return. My reference to his return as 'bodily' coincides with an extremely 'metaphysical' stunt Yasha performs at the end of the novel. After ending his wandering and indulgent life as a magician, Yasha has become a 'saint,' self-imprisoned in the cage built by himself. The Jewish men and women once watched Yasha performing his feat of walking a tightrope but now, around the stone hut, they're watching him perform another feat, namely making himself a self-imprisoned penitent. By now, the magician of Lublin has completely returned to Lublin, both bodily and spiritually. Even his morality and desire have returned as well. Only that, as readers notice, all he has done is attached the cruellest condition: the loss of his freedom.

It is shameful to record another voice, but I'm convinced that some have doubted Yasha's inner voice: doesn't fate dictate I become a good person or a saint? Okay! Okay! Let me lock myself up then!

Yasha used to be famous for walking a tightrope in Poland but readers see him walking on the blade of human nature with blood splattering in all directions. Following the trail of the magician is following a sharp tingling sensation which the magician's soles transmit to us. Of course, the magician, who used to conjure up things, has now produced a humorous pain by magic.

"Wandering for the first half of your life, you've just made a joke with yourself and the entire world." This is the wise and graceful Emilia's assessment of Yasha. To my mind, this is exactly what Singer tries painstakingly to insinuate. Tossing Yasha into the history of literature, Singer not only practices shooting with his Jewish brothers and sisters as targets but also fakes a punch at the evil deeds and moral principles of the universe, thus playing a well-meaning, tragicomic joke on us and the world.

ABOUT THE AUTHOR

Su Tong was born in Suzhou, East China in 1963. He rose to international acclaim after his book *Wives and Concubines* was adapted into the BAFTA-winning film *Raise the Red Lantern* by director Zhang Yimou. His novel *The Boat to Redemption* won the Man Asia Literature Prize in 2009, and in 2015 he was joint winner of the prestigious Mao Dun Literature Prize for *Shadow of the Hunter*.

Having grown up in the Cultural Revolution, Su Tong's novels and short stories depict everyday life in 20th century China with a dark twist. In addition to his many striking novels, he has also written hundreds of short stories, many of which have been translated into French and English. He currently lives in Nanjing.

ABOUT THE TRANSLATORS

OLIVIA MILBURN

is professor of Chinese language and literature at Seoul National University. She holds a doctorate in classical Chinese at the University of London's SOAS. She has authored several books on Chinese history and co-translated two spy novels by Mai Jia.

NICKY HARMAN

has translated the works of many renowned Chinese authors including Jia Pingwa's *Broken Wings* and Yan Ge's *The Chilli Bean Paste Clan*. When not translating, she blogs, gives talks, teaches literary translation, and works on Paper-Republic.org, a non-profit promoting Chinese literature in translation.

JAMES TRAPP

has published numerous China-related books. His translations include new versions of *The Art of War* and *The Daodejing*. Much of his work revolves around integrating the study of Chinese language and culture, and breaking down cultural misunderstanding.

HAIWANG YUAN

is a professor at Western Kentucky University. He has authored and co-authored many books, including *Princess Peacock* and *This Is China: The First 5,000 Years*. Among his translations are *Different Carmela* and *Memorabilia in the Earth*.

About **Sino**ist Books

We hope you enjoyed reading this extensive collection of short stories by the masterful award-winning author, Su Tong, one of the giants of modern Chinese literature.

SINOIST BOOKS brings the best of Chinese fiction to English-speaking readers. We aim to create a greater understanding of Chinese culture and society, and provide an outlet for the ideas and creativity of the country's most talented authors.

To let us know what you thought of this book, or to learn more about the diverse range of exciting Chinese fiction in translation we publish, find us online. If you're as passionate about Chinese literature as we are, then we'd love to hear your thoughts!

SINOIST
BOOKS

sinoistbooks.com
@sinoistbooks

SINOIST BOOKS

Want to read more from the man behind Raise the Red Lantern?
We have just the book for you:

Shadow of the Hunter
SU TONG
translated by **JAMES TRAPP**

Prey, Predator, Predator, Prey.
On this street, the hunters are also the hunted.

The people of China tell of an ancient tale, where the mantis hunts the cicada, unaware of the yellow bird behind it. In a small corner of one of its many cities, a random act of violence sets off a spinning top, entwining the lives of three people.

Baorun, the compulsive bondage expert, is forever aided and abetted by Liu Sheng, a brash troublemaker, to indulge in his obsessions; and the lady Fairy Princess, ever-youthful, becomes the target of the pair's escalating antics.

As the years pass, many things begin to change, but in the dysfunctional world of a mental hospital at the end of Red Toon Street, just who is prey, and who is predator?

Often insightful and occasionally unsettling, *Shadow of the Hunter* is a memorable tale concerned with guilt, injustice, madness and the struggle not to lose one's soul to history. It is one of Su Tong's most acclaimed works, now available in English for the first time.

'His strokes are restrained but merciless.' – Anchee Min, author of Red Azalea

'Su is a master of implication…' – The Guardian